On Animation

The Director's Perspective

VOLUME 2

On Animation

The Director's Perspective

VOLUME 2

Editor

Ron Diamond

Interviewers

Bill Kroyer and Tom Sito

Associate Editors

James Brusuelas and Tom Knott

CRC Press
Taylor & Francis Group
Boca Raton London New York

CRC Press is an imprint of the
Taylor & Francis Group, an **informa** business

Associate Editors: James Brusuelas and Tom Knott
Cover design by Alan Bodner (bodnerart.com)

CRC Press
Taylor & Francis Group
6000 Broken Sound Parkway NW, Suite 300
Boca Raton, FL 33487-2742

Printed on acid-free paper

International Standard Book Number-13: 978-1-138-06656-4 (Paperback)
978-1-138-06709-7 (Hardback)

Visit the Taylor & Francis Web site at
http://www.taylorandfrancis.com

and the CRC Press Web site at
http://www.crcpress.com

For Lisa, Sara, and Anna

CONTENTS

FOREWORD

My love affair with animation started around 1962 not with a movie in a theater, but with an album on a record player. It was a 78 RPM of "Cinderella," with songs and story. I carried it around our house on a small portable turntable and listened to "Bibbidi-Bobbidi-Boo," "A Dream Is a Wish Your Heart Makes," the entire soundtrack really, ad nauseam.

Such is the magic of animated films. The great ones (and there are so many great ones) become so powerfully ingrained in our culture that a little girl can fall hopelessly in love with animation just by listening to the music.

I'm sure that, on more than one occasion, my parents were tempted to break that scratchy record, but instead they let my love affair deepen. I am forever grateful they were so tolerant because, improbably enough, 30 years later animation would become my career … and my passion.

In 1992, I began work as the producer of *Toy Story*. At the time, I had only worked in live action and had just come off of *Dances with Wolves* and *The Addams Family*. Live action and animation are very different expressions of the film art form (I describe it as the difference between a sprint and a marathon), but at the center of both is the director.

And now, as I start development on my eighth animated feature, I think about the creative team that will collaborate on that film, and I am excited to meet the person who will be the director.

The directors featured in this collection of interviews are masters of the art. Each has a different way of working and brings something entirely unique to the mix. Each has a specialty, whether it is traditional animation, computer animation, or stop-motion. Using imagery, words, and music, they have taken audiences on imaginative journeys to amazing worlds inhabited by unforgettable characters, and created some of the most beloved family entertainment of all time. We and our children, and even our children's children, have watched and re-watched these outstanding pieces of storytelling.

I consider myself very fortunate to know them all and have worked with most. We've been through it all together; the hard work, the long hours, the good days and bad days, the redo, the notes, and ultimately the anxiety-inducing opening weekend.

Thanks to this book, you'll get to know them as well. Bill Kroyer and Tom Sito have spent several years asking questions about how these animation directors got started, how their life experiences influenced their work, what is their process, how do they maintain their vision and still collaborate with their team, what are their biggest challenges, and what brings them joy.

I know that after you spend some time with these incredible individuals, you will have a greater appreciation for the role of the animation director in conjuring up the extraordinary magic of an animated film.

Bonnie Arnold
Producer
DreamWorks Animation

ACKNOWLEDGMENTS

Coming up with the idea for this book was the easy part; making it happen took the combined efforts and enthusiasm of many people over many years. For starters, if it weren't for Ed Catmull, former president of Walt Disney Animation Studios and Pixar Animation Studios, this book would have not have been possible. When I reached out to Ed and told him about the idea, he immediately expressed interest and gave the book his blessing. This opened the doors to meet with the directors who were currently working at Disney, and allowed us to license many critical images, since so many of the directors in the book at one time or another worked at what many referred to as "Disney's." From the beginning to the end, the next most essential person was my friend of over 30 years, animation and VR producer, recruiter, and former director of the Ottawa International Animation Festival, Tom Knott. Tom oversaw the lion's share of the image selection, clearances, and communication with the directors and the studios. Without Tom's significant support and diligent work, this book would not exist.

I'd like to thank Bill Kroyer and Tom Sito for their tireless devotion in researching and interviewing the directors, and for welcoming me as I'd chime in with questions of my own during the interviews. And for their participation, candor, and honesty in sharing their experiences and expertise and giving us a glimpse into their inner worlds, the directors themselves (in the order they appear in the book): John Musker, Ron Clements, John Lasseter, Andrew Stanton, Brenda Chapman, Nick Park, Tomm Moore, Chris Wedge, Roger Allers, Chris Buck, Tim Johnson, Bill Plympton, Brad Bird, Henry Selick, Don Bluth, Pete Docter, Chris Sanders, Dean DeBlois, Vicky Jenson, Rob Minkoff, Jennifer Yuh Nelson, Carlos Saldanha, and Kevin Lima.

Special thanks to our tireless editors James Brusuelas, Jon Hofferman, and Carol Frank, to Bonnie Arnold for a fantastic Foreword, and to Alan Bodner for beautiful cover designs.

Early in the process, we were supported greatly by Dan Sarto, co-founder and COO of AWN, Inc., editors Bill Desowitz and Rick DeMott, and interim coordinator Aria Stewart.

Sincere thanks to all of the studio contacts who facilitated the interviews and the clearance of images: Chris Wiggum, Maraget Adamic, Maxine Hof, Gregory Coleman, Wendy Lefkon, Heather Feng-Yanu, Michelle Moretta, Victoria Manley, Marguerite Enright, Leigh Anna MacFadden, Christine Freeman, Debby Coleman, Kiera McAuliffe, Alex Ambrose, Mary Walsh, Fox Carney, Michael Buckoff, Dave Bossert, Victoria Thornbery, Jerry Rees, Jessica Roberts, Katie Smith, Julia Reeves, Shelley Gorelik, Melanie Bartlett, Casie Nguyen, Andy Bandit,

Lucy Manos, Brook Worley, Laura Baltzer, Patrick Skelly, Jerry Schmitz, Richard Hamilton, David Hail, Beverly Moyer, Michael Garcia, Chase Schultz, Daniel Chun, David Hall, Cathleen Girdner, Kim Kline, Lillian Ritchie, Justin Melillo, Waiolo Shannon, Robbin Kelley, Shanna Robalino, Noreen Ong, Robbin Kelley, Gary Goldman, Kip Goldman, Gabrielle Ruffle, Angie Last, Deborah Rouse, Heather Koopmans, Megan Bradford, Rosemary Colliver, Jenniphur Ryan, Mark Shapiro, Yael Gabbay, Owen Miller, Lorne Mitchell, Julie Heath, Jacklyn Pomales, Margarita Diaz, Andy Jeyes, Roni Lubliner, and Desiree Meade.

A massive thanks to the Acme Filmworks studio crew and the interns for their dedication and support: George Khair, Misty Myers, Diane Schlactus, Masha Evans, Kaitlyn Cavanagh, Josephine Moss, Tara Beyhm, Kelsey Peterson, Hae-Joon Lee, Amy Lee, Christian Kemabia, Helen Shi, Kerin Amit, Nolan Nissle, Dhanesh Jameson, and Molly Tomecek.

And, last but not least, thanks to Lisa Frank, Sara Diamond, Anna Diamond, Mark Diamond, Debi Perluss, Isaac Diamond, Dan Sarto, Debbie Sarto, Becky Sarto, and Nikki Sarto for unbridled support, love, and encouragement.

Tom Knott also offers personal thanks to Will Ryan, Shannon Tindle, and Ann Knott.

Ron Diamond
Executive Producer

EDITORS

Ron Diamond founded ACME Filmworks in 1990 to create commercials, shorts, and long-form animated projects with more than 50 notable international animation artist storytellers. In addition to producing over 1600 commercials, Ron produced the TV Series *Drew Carey's Green Screen Show* for the WB Network and *Drawn from Memory* for PBS' American Playhouse. He is a recognized expert on international animation and lectures at schools and animation festivals worldwide. He curates specialty animation programs for festivals. Since 1998, he curates *The Animation Show of Shows*, a feature length movie comprising new notable international animated shorts; presents them at the major animation studios, tech companies, game companies, animation schools, and animation festivals; and releases them for the general public. He co-founded the Animation World Network (AWN.com) in 1996.

Bill Kroyer is an Oscar-nominated director of animation and computer graphics commercials, short films, movie titles, and theatrical films. Trained in classic hand-drawn animation at the Disney studio, Bill was one of the first animators to make the leap to computer animation as computer image choreographer on Disney's ground-breaking 1982 feature *TRON*. He pioneered the technique of combining hand-drawn animation with computer animation on projects such as his theatrical animated feature film *FernGully: The Last Rainforest* and his short film *Technological Threat*. As senior animation director at Rhythm & Hues Studios, he directed animation on scores of commercials and many feature films, including *Cats and Dogs*, *Garfield*, and *Scooby Doo*. Bill served as co-chair of the Science and Technology Council of the Academy of Motion Picture Arts and Sciences and is a governor of the Academy's Short Films and Feature Animation branch. He is a tenured professor and is director of digital arts at the Dodge College of Film and Media Arts at Chapman University in Orange, California. In 2017, Bill and his wife Sue received the prestigious June Foray Award from the International Animation Society (ASIFA) for significant contributions to the art and industry of animation.

Tom Sito is an animator, animation historian, and professor of animation at the University of Southern California, Los Angeles. His movie credits include Walt Disney's *Beauty and the Beast* (1991), *Who Framed Roger Rabbit* (1988), *The Little Mermaid* (1989), *Aladdin* (1992), *The Lion King* (1994), *Pocahontas* (1995), and DreamWorks' *Shrek* (2001), and *Osmosis Jones* (2001). He has worked on television series such as the *Super Friends* (1978) and *He-Man and the Masters of the Universe* (1983). He is president emeritus of the Animation Guild, Local 839 Hollywood and on the Board of Governors of the Motion Picture Academy of Arts & Sciences. He received the June Foray Award in 2011 and the Dusty Outstanding Alumni Award in 2016. He is the author of several books: *Drawing the Line: The Untold Story of the Animation Unions from Bosko to Bart Simpson* (University of Kentucky Press, 2006), *Timing for Animation,* 2nd Edition (CRC Press/A Focal Press Book, 2009) *Moving Innovation: A History of Computer Animation* (MIT Press, 2013), and *Eat, Drink, Animate: An Animators Cookbook* (CRC Press, 2019). In 2014, he was featured in the PBS American Experience documentary *Walt Disney.*

INTRODUCTION

Animation. Not a day goes by that I don't think about it. Animated images dance through my head: memories of favorite films, snippets of past projects, abstract shapes, and evocative faces. While I work in animation, I don't believe I'm alone in this obsession. For vast numbers of people throughout the world, animation is a singularly rich art form, encompassing some of the most profound and pleasurable cinematic moments we have experienced.

As with all forms of artistic expression, each creation is measured by the success of its realization. However, in animation, the road to a finished product is especially daunting, and the challenges facing an animation director must be met with an especially high degree of resourcefulness, insight, and endurance. In feature animation production, a director must collaborate with multiple teams of highly skilled artists, storytellers, engineers, composers, lyricists, musicians, and producers in an immensely labor-intensive undertaking. To carry forward a personal vision in a process that can take 5 to 7 years, sometimes even longer, requires extraordinary persistence, tenacity, and commitment.

The demands on a director, or in some cases a two-director team, frequently include an in-depth knowledge of fine art, literature, theater, animation, and cinema history, as well as highly refined skills in communication, writing, humor, stagecraft, performance, design, painting, draftsmanship, visual effects, music, camera, lighting, and editing. They must also have the ability to helm a nine-figure production employing the skills of dozens—if not hundreds—of experts and to draw out of them the best they have to offer. And, on top of all that, they must tell a great and beautiful story that appeals to a large and diverse audience.

They must be able to defend their ideas and to challenge them as well, to construct a formidable production plan, and also be ready to tear it down and rethink it if the story isn't working or the characters aren't just right. This is what it takes to be an animated feature film director—as well as to be able to retain a sense of humor, to keep working when exhausted, and to meet crazy deadlines imposed by others or, worse yet, by oneself.

This book is about the blood, sweat, and tears of the craft of animation direction at the most complex levels—but it's also about inspiration and faith in oneself. I believe that by learning more about these artists' personal histories—what grabbed them, often at a very early age—and compelled them to follow the path of animation, we can acquire a deeper understanding of their art and find greater enjoyment in their artistic creations.

For this book, we followed a few basic guidelines. The first was that, to be included, a director had to have directed at least two animated feature films. Apart from providing a baseline qualification (since, unfortunately, we couldn't include everyone), the idea was also to explore what it was like to direct a feature for the first time and how that experience differed from successive directing experiences. We were very interested in this learning process, and we hope you'll find it as fascinating as we did.

In addition, we wanted the directors to speak freely, to be unbridled in the telling of their experiences. We then worked with them to edit the work down to convey an honest and revealing story that clearly leads us through their journeys.

Finally, it was decided that fellow feature film directors should conduct the interviews, since who is better suited to ask informed questions and discuss the ins and outs and nuts and bolts of animation? This turned out to be an inspired idea; our two interviewers, Bill Kroyer and Tom Sito, were exemplary in drawing out the directors and in producing remarkably insightful discussions that have the pleasant familiarity of colleagues talking to colleagues.

I have been fortunate to have known several of these directors since their college days and others along the path and have stayed in touch with them throughout their careers. Their unmistakable glimmer of greatness was visible early on, and we are all the beneficiaries of their brilliance as they went on to direct some of the greatest animated features of our time. These interviews reveal commonalities of the collective experiences of some of our finest contemporary minds, and the lessons they learned. This is not just a book about approaches to animation production but also a primer on how to live a life filled with art, passion, giving, friendship, love, and contentment.

I am truly pleased to present this collection of 23 interviews in two volumes for you to enjoy. As for those directors who couldn't be included, we look forward to publishing future volumes in which we can get to know them and their stories as well.

Ron Diamond
Executive Producer

1
Brad Bird Interview

Brad Bird © Disney/Pixar.
Photo: Deborah Coleman.

I recently asked Brad Bird a question: "What do you know now that you didn't know when you started directing?" He said, "I know I'll never spend four years making a film again. I have too many stories and not enough time to tell them."

That doesn't mean he won't direct animation again, but if he does, he'll be searching for a way to do it that won't require the four-year schedule of *The Incredibles*. Brad didn't get a chance to direct his first feature until he had been in the business for almost two decades. Ironic, considering he was animating in his early teens—earlier than any of us.

Why the late start? Brad started at Disney when he was barely in his twenties, but even then he had a passion for animation and knowledge of film that was unsurpassed. That passion, the insistence on excellence and an aversion to compromise, got him in trouble, got him fired, for simply insisting that the studio hold to the very standards of Walt Disney they claimed to be preserving.

While the rest of us young, struggling animators bought furniture, Brad bought laser discs, which he studied incessantly (while sitting on the floor) on the biggest TV screen he could afford. He is the greatest student of—and lover of—films that I have ever known. When his film career stalled he switched to TV and brought innovation and cinematic excitement to *The Simpsons*.

He finally got his shot helming *The Iron Giant* and hasn't looked back. The innovations, Academy Awards, and record revenues of *The Incredibles* and *Ratatouille* have secured his place in animation royalty. His worldwide hit *Mission: Impossible—Ghost Protocol* proved that his directing skills reach beyond animation.

There are some big stars in Hollywood that have huge success, but when you meet them in person you wonder, "Is that really the guy who did all that?" You never have that doubt with Brad. Whether you are student or an industry icon, spend three minutes talking with him and you will come away with a memorable moment, a story, anecdote, or an observation about the art that will get you thinking, get you laughing, get you inspired.

We interviewed Brad at the Pixar Animation Studios in Emeryville, with a follow-up by phone.

Bill Kroyer

Bill: Tell a little about when you first had the inkling that you might be interested in animation.

Brad: If you'd asked me this question fifteen years ago I would have given you a different answer. I would have said I got interested in animation around the time I started my first animated film at age eleven. But I've since realized that the very first drawings I did were sequential. They weren't very good drawings. They weren't animation; they were more like a storyboard or a comic strip. They showed a character entering a scene, doing something, then exiting a scene or something like that. I'd hold the drawing in a stack, and—as I would tell the story—I'd take the front one and put it in the back, revealing the next drawing, and so forth. I was doing that at three.

Bill: You were pitching to your family!

Brad: Well, the drawings were meant to be viewed in a certain order, and I would tell the story verbally while I was showing the pictures. I think in my own way I was trying to make movies right from the very beginning.

I was considered odd at the time because I wanted to see animated features more than once. Nowadays, you buy them on DVD or whatever and kids see them probably a hundred times, but back in the day the only way you could see them was to go to the theater. My friend's parents and my grandparents thought my mom was a little indulgent, letting me see films more than once. I'm talking about like three or four times.

Bill: Did you go by yourself?

Brad: I'd go with my family once, and then I'd go with friends, and then I'd go with a different group of friends, because the same friends wouldn't go back twice with me. Sometimes my parents dropped me off at the theater and picked me up when the show was over. I sort of knew from the encyclopedia how animation was done, that they were drawings that were slightly different, and at a rapid speed they looked like they were moving.

Bill: What happened at eleven that made you want to make an animated film?

Brad: Something clicked in me when I saw Disney's *Jungle Book* at eleven. I remember watching the panther jumping up on a branch and thinking, "That really looks like a panther. It doesn't just move like a cat; it looks and moves like a panther."

And when that same panther began to talk, I thought, "well this is a rather *stuffy* panther, you know?" Someone was making very specific observations. It's not just any animal; it's a cat. Not only is it a cat, it's a panther. Not only is it a panther, it's a stuffy panther.

And then I realized: adults made this. And somebody's job is to figure out how a stuffy panther moves. This is a person who gets a paycheck and is considered a part of society. Up until then I was dreading becoming a grown-up because I'd see them at my parents' parties milling around, talking about stuff I wasn't interested in, and that was the moment where I realized there are really weird, cool, interesting jobs out there. Suddenly, growing up seemed like a really fantastic destination.

Bill: **So up until this moment, when you had that revelation, what were you thinking when you were watching a movie more than once?**

Brad: Well, I enjoyed it. I was drawn to it, but if you'd asked me why at the time, I probably couldn't explain more than "I like it." But I think that there was something about animation being like the magic trick that could never really be explained.

You could explain that each drawing was different. You could explain that they were put on pieces of celluloid, placed over backgrounds, and photographed. You could explain the process, but you couldn't explain the magic trick. In other words, it was like explaining a joke; you can sit there and dissect it, but the reason it makes you laugh remains wonderfully mysterious.

With animation, it was like: why do I care about these things that are announcing their unreality every moment? They're not real; they've got flat colors and lines around them. And yet you're getting dramatically wrapped up in them, as if they have lives and feelings. You care about them. You're worried about them. When something dangerous happens to them, you're concerned about their well-being. How does that happen?

When I started making animated films, I had to figure out not just how to move characters around, but filmmaking: Is this moment in a close-up? Or is it in a wide shot or is everything eye level? Or do I cut to a new shot? I started noticing filmmaking in live action films, which got me interested in film in general. So animation was my gateway drug to the entire film medium.

Bill: **This film you were making when you were eleven, how did you make it?**

Brad: I saw *Jungle Book* and I came out of it and asked, "How did they do that?" And my parents said, "Well, you know how they do it. Each drawing's different, etc." And I said, "Yeah but how could *I* do it?" And there was a guy who was with us that one time, and I'll never forget him. He's a family friend named Marty Dowling, that was the *only* time that I was ever in his presence, and he happened to have taken an animation class at UCLA. So he knew how to do it! And he talked me through all the things I'd need: like a movie camera that could shoot one frame at a time, a camera stand, etc. It was the weirdest serendipity that I asked the question at the one moment that there was somebody around me who could answer it. Because I lived in Oregon and nobody knew anything about animation.

Bill: It wasn't long after this that you started to contact the Disney guys, right?

Brad: A friend of my parents went to Oregon State with George Bruns, who was the composer for Disney. So I met him and he said, "Come down to LA and I'll take you through the studio." So I went down to LA and I met everybody.

Bill: How old were you then?

Brad: Eleven. I met Frank and Ollie, Al Dempster, and Ken Anderson, I met the key people who took me through every department. I remember George introducing me to Frank and Ollie, saying, "Brad just started making an animated film," and they kind of gave me this little smile, very much like, "You're gonna lose interest in two weeks, kid." So, they were shocked when I showed up three years later with a finished film that was fifteen minutes long.

Bill: Was it in color?

Brad: Are you crazy? Fifteen minutes of color?

Bill: I'm just asking!

Brad: I was a *kid*! I've gotta go to school! You're making me feel like a slacker because I didn't do color! The film was my version of *The Tortoise and the Hare*. The tortoise is more of a bad guy and the race ends in a five-way tie. The animation and the design get progressively better as the film goes on.

Bill: Here's the thing I was always wondering about: you talk almost immediately in your career about analyzing filmic aspects of animation, but you're a kid who's eleven who had no one personally teaching you.

Brad: Well, my parents were unbelievably supportive; my mom prodded me along, got me focused on entering a Kodak contest, and even helped me physically assemble the film to make the deadline. My dad built and set up my camera stand. In addition to great parents, I had three books, two of which my parents bought at Disneyland. One was *The Art of Animation* by Bob Thomas, and I wore that thing out. Man, if you look at my copy of that book, it just feels like the juice has been sucked out of every page by just eyeball wear. How that book even retained its spine I can't even tell you. Another one was a very simple book on how to do Disney animation. And then there was the Preston Blair book, which was the best book in terms of basic animation technique.

Bill: Everybody's bible.

Brad: Yeah, the Preston Blair book helped a lot. So when I finished I sent that film to Disney and they responded. They were just starting to get the idea that their animators weren't gonna live forever and they realized they didn't have anybody trained to replace them. So they said, "Any time you're in LA, come in and you can work with one of our animators." I turned to my parents immediately: "We have to get to LA!"

Bill: You're a junior in high school!

Brad: I was in seventh grade. So I came down and they didn't have any training program in place, so they had Milt Kahl be my mentor.

Bill: He's the last guy to train a kid!

Brad: Exactly! [laughter] Because he's not verbal, he's not exactly the most patient guy. You'd think he wouldn't want to be bothered, but he was incredibly generous to me. You know, I somehow had the right constitution for him. He was intense, and in my own kid way, so was I!

Bill: How exactly did you work with him?

Brad: Well, they cleared out a room and just put an animation desk in there. Milt was right down the hall; you went through Johnny Bond's room and turned left and there was Milt's office. Milt was in what was, years later, the largest of the two rooms that made up the "Rat's Nest"!*

Bill: What did he give you to do?

Brad: It wasn't an assignment for a film. It was a teaching exercise. Goofy's late for work and he's running, and he grabs his brief-case and is suddenly surprised because it's filled with anvils. There's no reason why Goofy's briefcase would be full of anvils; I mean, we don't go that deep into it. The idea is to show something where he's got an attitude and then suddenly reacts to something unexpected. So, I would animate it, then Milt would flip it and audibly react. Whatever reaction he had on his first flip-through was the only unfiltered reaction I'd get. Then he'd kind of reset his body and flip it again, and then he'd start going into all the things that were not right about it.

* The "Rat's Nest" was two connecting rooms in D-Wing, originally inhabited by Milt Kahl, Frank Thomas, and Ollie Johnston. When they retired, the next occupants (Brad Bird, John Musker, Henry Selick, Bill Kroyer, Jerry Rees, and Dan Haskett) were given the name "The Rat's Nest" by Don Bluth. Meant as a put-down, the term was embraced by the group, who shared an alternative vision for the future of Disney's animation department.

Bill: You were the only kid in the studio, I'd have to guess.

Brad: Yeah. I would get some double takes, too. I would just go down on vacations or during the summer, whenever I could get down to LA and the door was open.

Bill: So even when you were back home, you'd be sending stuff down to him for comments.

Brad: Yeah, and I started a new film, which was even more complicated than *The Tortoise and the Hare*, and it was in color. For you, Bill.

Bill: In ink, I would assume.

Brad: Hand colored with felt pens! I got like forty seconds into it, and I sent the Disney guys that forty seconds and they loved it. And I suddenly realized: this is going to be the only other film I do, for the rest of my time as a kid!

Bill: Because it was taking you so long?

Brad: It was long and more complicated and in color! I basically realized that I would have to miss the rest of my youth! I said, "I don't think that I can finish this!" Because already I was flirting with outcast geekdom. I only wanted to talk about animation, and my friends could feign interest for maybe thirty seconds, and then their eyes would glaze over. I couldn't say, "I went down to Disney and worked with Milt Kahl!" because that name didn't mean anything to anyone in Corvallis, Oregon, except me!

I was into this world, but no one else was. So I just said to Disney that for my own mental health I have to do something else. They were disappointed, but they understood. So I stopped animating, discovered girls, played football, got into photography, got into theater ....

Bill: Weren't you a pretty good basketball player?

Brad: [dismissive laugh] But I had a childhood. I got serious about theater, and I was going to go into it in college. But then Disney offered me a scholarship to CalArts, and I went. I was the only student in the animation program at CalArts that was getting *back into* animation after a four-year layoff.

Bill: Totally unique.

Brad: And I thought, "Well, okay ... I'll go back into animation and learn a trade. And then I can go do theatre." Then, of course, the moment I got back into animation, I got really interested in it again. Which is ultimately why I love film. I love all of the arts, and film is the only medium I know where all the arts come into play: photography, acting, writing, color, design, movement, music—all of it is in film.

Bill: How did you advance your ideas and your craft in your two years at CalArts?

Brad: The weirdest and greatest thing about CalArts was suddenly I was surrounded by people who were as interested in animation as I was, and I could actually discuss it with others my age for the first time in my life. You had all these thoughts bottled up and suddenly you find yourself with people who could keep up with you, because they had been thinking the same thing in some other remote small town.

One of the weirder things about the Disney program was that the weakest class was animation! Every other class was absolutely topflight: the life drawing class, the caricature class. Bill Moore was the greatest design teacher, probably the best single teacher I've ever had in anything.

Bill: Everyone says that about him.

Brad: Yeah, he was extraordinary, and I learned more from that class than any other single class. But the guy who taught the animation class at the time was really more of a director. He had only animated a tiny bit, so his notion of actually animating a scene was pretty limited. We ended up compensating for that by putting together our own class unofficially at night.

Bill: Self-critiquing.

Brad: Right! CalArts had sixteen-millimeter prints of Disney features, and of course we wore them out. We would run them at regular speed, and any one of us at any time could say, "stop," and we'd stop. Then whoever called the stop would point out some specific observation about a particular piece of animation. It was really illuminating, because each student was spotting different things. So we all benefited from each other's eyes. And we taught each other.

Bill: Why did you leave after two years?

Brad: I was offered a job, along with John Musker, Henry [Selick], Jerry [Rees], and Doug Lefler.

Bill: So then you go to the Disney studio and start the training thing.

Brad: You know the story. You were there. That's where we met. It was not a great period at Disney. All the guys who really were the masters were out the door when we arrived, and the people who were being elevated into the top positions were people who had been there for twenty years and weren't good enough to rise to the top under the masters. They were interested in holding on to their jobs, and they were threatened by anyone who was talented, I think. As far as the future of Disney feature animation, it was up for grabs, and the young people were divided into two camps: Don Bluth's camp … and the rest of us. I was learning, but half of what I was learning was how *not* to make films.

Jerry Rees, Dan Haskett, Bill Kroyer, Henry Selick, John Musker, and Brad Bird.

Bill: You were there how long?

Brad: A couple of years. I got fired.

Bill: Had you thought of being a director?

Brad: You know, my plan was to animate for fifteen years, or something like that, and then move into directing. So yeah, I animated for a while, but I was very unsatisfied with the kinds of films that were being made and the lack of quality. I felt like I got fired at Disney basically for standing up for the very principles that Disney's master animators had taught me to care about and fight for! Surreal.

Bill: So you left Disney, and am I wrong in guessing that maybe the first thing you directed on screen was your ice skating thing in *Animalympics* … ?

Brad: Yes, yes … and that was a wonderful thing to go into. Thank you, Bill Kroyer, for inviting me to join you on that. That was a wonderful thing to go into after Disney, because it was the opposite of Disney in many ways. They encouraged you to do whatever you could. It was about how much work you did, and how good it was, rather than punching a clock at exactly eight o'clock in the morning … and "behaving" … which is what Disney had turned into as the masters were retiring.

Bill: **You storyboarded it, you did the layouts, you did all the animation.**

Brad: I cut the music ….

Bill: **I think you even inbetweened, most of it.**

Brad: A lot of it, because it was kind of funkily timed.

Bill: **Is that the only sequence that's ever been in a film where you did it all—board, animate, direct?**

Brad: Well, it's very basic staging, but yeah. I animated scenes in *Family Dog*, and I had one scene in *Iron Giant*, but yeah, it's the only sustained piece of animation that I did.

Bill: **Your next real directing assignment was *Family Dog*, right?**

Brad: It was a key moment for me because I was in my early twenties, and I had already been at the best place in the world for feature animation … and it sucked! All the masters had left Disney, and the people running the studio weren't empowering the young animation talent, and every other studio was worse! I was seriously thinking about quitting animation. But then I thought I should take one last shot. Make a film pitching the kinds of things *I* wanted to see animated and see if anyone would go for it. I sunk my own money into a short film called *A Portfolio of Projects*. Two of the projects were shorts (which included *Family Dog*), and one of them was a feature based on Will Eisner's *The Spirit*. Gary Kurtz got interested in *The Spirit*, and then Jerry Rees and I spent years trying to get a studio to back it. And I could not get that sucker backed, even though I had the producer whose last two films at the time were *Star Wars* and *The Empire Strikes Back*.

We were told repeatedly by the top people in Hollywood that no animated feature would ever make more than fifty million dollars, and Disney would be the only one that would come close to that. So now when I hear some executive gassing off about what will or won't work, I've absorbed way too much nonsense to give it any credence. Don't listen to anything anyone in a suit tells you about "the business," because the only thing true is what William Goldman says, "Nobody knows anything."

Bill: **So *The Spirit* doesn't go but *Family Dog* does?**

Brad: That's a complicated story. The simple version is: I wrote an *Amazing Stories* script for Matthew Robbins to direct, and Steven really liked it and had me come down. Tim Burton and I had done storyboards for *Family Dog*, and I showed them to Steven. He said, "Can you do a half an hour of this?," and I said, "Sure." And he said, "Let's do it as an *Amazing Stories*," and so that was my first real directing thing. And that was fun.

Bill: **Talk a little bit about that production you set up on Traction Avenue.**

Brad: *Amazing Stories* was an anthology show like *Twilight Zone* but with a much bigger budget. Steven got an unprecedented commitment from NBC for forty-four episodes. Our episode was the only episode that was a negative pickup, meaning that they gave us the money and we went off and made it, because neither Amblin nor Universal had an infrastructure for animation.

One of the great things about a negative pickup is that you're given a lump sum of money, and how you spend it is up to you. So I didn't spend anything on the surroundings. Every dime went to what was up on the screen. We were part of a floor of a building that was formerly an open parking lot. They decided to just put up walls, so you could still see the parking spaces painted on the floor. I'm not kidding. In spite of the fact that we were full animation, we delivered well under the average budget of an *Amazing Stories* episode.

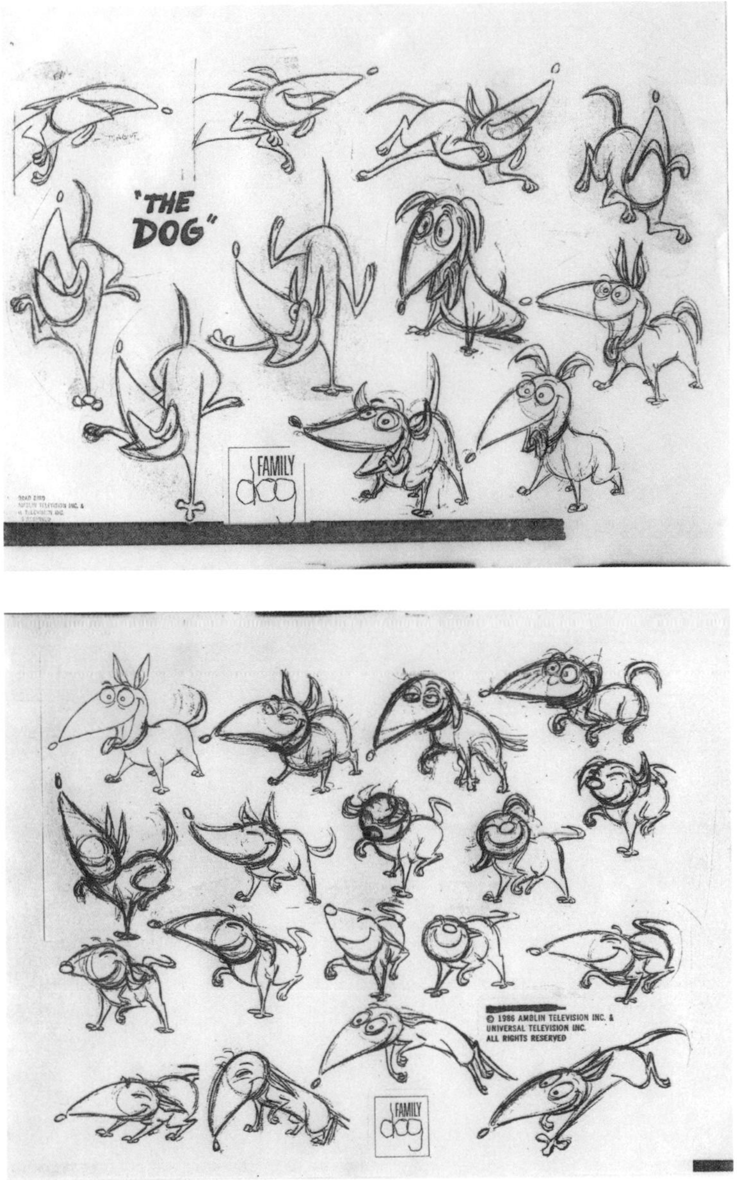

Model sheet "The Dog", *Family Dog*, 1987 © Universal.

Bill: Where'd you get the furniture?

Brad: Well, the furniture was very cheap stuff. We were all in one room. So we had a very family sort of atmosphere. The bad thing is that we were under a lot of pressure, and if anybody flipped out or got into an argument, everybody else heard it. We had to go up to the roof to have fights.

Bill: Two things on that show that I think have been kind of typical of your experience as a director are, number one, you had a pretty strong vision in the story reel stage of where you were headed, and number two, you had an amazing ability to recognize and cast talent and to be very inspiring to your team. Those are things that have seemed to be a real trademark. Can you talk a little bit about your first experience with those things on *Family Dog*? You really worked hard on that reel, right?

Brad: Right. We gave a lot of top talent their first animation jobs. Several people who couldn't get into Disney got in after they did *Family Dog*. And production-wise, we were very lean. We didn't do any animation we didn't use. I'm fairly proud of the fact that that's been pretty constant in my career, that I've had very little animation on the cutting room floor. I try not to waste people's energy. However, I will go back and I'll fix animation probably more times than some people like me to do. They always like it later, though.

I think that what people respond to is the fact that I respect talent. I think that people often underestimate their own talent. There were people on *Family Dog* that thought they were gonna get jobs as inbetweeners and I'd say, "Well, I saw your reel, why don't you animate a scene instead?" They all did really great work. I think often people are capable of more than they think they are.

Bill: How did you strike the balance, and *Family Dog* was a good example, of getting a really talented animator inspired to do something that is primarily already in your own mind the way you want?

Brad: I think that I have in mind who the character is and what I want the moment to feel like. You want to get a 100 percent of the entertainment, but there are many ways to get that 100 percent, as long as it's true to the character. But it's directed toward letting the animator be an animator. I mean, that's the joy of it.

Bill: And an innate skill is that casting, right?

Brad: I learned a lot on that film because we were in one room, and you didn't have walls to diffuse the vibe. Here's a good example: Ralph Eggleston, later a top designer at Pixar, had this manic sort of energy. I mean, he would get a scene and three hours later he would have it roughed out completely, done in a ridiculously short amount of time, but it would be sloppy. I'd say, "If you slowed down a little bit, Ralph, you wouldn't have these problems." I'd give him like twenty fixes, he'd be back two hours later, all twenty fixes done, but with ten other problems.

Tony Fucile, even as a young guy fresh out of CalArts, had a kind of sleepy but precise energy. So I saw Ralph over here spinning like a top, with sparks flying everywhere in uncontrolled spasms of energy, and then I had Tony who's practically falling asleep. So I decided, I'll put 'em next to each other. I moved Ralph right next to Tony. Ralph calmed down and Tony woke up. And it was perfect!

Bill: That's more psychology than casting.

Brad: Well, you need that as a director, too.

Bill: So you finished *Family Dog*, it's a fantastic thing, Amblin wanted to do it as a series, but you decided not to do that. And then you ended up spending your next years in television.

Brad: Well, yeah. No one has better commercial instincts than Spielberg, and I think he was seeing that the time was ripe for a primetime animated cartoon. This was before *The Simpsons*, and as usual his instincts were dead-on.

But *Family Dog* scripts are difficult to write, because the dog doesn't talk. The dog's a dog, and crafting situations so that you see it from the dog's point of view, that all has to be done carefully. We also couldn't do the *Garfield* approach, where the cat can look at the camera and you just hear his voice telling you what he's thinking. Our dog was a dog; he only made dog sounds … which meant it was entirely up to animation to tell you what he was thinking. That takes real craftsmanship. Even though the designs were simple, the animation was not. We could do six seven-minute shorts a year theatrically, but we couldn't do twenty-two half-hour episodes and maintain the quality.

I didn't want to fail Steven Spielberg. I didn't want the second thing that I did to be a bad, pale imitation of the first thing that I did. So, we parted ways, and they went off and did the TV show that they had in mind with Tim Burton and I went off onto *The Simpsons*, which was an idea I thought *could* be done well on a TV schedule.

Bill: How did it come about that you went to *The Simpsons*?

Brad: Jim [Brooks], [Sam] Simon, and Matt [Groening] liked the fact that *Family Dog* had unusual filmmaking in it, that the filmmaking was more like a live-action film. So they invited me to come on *The Simpsons*. What was weird for me was going from doing something that was mine to being a team player, and just helping someone else with their vision.

People thought I was crazy not to lead a series with Steven Spielberg, a series I had created, in favor of taking a supporting role on *The Simpsons*, a show that I had had nothing to do with. But for various reasons (I was also going through a rough time with a tragedy involving my sister), it seemed like the right thing to do at the time. It also allowed me freedom to work on all these episodes, make a lot of contributions that got to the heart of what was or wasn't working with a given episode. I could fix it and improve it without having to do the heavy lifting.

Which also allowed me enough time to go out and try to get movies made, which is what I really wanted to do. So all during the time I was on *The Simpsons* I was trying to get films made. I got films that are still to this day stuck in the catacombs of various studios.

I had no trouble selling ideas to Hollywood; the problem was getting them out of development hell, and I've learned a lot about that since then. I think if they can smell that you are willing to wait to get your dream, they will keep you waiting forever.

My attitude toward trying to get projects financed in the film business has changed. I entered the business loving "yes," and liking "maybe," and hating "no". Now I love "yes" and "no," and I *hate* "maybe". Because "maybe" will suck your life away.

Hollywood is basically a fear-based town, and "maybe" allows them to keep a project from slipping away from them, but they don't have the risk of committing to it, either. So they will load up their trays with "maybes." And the coffers of these companies are rich enough for them to support a lot of "maybes."

Bill: **So to get to *Iron Giant*, didn't you give them an ultimatum?**

Brad: Oh yeah. I was so sick of the usual cowardice, not saying they didn't want to make it but not backing the idea either. And you'd ask, "Can I have it back?" And the answer was, "No. Because you might make it a hit for somebody else, which makes us look bad," you know what I mean? So by the time *Iron Giant* came around, I fought for a bunch of things in my contract and I would not budge on them. They were not money issues. They were all about creative and time issues.

And one of the things that I insisted on was if they didn't greenlight it in six months, I was out.

Sure enough, they went to six months and one day. I was ready to walk and they greenlit the film. You could absolutely feel that they wanted to stay in "maybe," though. They wanted to see how *Quest for Camelot* did before committing to *Iron Giant*. But because they greenlit us and we were too deep into production by the time *Quest* came out, it was cheaper to finish us than to cancel us. So the only reason that *Iron Giant* actually got made was because I had that one requirement in my contract.

Bill: You finally get your opportunity to direct an animated feature, and it's in this very trying situation.

Brad: I finally get the ticket to board a luxury liner, and it turns out it's the *Titanic*.

Bill: And it's already sinking …

Brad: But the way I looked at it was, we can run around first class, we can have all the brandy and cigars we want, as long as we know that we'll all be dead on the bottom of the ocean in two hours. Part of the deal was that we had to be an incredibly tight and efficient production. Warner's had terrible experiences with their feature animation division before we arrived—it wasted a ton of money and had little to show for it. So we had a complicated film and a tight budget. We struggled every week to hit the productivity numbers, which were aggressive, and the way I said it to the crew was, "As long as we hit the numbers, they'll stay away. If they stay away, we have a shot of making a really great movie here. If we don't hit the numbers, they are gonna start to question everything. And, we don't want them to question everything. It'll kill us … we want to make our film."

Bill: Your experiences as a director are so filled with political and economic intrigue and stress. Try to set that aside for one instant and talk a little bit about what were you thinking of doing when you started *Iron Giant* that you felt might be fresh and different, that would be something that you personally had always wanted to see and had never seen.

Brad: I saw an opportunity to do the kind of animated film *I* wanted to see, something smart and dark and touching. Something that was paced confidently, not the sort of hyperactive rushing around that had become the new norm, this desperate busyness that seemed to suggest a fear that the audience would go for popcorn or grab a remote to change channels if you weren't shrieking at them all the time. I have always been kind of interested in animating humans. Milt was interested in humans, but Disney …

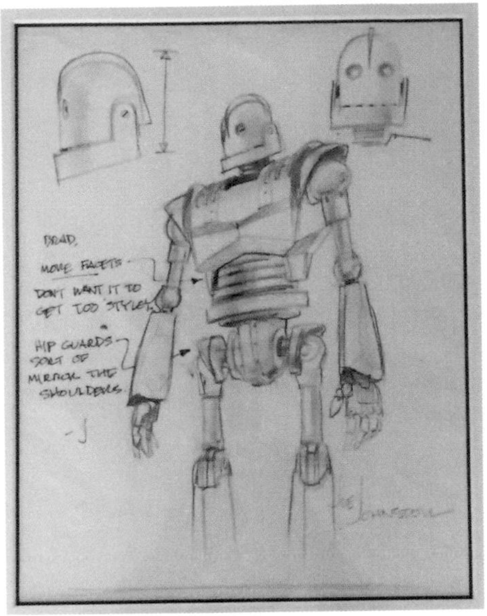

Early model sheet "The Giant", Joe Johnson, *The Iron Giant*, 1999 © Warner Bros. Licensed by Warner Bros. Entertainment Inc. All Rights Reserved.

Character development, Mark Whiting, *The Iron Giant*, 1999 © Warner Bros. Licensed by Warner Bros. Entertainment Inc. All Rights Reserved.

Bill: Lots of talking animals ...

Brad: Yeah, I have no problem with talking animals. A lot of my favorite films have talking animals. Remy is a talking animal. It's just that a lot of stories that featured humans weren't being done because the thinking was if it has humans in it, it could be done in live action and therefore shouldn't be done in animation. Well, I even knew when I was starting out that that was idiotic thinking. If the only reason to animate something is because it can't be done in live action, animation would've gone extinct decades ago. Because live action can now do anything. The reason to do something in animation is caricature, and I use that word in a good sense, to get through to the truth of something. The truth can be really unreal-looking. I mean, *The Simpsons* in its own weird way gets at a lot of truth that people couldn't face if it were in live action.

Visual Development, Mark Whiting, *The Iron Giant*, 1999 © Warner Bros. Licensed by Warner Bros. Entertainment Inc. All Rights Reserved.

I got *Iron Giant* going with this pitch to Warner Brothers: "What if a gun had a soul and didn't want to be a gun?" That's an unusual pitch for an animated film. I mean, you don't hear that sort of idea in the halls of a lot of the animation studios. I think *Giant* had enough of the recognizable "family" elements in it to make Warner's comfortable with making it. But we also were able to squeeze in some darker and headier stuff, which was interesting.

Bill: I think the cinematics of that film are very different from almost any other animated film up to that time, and it had certain live-action style camera moves, cutting and staging, effects, rack focus, that were a very bold cinematic style.

Brad: Thanks.

Bill: Which I think has been sort of a trademark of yours. But the other thing that is, I think, the most remarkable was that as innovative and exciting as they are, they're never what I would call "gratuitous." And I think most agree that people who watch your movies are never conscious of wild camera moves or a wild kind of directing.

Brad: There *are* some wild camera moves …

Bill: But they seem to fit, they seem right for the moment.

Brad: I paid attention to live-action filmmaking when I started making films. I realized that people wouldn't notice flamboyant camerawork if it were psychologically right. The only times that you notice it is when it pulls you out of the movie rather than pulling you into the movie. So, if you can bury the technique in emotion, so that it has an emotional grounding … You're home free.

Some directors view camera work as almost a chore, and they kind of turn it over to their DP: "You figure out a good place to put the camera, I'm worried about the performance here." To me, where the camera is placed is part of the performance. It's an observer in the room who also has a brain, a take on the scene, and a point of view. The shower scene in *Psycho* is very stylized, very fragmented, but at that point, your own psyche is jagged and you're in a confined space, and you want to get out of there. So, psychologically, it's right to have fragmented, jagged shots.

Bill: I remember going to your house and you had the biggest TV of anybody we knew. And you had scores of laser discs, and you'd just keep popping the laser discs in and saying "watch this move, watch this cut, watch this …" I know you still do this, you watch so many DVDs at your house. If somebody who wanted to be a good director wanted to mimic you, is there a way to watch and learn?

Brad: I think for students there's never been an easier time to study film. In some ways DVDs are making it too easy, because they have the commentaries and all these extra materials at the end explaining everything. I'm almost starting to react against commentaries, because it's breaking down a movie before you've even had a chance to digest it, if you go straight into it.

The problem with commentaries, and I've done several of them, is that they tend to make people think that the things you're pointing out are the only things worth noticing or the only way to see a particular film. It's probably better to not say anything and let the viewer get their own stuff from it. Because the viewer is gonna make connections that have nothing to do with connections that may have caused the filmmaker to do a moment. And that doesn't mean that they are any less valid.

Bill: So, you finish *Iron Giant*, everyone loved it, but it had a disappointing box office. You've finished your very first big feature film and you've got this kind of odd dichotomy of reactions, but fortunately along comes the Pixar offer.

Brad: It became clear that Warner Brothers was not the best place to do animation. Even after *Iron Giant*, they were kind of asking me to audition again. I pitched *The Incredibles* to Warner, and essentially they said, "Well, we like the idea; if we like the script we'll make it." Well, basically you could say the exact same thing to any cab driver. That's no real commitment, particularly after the hell we had to go through on *IG* … and I felt we had more than proven ourselves.

When I saw *Toy Story*, I had called John Lasseter 'cause I just flipped over it. It was everything that I had been waiting for our generation to do. It honored everything that the old guys taught us that matters, which is: characters, and story, and character, and character, what is your character thinking, what is your character feeling, character, character, character, character, character—that's the reason you do character animation, that's the beginning and end of it.

Toy Story was both absolutely fresh and absolutely classical. It got at the heart of all the things that mattered most, but in a whole new way. The technical stuff was very interesting, but not nearly as interesting as the story that was being told. It was contemporary, it had original characters, but it was far more sincere in how it approached them.

The Incredibles, 2004. © 2004 Disney/Pixar.

There's very clever direction in the opening of *Toy Story*; you begin from the point of view of a kid. Everyone knows what it's like to be a kid and play with a toy. And very subtly, they start to shift to the POV of the still-inanimate toy. As if the film is saying, "You remember how it was to play with a toy? Well, now we're going to show you a toy's point of view." It's subtle, it's sophisticated, it's simple, and clean, and the whole movie is like that.

I had seen John at a Disney premiere party when he was making *Toy Story* and he said, "You know, we should stay in touch." And we did while John was making *Bug's Life* and I was doing *Giant*. So I pitched *The Incredibles* to Pixar and their reaction at the end of the pitch was, "No brainer, let's do it." And I was like … "Really? That's it? Don't I have to walk over coals or give you my first child, or … you know … pay you something?" Pixar was going, "Come on up! Make a film!" The whole mindset was different from Warner's. It couldn't have been more opposite.

I would not say *The Incredibles* was easier than *Iron Giant*. But it was easier in the sense that I had complete support from the studio. It was a really ambitious, really complicated film.

Bill: **It was all pretty new to you, because you had not yet worked in 3D.**

Brad: It was new to me, and we were pushing them to do something way bigger than they'd ever done before—but with the same amount of resources. A lot of that *Iron Giant/Simpsons/Family Dog* TV training came in handy, because we were trying to do a movie that was three times bigger than anything Pixar had done but didn't cost more or take more time to do. So being very specific about what we were doing from moment to moment became important because we couldn't waste a dime.

The difference was, on *Iron Giant*, I was spending about 30 percent of my energy protecting what the other 70 percent of my energy had produced, flinging my body between the studio and the film, whereas at Pixar, I was spending 100 percent of my energy on the movie itself. And that's the way it should be. I mean movies aren't easy, even if you have support. But if you have real support, you can spend all of your effort on making the movie as good as it can possibly be and not just spend energy keeping your decisions from being undone. That's exhausting.

Bill: **Pixar is maybe the best environment for that to happen.**

Brad: You can feel it when a filmmaker and a crew are invested in their work and really are excited about the idea of realizing it. You can feel it. These are films that we want to see. If you start defining a filmmaker's job as you would a private sector job—"okay, you're to figure out what would make people of all ages and all different cultures be affected and entertained two years from now"—if you think about it logically like that, you'll go crazy. You'll just go into a fetal ball and curl up in the corner, because it's impossible. You can't know what's gonna entertain a wide spectrum of people all over the world two years from now.

The only way you can even begin to approach it is to say, "What would entertain me? What would I be interested in? What would I find funny? What would I find scary? What would I find dramatically involving?" And then, proceed from there. Because that's something that's possible.

That's one of the things that I object to in a lot of quote unquote "family entertainment." You have a feeling that many of the people making it would not want to sit down and actually watch the film that they're involved with.

I don't think any of the Pixar films feel that way at all. They feel like they assume that people are reasonably intelligent, that they want a story that's well constructed and characters that are engaging. They don't feel focus grouped. Because they aren't.

If you load your slate up with sequels, they suddenly get very happy on Wall Street and say, "This is gonna be a great year for Hollywood because I recognize every single film that's coming out! I know what I'm gonna get!"

Bill: **Right, no "old man with a balloon-lifted house" film.**

Brad: Right. And no film with cooking rodents. Or silent robots.

Bill: **Your films have a lot of live-action influence, like cinematography. Do you think good live-action directors can direct animation?**

Brad: A lot of people who don't know animation are directing animation films. That's what you're talking about, really. Gore Verbinsky did one …

Bill: **Wes Anderson …**

Brad: Wes Anderson made *Fantastic Mr. Fox*. I guess *Tin Tin* is sort of one, right? So it's Spielberg and Peter Jackson and Zemeckis doing mo-cap films. And there are other people, Gary Ross, *Tales of Despereaux*, Zack Snyder, et cetera. It's fashionable now, animation. The technology and the continued success of the animation medium has made it suddenly attractive to the live-action community.

I think, for me, the advantage of an animator directing an animated film is that when you don't get it the way you want you can break it down and get to the absolute pinpoint of what's not right.

We ran into some weird stuff on *The Incredibles*, because we had to convey that Mr. Incredible is strong, but that things he was lifting were really heavy. How do you convey that something is heavy but that somebody is strong enough to lift it?

If you want to see an example of that idea done badly in a live-action film, there's a Jet Li film called *The One*, where he picks up a couple of motorcycles in his hands and smashes 'em together. They look like helium balloons. They do not look at all like he's picking up motorcycles. And rather than being an impressive thing to watch visually, you go "Oh, that's so phony. That's not cool; it's dorky looking." Jet Li should have been lifting real things with some weight, but you can see that that they basically told him, "Okay, you're holding a motorcycle in each hand, now just lift them up and smash them together." But since he was holding no weight, his body reacts as if the motorcycles are like helium balloons.

On films I've directed, because I've animated, I can get in there with the animators and analyze problems on an animation level, you know, "maybe the knee would take a little more of the weight." Now that sounds tedious, and I can understand why a lot of live-action directors wouldn't want to bother with that, and probably you can lean on a good animator, but I feel, if you know the animation, you know how to play to animation's strengths. You're cognizant of what the medium's weaknesses are, so that you can somehow use that to overcome them.

There are certain occupations where people more readily move into directing than others. You see a lot more actors and writers being good directors than you see editors. I view animators on an animated film the way I view actors on a live-action film. In an animated film, the animation is front and center, all the other departments—and they're important, every single one of 'em—are kind of setting the stage for the animator. Animators are kind of center stage. They're the characters, so I think that it helps for a director of animated films to speak that language.

Bill: **It's a different way to do a performance than a live-action actor would do. And it will always be different.**

Brad: I agree, at its best I think it will always be different. I don't consider mo-cap animation. I'm not against the use of mo-cap; I think that it has a very valuable place in the filmmaking arsenal. I think that Andy Serkis and Weta's work on Gollum and Kong is a testament to that fact that mo-cap can give you a very good basis for performance.

But make no mistake that animators helped make those performances possible as well. It wasn't just wires hooked up to an actor; it was animators finessing it, after the fact. Even on *Avatar*, which had a more sophisticated rig to capture actors' movements, animators took it that last 10 percent. A good animator has the eye to detect what's missing. Even if the mo-cap is really great mo-cap, an animator can really readily discern what's missing, to take it to that full level of life.

Bill: **That being the case, do you think it should be called "animation"?**

Brad: No, I don't. In mo-cap, animators are not creating a performance from scratch. They're being a performance preserver. You know how energy, like electricity on a grid, diminishes when it's transferred? That's what those animators are doing. They are compensating for nuances of the actor's performance that are lost in transit by boosting the energy back. But just because that's their function on *Avatar* doesn't mean animators can't also turn in beautiful fantastic performances, all by themselves, you know?

Look at the non-Navi creatures in *Avatar*. They're 100 percent animated, and they look absolutely convincing. Then look at a film like *Coraline*. It doesn't look remotely realistic, but it absolutely is engaging. It draws you in. That's the work of animators.

And you care about it. I look at *Wallace and Gromit*, and the dog Gromit doesn't even have a mouth, and yet I know exactly what that dog is thinking, every single second. And I feel for that dog. I feel like I know that dog.

Bill: **Gromit is one of the great appealing characters of all time.**

Brad: Absolutely. And he doesn't even have a mouth. So I would love it if actors could see animators as brethren, rather than competition. I keep wanting to give a talk to the Screen Actors Guild and tell them to stop viewing animators as the enemy, you know? Put 'em in the Screen Actors Guild!

Muppet puppeteer Frank Oz is an actor. Milt Kahl is an actor. Frank Thomas, Brando, Meryl Streep, they're *all* actors.

Bill: **In your story reels, you have a really strong idea of where you're going with story and acting and content. At what point do you start getting an idea of how it should look? How do you collaborate with your designers?**

Brad: Although I had a pretty strong visual idea for the way I wanted *The Incredibles* to look, it didn't mean that I was looking for people who would just do my bidding. You go after people who you think can capture something new to expand your vision beyond what you're seeing in your mind. You cast graphic talent the way you cast an actor.

In the case of *Ratatouille*, the film was already going and most of the crew was in place when I took it over. I had admired Harley Jessup and Sharon Calahan's work for years. But the sets were not very well defined because the story kept shifting. And beyond the kitchen and dining room of Gusteau's, they could never figure out what the sets were.

When I got onto it, we had to do a whole new story reel in a very short amount of time, and twenty-two of the film's twenty-five sets. We had to figure out Linguine's apartment, that it had to be both a tiny, borderline-poverty apartment, more like a glorified broom closet, and at the same time be romantic; you had to look out the window and be able to feel that magic of Paris, you know?

It was fun to work with Sharon because we're both ardent fans of cinematographers. She could mention a name and I'd know who she's talking about. "Well we want bounce-light here like Robert Richardson," you know, and she'd say "Okay, got it." That's all I'd need to say. Or she'd pull up some shots from different Conrad Hall movies and say, "A little more like this?" It's like talking about rock 'n' roll with somebody who loves rock 'n' roll. You can just say, "the Byrds," and they know who you're talking about.

Visual development, Dominique Louis, *Ratatouille*, 2007 © Disney/Pixar.

Bill: When you're thinking of a sequence, do you ever think, "Well, the lighting or the art direction's gonna dominate this, as opposed to the acting or the dialogue."

Brad: I don't think about it a lot, except specific scenes. I always knew that the interrogation scene in the barn between Kent and Hogarth was gonna be weird in *Iron Giant*, because I wanted there to be only one too-bright light on Hogarth, with darkness everywhere else. I knew the transition from when the kid gets chloroformed and comes back to reality was gonna be an unbroken transition.

Every once in a while, I'll be shocked because something will so *not* be what I'm imagining that I thought, "Did I not communicate this?" Those times are relatively rare but they happen on every movie. Normally, if you get good people you don't have to manage them a lot; you just have to touch base with them and talk about where you are psychologically.

And you can make little suggestions. In *The Incredibles*, the scene where Bob gets let loose by Mirage and then grabs her throat, that was not lit at all the way I imagined it. I had to get Lou Romano to do a little sketch of the top rim light, so the characters are kind of dark with the hard light, and then, when he lifts her up, he has hard light on him. It's less soft and sleek looking and more hard-ass.

Sometimes I have ideas while I'm writing. I love the whole filmmaking process; I basically could be assigned almost anyone's job filmmaking and be interested in it. I am kind of a geek, and I have fun going from department to department. So sometimes when I'm writing I'm imagining a specific department and where we're gonna be leaning more on it.

On *The Incredibles* I'd noticed that modern action films had lost the tease. I'd always loved sneaking around scenes in the Bond films. And I realized that they didn't have that in the new Bond films anymore. Sneaking around is fun, you know? Now, you just cut, and the character's where he needs to be for the next action scene. So I thought, I'm gonna get some sneaking around in this movie.

Bob starts to penetrate Syndrome's base, and it's cool to show what obstacles he has to overcome. What if a couple of things go wrong? What if you're leaning up against a door, and suddenly it lifts up and you with it? I told everybody involved with those scenes, "Have fun with sneaking around." Even the lighting was all keyed by asking, "What's good sneaking-around lighting?"

It doesn't sound very intellectual, but I trust my people. I don't feel the need to give notes just to give notes. I can't stand that. And I worked for directors that did that. They loved having people taking their notes down and people scurrying after what they want, so they think of meaningless stuff for people to do. I don't enjoy meetings. They're functional, but I don't like drawing them out.

I'm in a meeting to get stuff taken care of and move things out the door. When I first got involved with *Ratatouille*, they were shocked because they'd schedule an hour and a half meeting, and I would deal with it in like twenty minutes and go, "okay, what else?" And they'd go, "Th– … that's it."

Some people want to become directors because they can get people to bring them tea, and they get to point and have people run off in directions that they point to. That's the stuff that they're interested in; they're not that interested in the story or achieving a moment on film. For me, those people aren't really directors. They're people attracted by the *power* of directing and not the filmmaking part, which is the whole point.

I've run into students who talk to me about directing, but they want to talk about making the deal, or what it's like to work with famous people. That's not what's exciting.

Some people will cast famous actors that are wrong just so that they can have the experience of working with that famous person. I would rather have a nonfamous person that's absolutely right for the role … that's more exciting to me. It's more about getting something on film that is … electric, or memorable. The medium is what's exciting, not the other stuff.

Ratatouille, 2007. © 2007 Disney/Pixar.

Bill: I think you convey that sense of energy and excitement to your crews by your ability to not take them down the wrong road.

Brad: Right.

Bill: That's how you kill a spirit in a film. By always changing and fixing it.

Brad: Well, yeah, at least if you're changing stuff and *not* fixing it. And I've said this before, but I really believe it: I learned as much from working on bad films as I did from good experiences like working at Lisberger Studios, where the studio was a fun place to be. But the one line that no one ever puts on a budget, that's absolutely *crucial*, is morale. If morale is bad, you get twenty-five cents out of every dollar you spend. If morale is good you get three dollars out of every dollar you spend.

So whipping people up and getting them excited about what we're doing together is absolutely essential. Films are hard; people work hard. You want creative people. You want people who have their own ideas and who bring them to the table every day. But the challenge is like having an orchestra. You can't say to each player, "Play whatever you want." Individually, each member of an orchestra could play a wonderful thing. But if they all do that at once, it's a mess.

Somehow, without limiting them, you must get them all to weave through each other and support each other, and lift each other up. The film is the goal. The weird thing about directing is that if you do it right, you're only in control maybe a little over 60 percent of the time.

And that's actually good. It's more like a tennis match; you take the first shot, but then the film hits it back to you, and it may push you over into the left side of the court, where you didn't necessarily want to go. But if you go there and hit it back, then it becomes this new thing. And I've tried to force my original thought sometimes, when the film didn't really want to do what I wanted, and it wasn't good.

You can't let the film go out of control, but the best thing is to constantly be asking the film what it wants to be. Or being aware, being open to seeing what the film wants to be, because the film, once you start to create it, starts to have its own momentum.

It's more like martial arts, where you're redirecting energy, rather than blocking energy. You know, if you try to stop it, it'll knock you over. It's about taking the energy that's there and channeling it. Ideas come out of the ether that are better than what you could imagine, and if you're locked on to what you were originally imagining and don't take advantage of gifts that arise, you're limiting what the film could be.

You're doing a dance with a movie. You have to initiate the dance and kind of get the movie up on its feet. But once it's on its feet, you can lead, but you're not the only dancer. The movie's also telling you what it wants to be. And you better be ready to respond to it.

Bill: **And by "it" and "the movie," you're also referring to the larger energy of all the people supplying their creative input.**

Brad: Absolutely.

Bill: **It's a really interesting approach. I think a lot of directors don't do that. They have a rigid idea and I think the films suffer for it.**

Brad: And then there are some directors who absolutely have the barest idea of what they want to do and are willing to just trust the storm of the process. Sometimes it yields a good film. It doesn't yield it often enough for me, though.

Bill: The "fix it in post" school?

Brad: Well, it's the "controlled chaos" school, and great films have been made that way, but usually if you look at the filmmaker's entire body of work, it's really inconsistent, you know? I think that my favorite directors are the ones who are strong lead dancers.

Bill: You're a real proponent of people coming with something other than animation to their experience.

Brad: Yeah, particularly when young people ask, "What should I do?" I basically assume that if they're in animation, they're relatively obsessed, because it's not an easy thing to do. You can't do it casually, really. A lot of work yields very little screen time.

The greatest thing for someone trying to learn animation right now is that you can look at the entirety of all the work that's been done; you can buy it or rent it and study it to a degree that we would have died for when I was first learning.

The weakness of having all this work so readily accessible is if you become a library of other people's solutions, it often limits how you solve problems. Don't get me wrong. I think it's valuable to study how other people handled problems. But try to look in your own life for inspiration. Frank and Ollie (and all the great animators from that earlier era) didn't have any animation to look at, so they had to pull from their lives and pull from plays and pull from other areas. The weakness of animators now is their tendency to only look at animation, because that's all they're interested in. And that means all that they're bringing into the medium is what we've already seen.

If they look to their own lives and look to other art forms and other ways of seeing, then they're bringing something into animation that keeps the medium fresh. Nick Park's dad is a tinkerer, an inventor, and that's one of his influences on *Wallace and Gromit*. And those films are incredibly specific to Nick Park. You feel it.

And that's new. If you asked who's the predecessor to Nick Park, I can name some people that did films in clay. I can name people that made films with British humor, but there is no other Nick Park. Nick Park is the only Nick Park. And that's how it should be. Tex Avery was the only Tex Avery. And so if somebody's interested in revitalizing the art form, I think that they have to absolutely look outside of it. And let the larger world feed them, and then they can feed animation.

Bill: You're one of the great students of directors and directing. Having directed three successful animated features, as you started your first job as a director of a live-action picture, did you bring any notions about directing that ended up changing or turned out to be different than what you expected?

Brad: I think the first thing that I did was I kept thinking that I only needed the bit of film that I was shooting. In other words, the shot begins at precisely this point and it ends at precisely this point. I tended to yell "cut" as I imagined a cut, rather than letting the scene play if it was working. We were starting the scene with a few lines to ramp up and ramp out and be a little looser about it. I would call "cut" and everybody would look at me like, "what is he doing?" I started to get the idea that I can shoot extra.

My brain was wired for "the shot begins here and it ends here," which is how somebody thinks in animation. There's no such thing as coverage, although that's changed a little bit with CG. It's not a coverage thing, where you're shooting something from a lot of different angles. You're tailoring. You're blocking for a specific shot, and a shot begins on Frame 47 or whatever and it ends on Frame 134. My first training in all this stuff was all animation, so I was used to having a stopwatch, which is the old-school way of doing animation, where you imagine how long things take and you hit a stopwatch, and you get your basic feeling for timing that way.

While I think that's a good way to do it—and it does give you a good sense of time—it doesn't really have a heck of a lot to do with how you approach things in live action. That was one of the things that I had to wrap my head around, being a little bit looser. Sometimes what happened, too, is if I cut too soon, a piece of film that I really could have used wouldn't be shot because I didn't let the camera roll a little bit more.

When you go into the editing room—which of course, I didn't do until after I finished shooting *Mission*—and you thought that what you wanted in a certain shot, you realize if you had it in another angle, it would be the perfect thing for a certain point. And if you don't shoot it in that other angle because you cut too soon, then you're hosed. A few members of the crew, and even Tom [Cruise],had to remind me, "If you keep rolling, you'll have something you could use. So why not do it?"

I learned pretty quickly to be a little bit looser about all that stuff. It eventually gives you a feeling for how you can orchestrate moments that you will want to have. It's a little looser than animation. You can still be very precise in live action, but there is the luxury of trying things a few different ways and then mixing and matching a bit later.

Bill: **Were there other big differences in getting into live action, other things you really enjoyed about it?**

Brad: It's not a physical thing. You can't move it as fast as you imagine in animation sometimes, because the camera is not a physical thing in animation. It has no weight. It has no presence in the room. In drawn animation, it's simply another drawing. There is a camera, but it's just moving closer, farther away from flat artwork.

In the case of CG, the camera is like a video game camera, meaning it can be anywhere and move and as fast or as slow as you want it to. While that is a nice thing, I think that it makes a lot of people who direct in CG move the camera incessantly, like a video game camera. It's not anchored to a point of view.

I think that the human eye likes camera stuff that feels a little more physical. ILM, when they first started special effects, started introducing imperfection into camera moves so that it felt more natural with the live action around it. So when an explosion happened, the camera would jar just like it would in real combat footage. Even though the camera in a special effect is not a physical thing and you're dealing with effects that are often not physical as well, if you mimic the physical aspects of that, it makes it feel more real.

When you deal with a real camera in real space, there are limits to how fast you can move. If you want it to move really fast, you have to get up to speed before your shot can start. That is a physical constraint that you don't have in CG.

We were shooting on the Burj Khalifa, which is the tallest building in the world. We were shooting in IMAX, so the camera was huge and heavy, and we needed to control and do these elegant camera moves. It's a lot of trial and error, because you're physically moving a very large, cumbersome camera in space. One part of the shot might be too slow, and in another spot the actor gets ahead of the camera and you don't want him to.

You're trying to choreograph this dance between the camera and the actor and what's happening around the actor. It's performance by camera operators that have to interface with performance by actors. The more complicated your camera moves get, the more ways you have of screwing up. If the actor does this perfect take, but the camera is not in the right spot, that's going to be a problem. Another time, if the camera is perfect but the actor is not so hot, that's equally a problem. You're trying to orchestrate the perfect harmony of all these different aspects.

In animation, you can simply change things until they're all right, whereas in live action you have a schedule that you have to keep. It costs *x* amount of dollars per minute that you have all these people doing this stuff. You don't get that many times at bat. You get a few, and if you schedule your day right, not all your shots are equally complex. You give yourself more time to do the more difficult shots. It's a little more nerve-wracking because things are a little more out of control. That can be a good thing, as well.

Bill: I would think as an animation director, you would automatically bring a more precise idea of frame composition to each shot than a live-action director might, who often waits to see it, whereas in animation you're always thinking of that. Like you're saying, this idea of coordinating a performance with a precise bit of staging seems very animation-ey.

Brad: That aspect of having to imagine shots and be able to draw them, to convey them to other people in animation was useful. I knew what I wanted. Yeah, it was useful. There are live-action directors, of course, who are very precise about camera and what the camera should be seeing at any given point. I would say that that is an aspect of animation that was helpful when I went into it. There are a lot of animation directors who don't care as much about staging as I think sometimes they should.

Bill: I would guess that before *Mission* you had never done a scene that you had not storyboarded first. Did you storyboard everything in *Mission*?

Brad: Actually, most of *Mission* was not storyboarded. There were only two and a half sequences that were pre-vis'd. One of them was the Burj sequence and the other one was the car park. Then I pre-vis'd about half of the sandstorm car chase. Those were the only ones that were pre-vis'd. We didn't have time to pre-vis the rest.

I was used to storyboarding and I think that I am more involved in the storyboard staging than most animation directors. I try to work that out very early, to a degree that some people think is a little over the top. I was already predisposed to think that way, so when I had to pull stuff out of my pocket, I had something in mind. I think there's a danger in relying too much on that.

When I got into the editing room, I was relieved to find that even if I shot coverage of the same scene on two different days, or even a week apart, I instinctively tended to move the camera the same way at the same point in the scene.

That made things intercut pretty well. The coverage all tended to have the same tone, meaning that if I was shooting a lock-off shot, it would be a series of lock-off shots. Then movement would start at a certain point and it would start for a lot of my coverage, not just one angle. There was a similar quality to the filmmaking that made it easy to intercut. I was very relieved about that, because I was just doing it on the fly. We had a really tough schedule and a very large film that was filmed in a lot of different places on the globe, and stunts. We were shooting a big chunk of it in IMAX. There was a lot of trouble. It was a tall order. Even though the film was bigger than the previous *Mission: Impossible* in terms of the scale of it, we had a shorter schedule and a lower budget. We had to be moving pretty aggressively all the time.

Bill: It sounds like you were storyboarding in your head.

Brad: Yeah. What happened was, we didn't have adequate time to scout some of this stuff. I was arriving at locations and they were saying, "Where do you want to put the camera?", and I was like, "Can I look around first? Jesus!"

They said to me, "We have to have a shot list before you shoot." I was getting back so late and having to get up so early that, after a couple of days, I just said, "Look, I can't go home and do shot lists. It's sleep or shot list. Which one do you think I can do without?"

They said, "You have to get the crew going on something." I just said, "Look, I'll figure out the first shot before I arrive. I'll arrive with a shot. While you guys are working on that shot, I'll figure out the next two. Then I'll just stay ahead of you guys and try to keep my coverage doable in a day." That's how I had to do it. I knew that I had to cover *x* amount of pages of material in a day. I tried to plan out my stuff accordingly.

I had a very good crew. They were a very experienced crew. Very quickly, you start to learn the strategy of shooting one side of the camera facing one side of the room and then facing the other. You try to do all of your coverage on one side before you flip the lights around to do the other.

There's an efficiency, and your AD knows all these tricks on how to move efficiently so that you're not striking stuff and then having to re-put it into place. You start to learn where you can economize and move quickly. I don't shoot a ton of takes on every setup. On some of them, they're simple, so you don't do that many takes. You know you're going to hit something else that's going to take more takes than you want. You want to be able to accommodate that without falling behind schedule.

It was a lot to learn, but I was very lucky in that Tom was not only a very game actor, a wonderful, charismatic presence, but also a producer. Very experienced, and incredibly supportive of what I wanted to do. That makes [things] a lot more accomplishable, when you have somebody of Tom's stature on your side. He was very supportive from day one. That was a huge gift to me on my first live-action film.

Bill: **I remember when you were doing *Ratatouille*, I heard you talk about trying to get simulated spontaneity into some of it. It was just hard to do. Now, I guess in a movie like this, spontaneity is there all the time.**

Brad: Well, not all the time. *Mission* is a certain genre. There are a lot of action sequences that need to be very well planned out. There are just too many elements going into play. You have to know what you're going to do on set versus what you're going to later in effects, and where the line is drawn.

We built a large part of that car park, but it's supposed to look like a ten- or fifteen-story building and we could afford maybe three or four stories. It was a huge set. It actually worked. It lifted cars up and moved them around. We were designing it so that we could have those three stories be any one of the ten or fifteen stories that's in the movie. But you have to know where you are at any given point. You have to be able to move the cars around so that they look correct for being different stories. Some of them are CG and some of them are real. You have to know what all that stuff is going to be before you can even do a sequence like that.

I say "spontaneous," but it's the actors who are spontaneous within their given scenes. The kind of film that it is, it's not an improv-type film. It's not like a Will Ferrell comedy where they just roll and do 400 different takes of improv and then just pick the best stuff. This is much more tightly controlled than that.

In terms of comparing it to animation, yeah, you can get a running start. You can throw things in there and somebody can come up with a certain line that they say. We were shooting Renner and Paula and Tom was feeding them a line and he improv'd a line just to get a response from Renner. I thought the line was so correct that we went back and filmed

Tom saying it, because it was great. Renner came up with several lines that I liked better than what was in the script, so I just made sure to shoot them. That part was really fun, because it makes it a live thing that everybody can contribute to. You have to keep it so that it's always moving the story forward, but it's fun to let things slide a little bit.

Bill: Now that you had success in both live action and animation, how do you choose what to do next?

Brad: Well, really, you're just trying to be governed by what story interests you and you feel is challenging to you, that you can dedicate a certain amount of energy to, you think you're going to start to understand story really well, but the truth of the matter is, if you're mixing it up and trying different things, you're always a little bit at sea and you don't really totally know what you're doing.

I am far from feeling like I have story licked and all figured out. I feel like every time I start a movie, I'm back in the dark, feeling my way along the walls. Certainly, the film that I'm working on now is no different. I'm learning tremendous amounts. Like I've said before, I think that you have to stay in the attitude of being a student, because if you're doing it right, I think you're always learning something.

Bill: Are you learning something that you wouldn't have learned if you were doing an animated film right now?

Brad: Sure. It's a different way to make films. Some of the lessons are the same. You're still telling a story and still dealing with presenting characters on the screen and trying to do it efficiently and entertainingly.

Absolutely, the skill set is a little bit different than it is in animation. The heat is hotter. You have more pressure. Things are a little more out of control and you have to be okay with that.

Basically, both animation and live action are the medium of cinema. That's really what I'm interested in. I think animation is wonderful. I think the one thing that I would say is that I'm interested in doing animation more quickly. If I can do it quickly and still create the level of quality that I want, I'm going to try to do that.

Bill: If you go back and do another animated film, how might your directing be different based on these live-action experiences?

Brad: I don't know. That's interesting. I did do a couple of sections of *Ratatouille* where I planned them a little differently. It was because I needed them to feel a little more out of control. I didn't tell the voice actor exactly what he was going to say. I prepared a story reel that was elaborate, timed it with animation timing, then played it in the recording booth so the actor had to respond to it in real time. He had to react spontaneously because he was seeing it for the first time.

I did two takes where Linguini moves throughout the kitchen and is grabbing things from people and trying to explain himself—which I told to Lou Romano, who did the voice. I said, "If your character takes something from another character in the kitchen, try to cover for it. Try to make it sound—even though your body is jerking around—your mind is apologizing for what your body is doing." Lou just reacted. I did two takes and then just cherry-picked the best moments.

John Kahrs, the animator, animated a rough pass in 3D, without me telling him where the camera was going to be. When I got the scene back in rough, it had an out-of-control actor on the soundtrack with an animator who didn't know where the camera was going to be, and a camera guy who didn't know which angle I was going to cut to. That meant that I could edit it in a free-flowing manner and let the action determine the cut.

Even though it was still animation and wasn't really totally spontaneous or anything like that, it had a different feeling that it would not have had if it had been planned out from the outset. It had an out-of-control quality that really helped that part of the film.

Bill: **It seems to me like you get a feeling as a filmmaker of how a story should be told. It seems like no matter which medium you're in, you're going to find the right way to do it and sometimes they'll resemble each other. I'm guessing that your live-action films have certain animation things about them and your animation films have certain live-action things about them, because you're really just thinking about the story and the filmmaking, making the medium work for you.**

Brad: I think that's true. You have a lot of tools in film that you can use. There's the movement. It's not just the movement of people. It's the movement of camera. It's the movement of things in space. The lenses can give you a different feeling, whether it's a long lens or a wide lens.

The Incredibles, 2004. © 2004 Disney/Pixar.

I did a very strange thing in *The Incredibles* for animation. When Bob was in his office, I used the equivalent of really long lenses. Now, even though he was in a claustrophobic office and there was no way you could get those angles in a live-action film without crews putting it on a sound stage and getting way back from it and then zooming in on it. In other words, they were small spaces, but you were covering them with long lenses. It was giving you this very strange feeling of being compressed in a tiny space.

I was virtually building this very claustrophobic set and then moving the camera far away, and then eliminating everything between you and the character. It was continually slicing the set up virtually and getting very close to it. So whenever Bob was at his work, it was compressed and tight and feeling claustrophobic. At the point where he sees the guy getting mugged in the alley, suddenly it goes to wide angle because he's starting to move. He's feeling like his super-hero self—the feeling, suddenly, of space and movement.

Those kinds of qualities, that's like using cinema to get a certain feeling. A lot of my favorite filmmakers are aware of that kind of stuff. I've learned a lot from watching their work.

Bill: I think you're the embodiment of the crossover of animation and live-action, especially now, with CG. There are so many things that can be done; it's really just the cinematic vision that is needed in bringing the same ideas in development.

Brad: We'll see what happens. I'm learning a lot.

Brad Bird © Disney/Pixar. Photo: Deborah Coleman.

2
Henry Selick Interview

Henry Selick © Laika.

What's the toughest thing to do in Hollywood? Win awards? Get rich? Get famous? Be on a first-name basis with superstars? Many people do these things, but in my opinion the toughest thing to do is to be original.

Henry Selick has originality in his DNA. We could see it the first week in the old Disney training program. We were all slugging away on our pencil tests, as was Henry, but he was also working on a film none of us would have dreamed up: *Seepage*. Everything about it was different: the narrative, the design, the mix of mediums. It was hard to imagine Disney ever doing something like it.

And, of course, Disney did not. Henry Selick had to leave to find places to work his magic. Unlike the rest of us, and most of the directors in this book, Henry had an especially challenging path because he literally had to create and invent the entire production process for wanted to make them.

He has been a true pioneer. I remember visiting his studio in the old Pillsbury Doughboy days and seeing dozens of severed doughboy heads on shelves, because Henry was one of the first to use that innovation of interchangeable expressions. On his masterpiece *Coraline*, he was still mixing it up in ways no one else had dreamed of, using some CG while commissioning other props to be custom-cast in steel!

Henry even moves, talks, and gestures differently from other people! And it's not put on; he's always been that way. He has his own style. He's one of those people that make you feel that the magic of life has no predictable limits.

We interviewed Henry during a press junket on the rooftop of the Belage Hotel in West Hollywood.

Bill Kroyer

Bill: When did you first get interested in animation?

Henry: I was one of those kids who drew all the time, from when I was probably four or five until I was thirteen. Like most kids in the fifties and sixties, I enjoyed the old Disney shorts and Warner Brothers stuff that played on TV. I especially liked the classic *Popeyes* and those wild *Betty Boop* cartoons. Characters like Mickey Mouse, Bugs Bunny, and Popeye are some of the first drawings I ever made. But I was also a big fan of Ray Harryhausen after Mom took me, age five, to see *The Seventh Voyage of Sinbad* down at the Carlton Theater in Red Bank, NJ. I dreamed about his stop-motion Cyclops for years. I also loved the bits of Lotte Reiniger's cutout films that played on a local kids' TV show. The Disney Halloween TV specials that featured "Night on Bald Mountain" and "Legend of Sleepy Hollow" were quite memorable. As far as humor, I thought the *Rocky and Bullwinkle Show* was the funniest thing on TV and the *Peanuts* specials were pretty special. *101 Dalmatians* was the most impactful Disney feature I saw. I don't think I even knew there was a connection between the flipbooks I drew in schoolbooks and the professional cartoons and stop-motion I watched. It would be a lot of years before the light bulb went off and I became an animator.

Bill: Was anybody else in your family artistic?

Henry: My father was, in a way. Restoring old cars was his hobby, and he could make anything out of wood or metal. His shop was awesome and included welding equipment, metal lathes, and a sand blaster. He even knew how to do lost-wax castings. For years, my brother and I were his "helpers" and, while we never had his talent at making stuff, just getting to see how mechanical stuff worked and how to repair or replace it definitely influenced my love of doing stop-motion and all its handmade processes. My father also shot sixteen-millimeter home movies, and sometimes I'd be an actor in one of his gag shots. Despite him being a pretty macho guy, he and my mom encouraged my wanting to be an artist, making sure I didn't trace any images I drew.

In the third grade, I was taken under the wing of a local illustrator, the famous Stanley Meltzoff, and went to his studio once a week for free art lessons. He did paintings for *National Geographic* and *Life* magazine and worked from models, even having a dead horse brought to his studio for a Civil War series. Stanley was a great artist but kind of intimidating so, after a couple of years, I stopped going. Years later, when I told him I was going into animation he told me I was out of my mind, saying, "Animation is factory work!"

I switched from drawing and painting to music when I was around eleven years old—piano and clarinet and guitar, all through high school, along with English and physics because of some great teacher. It wasn't until college that my interest in the visual arts was reignited. I had a lot of catching up to do, but threw myself into life drawing, painting, printmaking, sculpting, and photography. Funny thing, I could never settle on one image in my photos. It was always a series of images that were telling simple stories. I even made a couple of full-size sculptures that had joints because I couldn't settle on a pose. I wanted to keep shifting them. When I was about 20, I saw an experimental animated short on TV. That's when I realized that all my various interests, including music, could come together in one art form. So I signed up for Bruce MacCurdy's course at Syracuse University.

Bill: What was your major at college?

Henry: At the time I was an illustration major. But I was also a musician, playing in bands, so there was a tug-of-war between the art courses and playing music. Honestly, I didn't know what the hell I was going to do.

Bill: Did you make your first film at Syracuse?

Henry: In class I saw a lot of animated shorts from the Canadian Film Board, which used all sorts of techniques like sand painting and pin screen and stop-motion. So I wanted to experiment a bit. My first film used animated cutouts of my artwork set to a pop song called "The Wall Street Shuffle." Then I got to direct other students on an original film of mine using traditional cel animation over backgrounds. It was called *Tube Tales* and, while it was pretty crude, it was nominated for a Student Academy Award. It was in '76 or '77.

Bill: From the Oscars? From the Academy?

Henry: Oh yeah. Got to meet Jack Nicholson and Warren Beatty and Buck Henry, Louise Fletcher and Jacqueline Bisset and Groucho Marx. My short ended up getting beaten by a film from CalArts.

Bill: Is that what brought you to LA?

Henry: The nomination came after I arrived. I'd gotten the animation bug and wanted to learn more from a school that had a full animation department. So, after seeing some excellent student shorts from the California Institute of the Arts, I applied to both the character and experimental animation programs. I got into both programs and ended up taking classes in both departments.

Bill: What was that experience like? You were probably older than most of your fellow students.

Henry: There were a few others who'd done undergraduate work; John Musker and Leslie Margolin come to mind. But most kids in character, like Brad Bird and John Lasseter and Jerry Rees, were right out of high school. The average age was higher in Jules Engel's Experimental Animation Department.

I grew up in New Jersey on Beach Boys and Disneyland promos, so coming to California in '75 was just incredible—it was the promised land. I had a Vespa scooter and I spotted a real roadrunner—the bird—my first week there. CalArts was like no other school I'd ever heard of, a place where you'd find incredibly great graffiti scrawled in the restrooms; world-class dance, music, and design classes and students. As the swimming pool was clothing optional, it'd be the first place to look if you needed a security guard.

Bill: Most of the animators say that they learned more from each other than from the faculty. How long did you stay at CalArts? And how did you develop and change during that time?

Henry: I had some great teachers for the two years I was at CalArts. In experimental, Jules exposed me to international filmmakers like Jan Svankmajer, Jiri Trnka, and Raoul Servais, and his incredibly good taste helped push my work to be better. Disney animator Moe Gollub taught under Jules and really helped me with some tough animal drawings for a film I was making. In character animation, I learned layout and perspective from Disney master Kendall O'Connor; design from Bill Moore; life drawing with Elmer Plummer; and caricature with T. Hee. And I took classes outside the animation programs from the likes of director Sandy McKendrick (*Sweet Smell of Success*) and lighting teacher Kris Malkiewicz. There were lectures by Maurice Noble, Chuck Jones, June Foray, Bill Littlejohn, and Bill Melendez. I got to meet Grim Natwick and John Hubley. And while all art schools have their share of poseurs and frauds, the overall community at CalArts was wonderful. If you needed music for your film, you could hire some of the best musicians in the world—guys that played with Frank Zappa—for a case of beer.

Bill: **Did you make films for both the character animation and experimental film programs?**

Henry: For character, I mainly did storyboards under Jack Hannah, no finished animation. In experimental, I did a lot of tests and completed one seven-minute film called *Phases* and started a second film, *Seepage*, my first feature stop-motion. I completed that film when I won a grant from the AFI/National Endowment while working at Disney. *Seepage*, using drawings and color, was about an individual whose inner self emerges to battle him as the two transform from one animal to another. In the end, they basically shake hands and merge back together. That was shown at many festivals, won a lot of awards, and was a finalist in the Student Academy Awards.

Seepage, 1992.

Bill: Your CalArts path seems very ironic. You start out with this independent drive, yet you also commit to the more conventional Disney character program.

Henry: I was really clueless about making a living. I never had a master plan; I just wanted to learn all I could. I did have this crazy idea that you could make short films and somehow people would pay you enough to make a living doing that. There was a film that had come out that was hugely successful. Was it Frank Mouris?

Bill: Yeah, Frank Mouris' *Frank Film*.

Henry: Yep, and no one told me how rare that kind of success was or that if you wanted to survive doing animated shorts, you needed to go work at the Canadian Film Board or become a teacher or become a master grant writer. Anyway, after my first year at CalArts, I went looking for a summer job. I failed the inbetweener test at Hanna-Barbera; too slow. Then I went over to Disney and met Eric Larson, one of the nine old men and the guy in charge of trainee animators. Because of the connection between Disney and CalArts, Eric gave me (and John Musker) a job. I spent the summer pretty much doing my own stuff with his amused input.

I returned to CalArts and, after graduating a year later, I went straight back to Disney. But this wasn't like my summer where Mr. Larsen had indulged my personal taste; now I had to deliver Disney-style character animation. And the other people in my group, like Bill Kroyer, John Musker, Brad Bird, and Jerry Rees, were light years ahead of me. Maybe I'd been enjoying *New Yorker* cartoons for too many years, but my sense of humor and character and storytelling just wasn't Disney. My first test was awful and I wasn't sure I'd survive. Good old Eric Larson saved my life, spending extra time with me, convincing me to use a Disney character and not one of my own, saying things like, "That might be humorous in a single frame, but it wouldn't work in one of our films." Under his guidance, I animated Mr. Toad shaving himself in the mirror and came out the other side of the process with a job.

Eric Larson at desk Left: Lorna Pomeroy, Heidi Guedel, Bill Kroyer, Dan Haskett (floor), Emily Jiuliano, Henry Selick, unknown. © Disney.

Bill: I have a really good photo of you and me from that time. It looks like you were really happy. How did you get assigned to *Pete's Dragon*?

Henry: They needed help with inbetweening, so I and some other animator trainees were tested. I could swear Brad Bird and John Musker purposely did poorly, but I passed. Anyway, my animation training was interrupted for a few months while I worked under Dale Oliver, one of the great animation assistants and a glider pilot in World War II.

Bill: How long were you at Disney?

Henry: About four years. The young talent there was phenomenal: Glen Keane, who could draw like Michelangelo, Ron Clements, John Pomeroy, Andy Gaskill. That's where I became friends with Tim Burton and Rick Heinrichs, and Joe Ranft. Frank and Ollie were still working there full-time, as was Woolie Reitherman, and both Marc Davis and Milt Kahl came around. Eric Larson remained my chief mentor; he was someone that I would continually go back to for feedback and suggestions. He taught me how to convey my ideas more clearly in my work and about staging and timing. Glen Keane deserves a lot of credit for my progress as well; it was while training under him that I became a full animator. I loved how he would rough things out with a thick pencil. It was really different from Don Bluth, who wanted us to draw with precision and leave very little room for cleanup.

Bill: What was it like working with Bluth?

Henry: Don was an impressive talent when I first met him, someone with a connection to Disney's past, having worked on *Sleeping Beauty*. And he was the heir-apparent, the guy who was going to lead the new generation at Disney. I never understood why he was working on another film at home, enlisting other Disney talent at night, when it was all going to be his candy store. And I still don't quite understand why he left Disney other than wanting his own name to be featured versus Walt's. Many of my roomies, including Brad Bird, Bill Kroyer, Musker, Jerry Rees, and the super-talented but reluctant Dan Haskett, had serious issues with Don—his directing style, story sense, leadership. I'll admit that when he called us a "Rat's Nest," I did challenge the guy.

"The Rat's Nest" – Henry Selick, Bill Kroyer, Jerry Rees, Brad Bird, and John Musker. ("Rat's Nest" is not a studio term.)

Bill: Was there a specific opportunity that led you away from Disney? Or did you feel it was just time to find something else?

Henry: We came to Disney from CalArts full of excitement and a desire to do great things. But that just wasn't going to happen, even when Don left the studio. The old guard was almost gone and the people now in charge were basically survivors. They might not all be A-list players but it was their studio now. Brad Bird got fired for simply talking like he knew more than one of the directors. Well, he did know more. But they were not going to take that from a twenty-year-old.

In 1981, an opportunity came my way through Jules Engel. A cutout animated feature was being made near San Francisco, with George Lucas as executive producer. It was called *Twice Upon a Time*, had a budget of about two million dollars, and was being directed by John Korty and Chuck Swenson. Compared with Disney at the time, it was a breath of fresh air. There was this Jay Ward kind of humor, with a lot of the dialogue improvised by local comedians. The completed scenes they showed me, featuring the work of Harley Jessup and Carl Willat, were really beautiful. So, I did an animation test for them, passed, and me and my wife Heather, who became a background designer on the film, moved up to the Bay Area. We fell in love with the region and it's been our home base ever since.

Bill: Were you just an animator on *Twice Upon a Time*?

Henry: I started as an animator, then did some background designs, and ended up storyboarding and directing a couple of sequences. My final credit was sequence director.

Bill: Did you do any designs?

Henry: My storyboards were copied pretty exactly, but I was following a style set by John Korty and his art directors. Man, Disney seemed like a country club in comparison to that low-budget show. We were shooting in this converted, three-story house, and if you were on one of the down-shooters pushing cutouts around, you pretty much lived there till your shot was done. It might last two or three days, just bathroom breaks and lots of coffee.

Bill: As a sequence director, were you applying things you learned from Eric Larson, in terms of storyboarding and storytelling? Or did you learn a lot about that during filmmaking?

Henry: I built on what I'd learned from Eric and CalArts and from doing my indie film *Seepage*. When I was being considered for *Twice Upon a Time*, they looked at both my Disney pencil tests and my indie films. It was the indie films that got me the job of sequence director. And I kept on learning during the making of *Twice*.

Bill: Stop motion can be quite different from hand-drawn or CG animation. There isn't the freedom to go back and simply correct scenes. How do you cope with that?

Henry: You have to learn to live with that. Some shots are going to be better than others; all shots are imperfect. You do your best to get good poses and timing in the story reels, shoot a rough rehearsal, and then hope that a great animator performing through one of these puppets in straight-ahead animation delivers something special. We do have the ability to pull frames in post or even create digital inbetweens to slow something down, but it's done very rarely.

Bill: What happened after *Twice Upon a Time*?

Henry: In '83, I got a gig doing storyboards and design for several effects sequences for Walter Murch, the amazing editor and sound designer. He was directing his first feature film, *Return to Oz*, for Disney with producer Gary Kurtz from the first Star Wars features. I got the job through Brad Bird and Jerry Rees, who were trying to get an animated feature, *The Spirit*, based on Will Eisner's comics, going, also with Kurtz. Anyway, I boarded all the Nome King sequences, which were animated in Claymation by Will Vinton's folks in Portland. It was great working with Walter, one of the best editors in the world. He wanted every possible version of a scene.

Bill: Like an editor!

Henry: Yes! He told me it was my job to make perfect "teacups." And it was his job to come in and smash them so that I could make another. I quickly got used to the idea that nothing is precious. And I learned a lot from Walter, still about the smartest guy I know. Afterwards, I worked on a laser disk game for Brad and Jerry as well as some ideas for an anthology show they wanted to do. And I started writing, starting work on a screenplay of my own.

In '86, I was intro'd to director Carroll Ballard (*The Black Stallion*, *Fly Away Home*) via producer Tom Wilhite, former head of production at Disney. Back at Disney, Tom, along with then–head of development Julie Hickson, had given Tim Burton the support to make both *Vincent* and the original *Frankenweenie*. Now, Tom had teamed Carroll with children's author Maurice Sendak to shoot a film of the *Nutcracker Ballet* that Maurice had designed in Seattle. Initially, I was brought in to storyboard the movie but Carroll liked my eye, so he had me shooting some seconds unit as well. I was shooting handheld with this unusual French camera of his, where when you adjusted the eyepiece the entire image would rotate. I remember shooting from the top of a ladder, praying I didn't drop the camera on these poor dancer kids! Additionally, I did some miniatures work. Carroll Ballard is another great filmmaker I learned firsthand from.

Bill: Is there anything specific you learned from Carroll?

Henry: He taught me a huge amount about lighting, about composition, about following and anticipating action with a camera. In my storyboarding work—where I was trying to find shots to capture the dancers at their best—he taught me about focusing on simple patterns of movement and not trying to show everything. Sometimes he'd have me stay up all night reworking a sequence I'd boarded to come up with simpler ways of staging things. The budget of the film was low and Carroll, the guy who wants to shoot a thousand-to-one ratio, was relying on the boards to help narrow his focus.

Bill: But I recall Eric Larson was always staging the shot to convey its emotion. Working as a painter you naturally think about lighting. So you didn't immediately apply that skill while working with Carroll?

Henry: While I'd lit the stop-motion figures in my short film with practical lights, most of the lighting I'd done was created with paint and pencils. Using real lights on real people was very different … Carroll must have thought I was an idiot and I had to learn fast.

Bill: Did you continue working with him, or did you move on to something else?

Henry: Carroll doesn't make a lot of movies. So when *Nutcracker* was finished, I moved on to other things. I worked on a lot of commercials. And I kept writing. My wife, Heather, was more continuously employed than I was.

Bill: Was she at Colossal?

Henry: Yeah, she was at Colossal Pictures in San Francisco, which started out as a very small studio. Then they became the top animation commercial house in the country, maybe the world. They were very innovative and explored a lot of different styles in commercials, special effects, and music videos.

Bill: She eventually became an executive producer, right?

Henry: After it split into two divisions, she ran the animation division. They were doing live action and trying to do a CD magazine at the time. Basically her division paid for everything else.

Bill: Didn't you do Doughboy commercials?

Henry: Yeah, I did. Nine in one season, 1989. I also directed some Ritz Bits stop-motion commercials that played forever on TV.

Bill: Was this your first stop-motion project after working with Caroll Ballard and doing cutout animation on *Twice Upon a Time*?

Henry: Yep. Then, almost simultaneously, I started to do a lot of work for MTV through my own company. I was doing design and direction, boarding things out myself, some of the lighting and animation. There were a lot of young people around who'd come out to work on Art Clokey's new *Gumby* series. I met a lot of great stop-motion animators via that show: Tim Hittle, Trey Thomas, Eric Leighton, Angie Glocka, Owen Klatte. I also started working with Pete Kozachik, who became the Director of Photography on three of the feature films I've directed. From the late eighties to the early nineties there was a burst of stop-motion projects, and the number of people I was working with kept growing and growing. When Tim Burton revived Tim Burton's *The Nightmare Before Christmas*, a lot of them became supervisors. This made the transition from small group to feature movie much easier.

Dollhouse MTV Ident, 1989 © MTV.

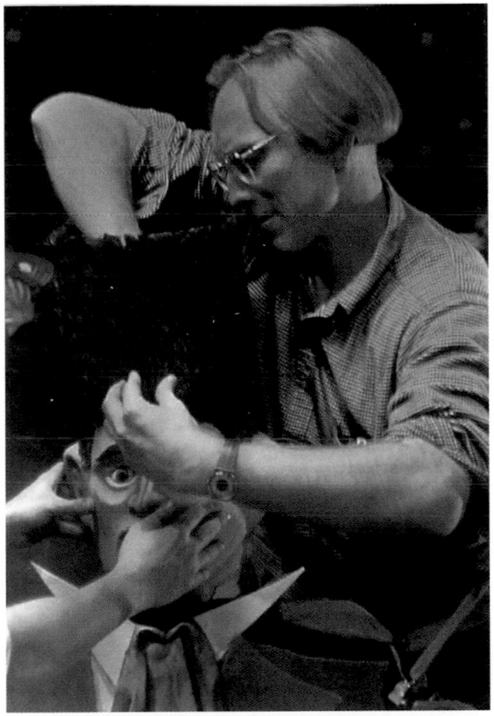

Henry Selick, *Taco M MTV Ident*, 1988 © MTV.

Bill: I visited you during the Doughboy commercials, and you had dozens of Doughboy heads lined up on shelves. I didn't know anything about stop motion; I couldn't imagine you'd use a different head for every frame! How did someone with no experience learn the genre? Who was teaching all these techniques for stop motion?

Henry: You'd study the films and commercials that existed, listen to people like Phil Tippet and Tom St. Amand, who had done stop motion for George Lucas. But there really weren't any teachers at the time.

Bill: What about the head-swapping concept? Was everybody doing that? Or did you just come up with that?

Henry: No, I didn't invent that. George Pal, a director known for his live-action films (the original *Time Machine*), was an animator first (*Jasper, Tubby the Tuba*) and is generally given credit for that. Back in the 1940s he came up with the idea of doing full-body replacements for a walk cycle, to give his puppets the same stretch and squash that Disney or Warner's was doing in drawn animation. He was creative director on the Speedy Alka-Seltzer commercials of the 1950s, where each of Speedy's mouth shapes was a new face. When we got the Doughboy spots, we got this kit from the ad agency that was under lock and key. When you opened it, you saw the original Doughboy body with no more than eight separate heads. The body reeked of some toxic substance, not the foam latex we normally used. I'm sure it gave somebody cancer!

Bill: They actually used that model for previous spots?

Henry: Yes, they did. We had to redesign and expand on the Doughboy, however, and completely rebuilt him. I was trying to bring in some stuff I'd learned at Disney, with extendable arms and legs, and we eventually sculpted about twenty-five more expressions. I was always trying to use things I learned at Disney. Funny, I just remembered this art class I used to take in Burbank. It was a night class and a few of us from Disney went there for life drawing. The teacher was this crazy guy …

Bill: The one they called Juicy Harvey?

Henry: His name was Harvey and there was a juice stand in town called *Juicy Harvey's*, so yeah, that was his nickname. He was a good teacher, full of enthusiasm, always saying, "You have to touch the model. Touching, touching, touching, touching, touching." It was a bunch of cool old ladies along with Tim Burton, John Musker, and a few other animators. That's when Tim and I first became friends. He was still going to CalArts. I also became close with Rick Heinrichs at the time, now a famous production designer, who was a CalArts graduate and the first person to take Tim's drawings and sculpt them as 3D beings. Ten years later, Tim had become very successful in live action, and I was doing more and more stop motion up north. That's when he sent Rick up to the Bay Area to ask me if I'd like to direct.

Bill: How did you set it up? Did you simply use your existing crew?

Henry: Yeah, my existing San Francisco crew became the core of the feature crew. As Peter Schneider of Disney explained to me, the film was a low budget gift to Tim from Disney in order to get him back to the studio. They wanted blockbusters, like Tim's *Batman*. So they didn't really care too much about the movie as long as we kept on budget and schedule. With Tim as *Nightmare*'s godfather, there were no studio notes to deal with, no politics; we could put all of our efforts on screen. So, while Tim directed *Batman Returns* and *Ed Wood* in Los Angeles, my crew and I spent three and a half years making *Nightmare* in San Francisco.

Bill: Those were all happening while you're making *Nightmare*?

Henry: Yeah. Tim managed to review all our story reels and animation. I think we only had to reshoot one or two shots in the film.

Bill: What did you get to start the picture? A storyboard? A script?

Henry: There was an original script by Michael McDowell, who had written *Beetlejuice*. And we had Tim's original designs of Jack Skellington, Zero, and Sandy Claws, which Rick had sculpted years earlier. But Tim didn't love Michael's script and so it was rejected. Yet we still had a deadline for delivery!

Bill: Where exactly did you start?

Henry: The one thing about doing musicals (*Nightmare* has ten songs) is that the songs are little stories in and of themselves. And Danny Elfman, meeting with Tim, had come up with two or three songs already. "What's This?" was the first, so we just started boarding it. It was clear Danny, with Tim's input, was going to come up with a song for each big moment in the movie that would pretty much tell the film's story. And we could certainly board those songs and bring them to life in animation. But how to coherently string the songs together? Screenwriter Caroline Thompson was brought in.

Bill: Did she write the story?

Henry: The core of the story was already there, but Caroline did a marvelous job of joining the songs together and expanding the characters. And she was wise enough to keep several of Michael McDowell's original ideas, like when Sally jumps out of a window, breaks apart, and then stitches herself back together.

Bill: When did you get started with the boards?

Henry: Because of our deadline, we jumped right in and started boarding the first few songs, despite there not being an approved script. I had Joe Ranft as head of story and talented board artists like Jorgen Klubien and Mike Cachuela.

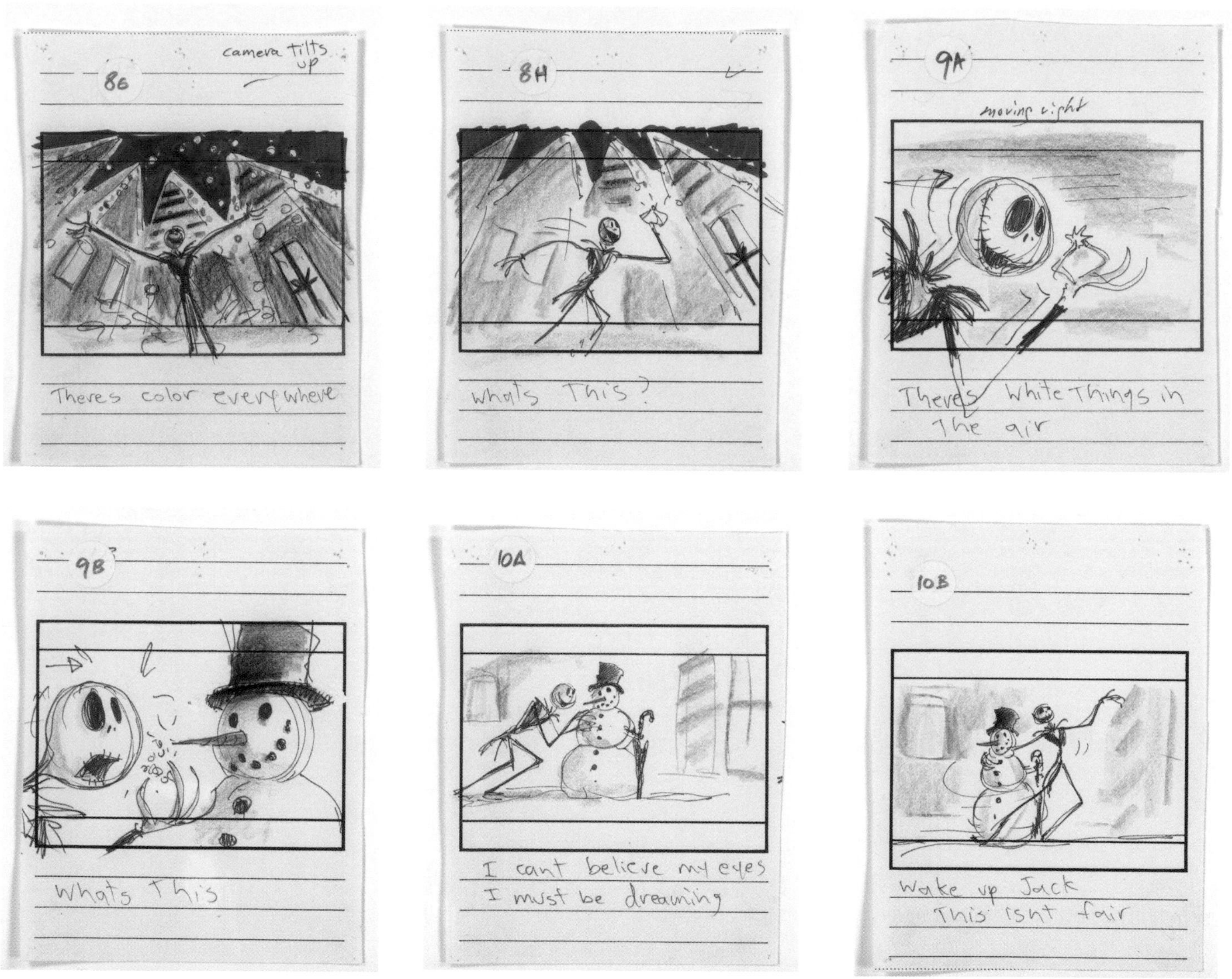

Storyboards, Joe Ranft,
Tim Burton's *The Nightmare Before Christmas*, 1993 © Touchstone.

Bill: I assume Tim was looking at the reels and giving you notes before you started animating.

Henry: Yeah, luckily he was very positive and had very few notes for us. We had a ton of other work to do at the same time, like making all the puppets, sculpting their different expressions, figuring out at least a couple of sets to build, cast voice actors and record them. And so much designing to do! Art director Dean Taylor and artists Kelly Asbury and Kendall Cronkhite gathered Tim's collection of other characters. We looked at anyone that had influenced him, like Edward Gorey, Charles Adams, and Ronald Searle. New characters often came from the storyboard drawings, like Joe Ranft's sweet little corpse boy and Mike Cachuela's wolfman.

"What's This?," the first song Danny had written, was the first thing we animated. It was set in Christmas Town, so we gave that location a soft, Dr. Seuss feel. And all those shots got finished without a hitch. When we got to the first shot in Halloween Town, however, Tim put on the brakes. It wasn't dark enough. There were too many colors. That's when Rick Heinrichs came in to consult as a production designer. He was brilliant, and we learned a lot from him about textures with a 2D and 3D feel.

And I still remember working on the final battle between Oogie Boogie and Jack. It was just down to me and Mike C. Everyone else had been let go from the story department, and Joe had moved on to *Toy Story*. Tim wouldn't approve anything we drew. But at a certain point I knew we had to go into production or miss our deadline. So I just put the sequence into production.

Bill: Was that the only friction you had with Tim on *Nightmare*?

Henry: I'd come up with a slightly different ending. When I tried to show Tim the story reel, he just put the flatbed machine on high speed. I said, "You don't want to see this?" He got angry and walked out of the room. Then he kicked a hole in the wall. I said, "Tim, you okay?" He pointed to his boots, said, "Yeah, they're steel toes."

Bill: He just didn't like the idea. That's his way of showing you.

Henry: Ninety-nine percent of the time, things were great with Tim and me. There were a few things we'd filmed that he wasn't in love with, like when Santa goes to set things right and gives one of the kids a puppy and takes back Jack's toy from hell. But when he screened it for his friends, they liked it, so it stayed in.

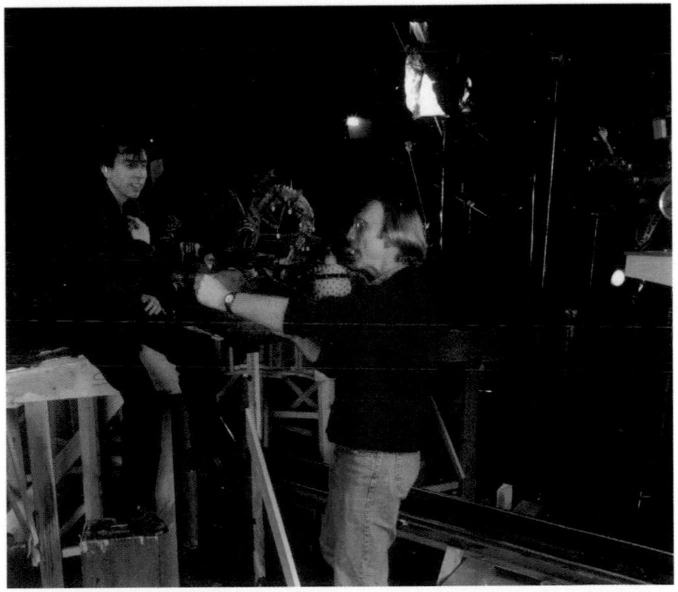

Tim Burton and Henry Selick
Tim Burton's *The Nightmare Before Christmas*, 1993 © Disney.

Bill: When that movie was released, it was a huge success, right?

Henry: *Huge* is a relative term; it came out and made double its cost right away.

Bill: How does that affect your life? What were you doing right after the movie? Were you looking for the next project? Did Tim offer you another job?

Henry: Yeah, my life changed a bit. I met with Steven Spielberg and was offered a live-action film, *Casper the Friendly Ghost*. But when I offered my notes on the script, I was told they weren't interested in my notes, "this is already a green-lit movie." The thing is, I loved stop motion and had already begun thinking of doing *James and the Giant Peach*, one of my and Joe Ranft's favorite Roald Dahl books. We met with Dahl's family, who were in charge of his estate. They came over to visit near the end of *Nightmare Before Christmas* and liked what they saw.

Bill: Did Spielberg's people ever look at your notes?

Henry: Who knows? They might not have been that good. Anyway, there were different opportunities post-*Nightmare* but *James and the Giant Peach* was the choice I made. It was also about keeping the studio we'd set up going.

Bill: Who was financing you?

Henry: Initially it was all Disney, and then the wonderful Jake Ebert came in with co-financing. He'd made remarkable films like *Chariots of Fire*, *Gandhi*, and *Baron Munchausen*.

Bill: Tim was attached to *Peach*?

Henry: Yeah, I asked Tim to produce again along with his business partner, Denise Di Novi. But, because he had no personal interest in *Peach*, he didn't protect the project. There was conflict between Disney live action and Disney animation over the film, and I ended up being stuck with a really angry studio executive who's only about power. He was the kind of guy who throws leftover tuna fish at his assistant. Amazing!

James and the Giant Peach, 1996. © 1996 Disney.

Bill: That says a lot.

Henry: The guy had no respect for our process. Brian Rosen, our line producer, and I'd give him a story reel to review, "We need to hear back on this by this date. After that it starts to cost money." And he always made sure to miss the date, then scream that it couldn't cost any more money.

Bill: And you were essentially in the same facility with the same crew, right?

Henry: Yeah, managed to hold on to most everything and get most everybody back when we finally went into production. Unlike *Nightmare*, where we had to start shooting and figure it out on the way, *James* was developed more traditionally, with many writers and many drafts of the script. By the way, Dennis Potter, the brilliant British TV writer, wrote the first draft but the Dahl family rejected it, as it strayed too far from the book. Anyway, we lost a lot of time and money in this process. And our Disney exec, from live action, didn't understand that the shooting script in animation is the story reels. That's where the real writing happens. No matter how good that initial script is, it becomes something else.

Andrew Birch and Henry Selick, *James and the Giant Peach*, 1996. © Disney.

Bill: One aspect of directing is studio politics.

Henry: Oh, I'm terrible at it.

Bill: You're an artist. But you have to deal with politics.

Henry: I've watched experts like Tim and my friend David Fincher deal with studio execs. Tim would never answer their questions directly; he'd become a warm, crazy, gesticulating artist and would always make them feel good without ever addressing their concerns. Fincher is more the manipulative, brilliant politician. He knows how to both terrify executives and to match their alarm with the same level so that it cancels out. Me, I'm not good at either approach.

Bill: When *Peach* was wrapping up, were you offered a multipicture deal?

Henry: [laughs, shaking head] Pixar's *Toy Story* came out between *Nightmare* and *James*, and the world of animation changed forever. Dick Cook (Disney head of production) told me stop motion just wasn't viable anymore. So, no, there was no multipicture deal.

Bill: What did you do?

Henry: I struggled a bit; did a few more commercials. Then a graphic novel, *Dark Town*, showed up, by a Canadian writer, Kaja Blackley. I liked the look and the story, about a puppeteer in a coma whose spirit lives as a puppet with a sidekick in the land between life and death. Eventually I hooked up with this writer, Sam Hamm, who had written *Batman*. He was also a Bay Area guy. We changed the puppeteer into a cartoonist, made his sidekick a cartoon monkey, and renamed the project *Monkeybone*, because *Dark Town* is a racist slang term.

We met with Bay Area–based producer/director Chris Columbus (*Home Alone*, *Harry Potter*), and, with his help, set the project up at 20th Century Fox with Bill Mechanic. The film was intended to be low budget (for a studio picture), with about 75 percent of it done in edgy animation. We were going to do the whole project in the Bay Area, give it an independent feel. But then the live action was moved to Hollywood and things started to transform. I met with Ben Stiller for the lead role, right after *There's Something About Mary*. He wanted to bring in a writer because the script wasn't funny enough. He was right. But my friend, Sam Hamm, was upset because I wasn't supporting him enough. But I can't alienate Ben Stiller either, because if he walks there's no movie. I stupidly chose friendship and we had no movie.

Monkeybone, 2001 © Twentieth Century Fox. All Rights Reserved.

Bill: **But you did solve the live-action problem.**

Henry: We ended up with Brendan Frasier. He seemed to understand the material and had just been in a great movie, *Gods and Monsters*. Once Brendan was cast, my "indie" movie changed again. They wanted way more live action, less animation. They were paying Brendan his full rate so they wanted him in the whole movie. I couldn't afford to composite him into a lot of animation, so everything that was meant to be miniatures and animation shifted to sets and lots of actors and costumes.

An animation director is a nobody in live-action Hollywood. They're a tight group and they're going to test you every hour of every day you're shooting. You have to be very macho and ultraconfident in your decisions, many made on the spot, because you'll have to live with them forever. Not like animation, where's there's always more time to think things through. I had a wonderful production designer, Bill Boes, who'd come from animation, and I really liked my DP, Andrew Dunn, and the top camera operator, Mitch Dubin. I mean, if you get through any project and you're still standing, you'll have made some friends.

Live action finally wrapped and I headed back to the Bay Area to shoot the animation. The Monkeybone character was probably the most complex and interactive stop-motion that had ever been done. Pete Kozachik, the animation DP, was instrumental in figuring out how to make it all work. We built a waist-up blue robot version of Brendan Fraser and matched its moves with the real Brendan's moves so our puppets had something real to interact with. It was fun. I was back in my world. Unfortunately, our champion at Fox, Bill Mechanic, was forced out by Rupert Murdock. The film was recut to pieces, and then it was dumped with no advertising. We got stellar reviews in the *New York Times*, the *LA Times*, and *Entertainment Weekly*, but, with no advertising, *Monkeybone* did terribly at the box office. It's not a great movie, but the stop-motion animation on that film might be the best or among the best that's ever been done.

Bill: **Who did the actual animation?**

Henry: Folks I'd always worked with: animators included Paul Berry, red-haired genius from England, Trey Thomas, Anthony Scott, Tim Hittle, and a few others. Puppet fabrication by Bonita DeCarlo and puppet sculpt by Damon Bard.

Bill: **What happened after *Monkeybone*?**

Henry: Well, it'd been an interesting ride so far. Now, it was like I'd gone off a cliff. I was in "director's jail." When your film bombs, you go to an imaginary jail—unless you're Andrew Stanton after *John Carter*—and sometimes you never get out. The best thing that happened near the end of *Monkeybone* was that I met author Neil Gaiman. I knew the *Sandman* comic books he'd written. Neil sent me the pages of his novella, *Coraline*. It wasn't even finished. It was something he had been working on as a side project for years. And he thought it might work as a stop-motion film. I read the pages the day I got them and knew he was right. It was a fantastic story about a girl who discovers another version of her own life where copies of her real mother and father existed, only with buttons for eyes. I took it to Bill Mechanic, who'd set up his own production company after his troubles at Fox over *Fight Club*. I convinced both Bill and Neil to let me write the script. In the end, it took five years to get a studio to back the project.

The Life Aquatic with Steve Zissou, 2004. © 2004 Touchstone Pictures.

Bill: Five years? During that time, were you just writing?

Henry: No, no, no. I probably spent a solid year writing several drafts, but no one would back the movie even if it was done in live action. Then Wes Anderson called and wanted me to do stop-motion sea creatures for his feature *The Life Aquatic with Steve Zissou*. That was a very good gig; in many ways it kept me going. I also got to spend time with Wes and see how he worked. He's got one of the best eyes in the business and I actually learned a lot from him.

Aside from *Life Aquatic*, it was the toughest period of my professional life. I had a great project in *Coraline* but I was coming off of a failed film. I still wanted to do stop-motion features but nobody believed in that anymore. Then there was the tone of *Coraline*—everyone thought it was too scary for kids, yet not scary enough for adults. It took Bill Mechanic announcing we were developing the movie to get a publisher to publish the book.

Bill: I always pointed out the animation in *Life Aquatic*.

Henry: Thanks, I'm proud of that work. One of the great moments of my life was when Ray Harryhausen came to visit our stage. We had just completed the jaguar shark, a huge puppet, seven feet long, that required mechanical model movers for its core swimming motion. The rest of its movements were all hand animated. Ray actually started to cry, he was so happy to see a stop-motion creature being used in live action.

Bill: Were you using motion-control cameras for that as well?

Henry: Oh yeah. We were using basic motion-control equipment as far back as the Pillsbury Doughboy days. Then on *Nightmare*, we went wild. Our DP, Pete Kozachik, with his ILM background, designed several boom cameras. He knew how to build stuff that was cheap and repeatable. On *Life Aquatic*, our DP was Pat Sweeny, and we actually shot everything at the old, predigital ILM. Martin Meunier built all the puppets, and Justin Kohn and Tim Hittle were the main animators. There was even a creature that could turn itself inside out, but that didn't make it into the film.

Bill: During this time were you writing, boarding, and designing *Coraline* all by yourself?

Henry: Yeah. There was no money for anything else. For the first two years I had to pretend it wasn't animation, because Bill had a deal that Disney would distribute his films as long as he didn't make any animated movies. I did meet with Michelle Pfeiffer, potentially the lead actress. But she said, "I don't know about those buttons." And I did meet Dakota Fanning, who was only nine. She was too young at the time, but a connection was made. When things finally got going, she was basically the right age and the right voice.

Bill: How'd this come about then? Suddenly it's on the market?

Henry: My rep, Ellen Goldsmith-Vein, came to me when my career was in the worst place possible. She said, "Henry, I love your work. I think I can make things happen and I'll stick with you." She told me that Phil Knight had been supporting the Vinton Company over the last few years and that he had basically taken over. They wanted to do a CG short film called *Moongirl* and they needed a director. They had a basic premise about a girl who controls the moon. So I grew their premise into a story, pitched it to them, and was invited to direct the short. I said I'd only come up if I could develop a feature: *Coraline*. They agreed, though they weren't actually serious at the time. Regardless, I said yes and commuted for a while from the Bay Area. Eventually my family moved with me to Oregon. The CG on *Moongirl* wasn't easy. While there'd been some CG on *James*, I had a learning curve and the crew I was working with was pretty inexperienced.

Bill: How did you manage?

Henry: We muddled along and the short turned out okay. And in the meantime, I kept pushing *Coraline*. I was also curious as to why Phil Knight was interested in animation. Turned out his son, Travis, is a world-class animator, both CG and stop motion, and the formerly known as Vinton Studio was going to be *his* studio. I basically got Travis' support on *Coraline* and things started coming together. Even then, it was still tough. Laika, as the company was renamed, was developing a more traditional CG feature, *Jack and Ben*, and that was consuming everyone's attention. Finally, Phil told me, "If you can find a distributor for *Coraline*, we'll make the movie." So I went out and found a distributor.

Bill: Just like that? You went out and found a distributor.

Henry: Yes. Although I don't think he expected that I would. *Coraline* was seen as the dark, weird project at Laika, whereas *Jack and Ben* was going to be their sunny Dreamworks-type film.

Bill: How did you find a distributor?

Henry: I was relentless, and I had some luck. I just happened to meet this mid-level exec, Michael Zoumas, on his last day of working for the Weinsteins. He loved *Coraline* and introduced me to Andrew Rona, an exec at Focus Features. Andrew took the project to the top, to James Schamus, and we had our distributor. Phil kept his word and we started the film. The irony is that *Coraline,* Laika's dark-horse project, was the film that got made, whereas the way-more-commercial *Jack and Ben* got shelved.

Coraline, 2009 © Laika.

Bill: *Coraline* was one of the most deluxe stop-motion setups ever. As the underdog film at the studio, how did you manage to create your dream set? Why did they even let you?

Henry: So there had been talk about whether we should use CG, stop motion, or both on *Coraline*. Ultimately, Travis Knight said he wanted to be an animator on this, and he liked stop motion better.

Bill: That's like Spielberg's son saying, "I don't like that movie." So the movie dies.

Henry: Just the CG version died. Since it was going to be stop motion, we needed space for all those sets. We found a huge, industrial building out in Hillsboro, fifteen miles from Portland. Thing is, you don't really *want* a place that's too big because your production will grow to fill it, and it'll cost more. On the one hand, Laika was inexperienced at making movies and we had a lot of growing pains. We worked our butts off but I couldn't say the studio was a well-oiled machine.

On the other hand, I got incredible artistic support from that company. At various times, Focus and Bill Mechanic would freak out about things in the movie. You know how it is. When the latest Harry Potter came out, they'd say, "You have to make it scarier, like that new Harry Potter film." But then a Pixar film would come out and now it was, "*Coraline*'s way too scary. What are you doing?" But Laika never wavered—as long as the ratings board gave us a PG, they were cool with what I was making. Crew-wise, I had an exceptional group of leaders to carry along the inexperienced first-timers. People like lead animators Eric Leighton, Trey Thomas, Brad Schiff, Phil Dale, and Travis; Georgina Haynes and Martin Meunier in puppet fab; Mike Cachuela and Chris Butler in story; Pete Kozachik and company in lighting and camera; Bo Henry and Tom Proust in sets; and on and on.

Bill: I suppose your process at this point amounted to everything you'd ever learned.

Henry: Exactly! And there was also new technology at our fingertips. Martin Meunier and I had seen one of the world's first 3D printers (rapid prototype machines) at Steve Perlman's company in San Francisco. We realized we could use it to print some of the replacement faces for our characters; we didn't have to hand sculpt every single one. So we started sculpting keys and scanning them into the computer.

Bill: Did you inbetween it as well?

Henry: Yeah, we did. Then we'd print them out, paint them, and put them in facial kits. We decided to split the faces horizontally to have separate replacement brows and mouth shapes, giving us thousands of facial expression possibilities. I'd wanted to leave the seam line in the final movie, but it made Phil Knight nervous so we painted it out in post. And we were the first stop-motion feature shot stereoscopically, something I'd wanted to do for years. For what it's worth, *Coraline* actually beat out *Avatar* for best 3D movie of 2009 according to the 3D Film Society.

Pete Kozachik designed new motion-controlled camera rigs that could do anything. Then, after a falling out with the production designer, I grabbed some set builders and quickly deputized them as art directors. I ended up supervising them, too. It was wild. It was bigger than *Nightmare*. There were a lot more shots, more complexities, and more subtleties in it than we'd ever done before.

Bill: So this was purely a Henry Selick film?

Henry: Yeah, and it's gratifying that people came to see it.

Bill: Working digitally, how did *Coraline* change your process?

Henry: To explain that, let's go back to *Nightmare*. Back then, we were shooting on film and we tried to do everything we could in camera. For example, to put Jack Skellington's ghost dog, Zero, in a shot with Jack, we used a beam splitter—a half-silvered mirror—in front of the lens like in the old *Topper* movies. You'd shoot Jack *through* the semi-transparent mirror while its reflective surface is picking up Zero, who's being animated off to one side. The digital breakthrough on *Nightmare* was simple but significant: we now had video tapes on those old Mitchell 35s and could capture two whole frames of imagery! So if a puppet broke its ankle and fell over in the middle of the shot, you could fix the puppet, line it up with the captured image and not have to start the shot over again. Additionally, the falling snow at the end of the film was CG. On *James and the Giant Peach*, we started using digital cleanup in a big way, and went from hanging an airborne character on boingy spider wire, to attaching them to a precise, controllable rig. Shoot a clean plate and paint out the rig in post. And we created an entire CG ocean for *James*, as well as a giant mechanical shark that attacks the characters on the floating peach. By the time I got to make *Coraline*, my first stop-motion feature in years, it would have been easy to throw all sorts of CG and digital work in the mix. But I asked myself, "Why do stop motion at all, if it's going to buried in CG?" and decided to try and create as much of the imagery as possible with hand animation. That includes a lot of the effects like the other world tearing apart and atmosphere like wind and rain and fog and leaves and stars and fire. Because stop motion's greatest strength is that it's a world of real objects, captured with real light.

Bill: Did you manipulate the character performance in post?

Henry: There was one shot where we experimented with software that could create digital inbetweens. But it killed the look and feeling of stop motion. So, aside from pulling some frames here and there to adjust timing, we did zero manipulation in post. I'd say 98 percent of what you see on screen is the original performance we shot.

Bill: When you developed your characters, were you consolidating the concept first and then casting the voices?

Henry: Well, I lived with the project a long time before it got made. I had been rewriting it and doing sketches and kept a scrapbook with image ideas. There was a newspaper photo I found—an old lady, a former child star I'd never heard of, had just died. And there she was in her heyday, back in the 1920s, holding a little doll that was an exact copy of her. Early merchandise, I guess. That gave me the idea for the Coraline doll the Other Mother makes in the film. Yeah, I went pretty deep during this time, thinking about the characters: who they were, how they would move, how they would sound. I knew we had Dakota Fanning as our lead and her voice was always in my head. Then when we got closer to making the film, I cast the other voices around her.

The Mother—Real Mom and Fun Other Mother and Wicked Other Mother—was the next most important character, and I probably considered eighty or a hundred actresses. I didn't go to them, of course. I just took clips from movies and cut their voices against Dakota's. I ended up with about three finalists, all strong actors with great voices that worked well against Dakota. Terry Hatcher worked best and wanted to do the part. It's funny, Terry didn't resemble the character design when we hired her, but her performance and presence so influenced the animators that the final Mothers and Terry became one and the same.

Bill: **In animation you have multiple animators creating one performance with the character. In stop motion, when it comes to creating the character through poses, is it harder to keep the consistency of the character's performance?**

Henry: It's not so different than drawn or CG animation; the director works with a supervising animator, building a vocabulary of poses and the all-important walk that help define a character. I try to be specific if I've something in mind. For example, I wanted the Other Father to be fun and silly but move really well. So I told them "He moves just like Danny Kaye." The voice actors really influence this defining stage as well. For the same character, I told John Hodgman to channel Dean Martin. He ended up channeling Bing Crosby, but it was perfect.

Anyway, then the lead animators come on and you try to cast them on what they want to do and what you think they're good at (not always the same thing). You've given them a foundation and they add to that, so that when the full crew comes on there's a lot of material for them to refer to.

Now, I really like the great shapes you get with facial replacements. But an added benefit—which goes a long ways toward keeping consistency between animators—is that

Coraline, 2009 © Laika.

they're all working from the exact same library of faces. It's harder when the character has a mechanical face and every expression has to be hand animated.

Bill: Do stop-motion animators thumbnail all those poses, or do they …

Henry: They're all different. For example, I really discourage shooting live-action reference and then slavishly copying it. Might be because I hated having to use rotoscope on that Christmas special, *Small One*, back at Disney. But on *Coraline*, there was one animator, Ian Whitlock, who was unbelievably good at acting out his scenes. He *became* Coraline. So he'd record himself and match that in his animation and it worked out wonderfully. Other folks would do thumbnails right on their exposure sheets. We always met one on one when a shot was assigned. There'd be puppets to pose. I could do a sketch or act it out, whatever it took, you know? Then all the animators would shoot a rehearsal before going for the take. Some rehearsals were nearly perfect; others were miles away from where they needed to be. But then we'd make adjustments, notes would be taken, and the final take almost always worked out.

Bill: That's quite different from your Disney days.

Henry: Yep, way different.

Bill: The fact that it's manipulated models, real lighting, and real materials gives it a unique kind of energy on the screen. It obviously doesn't have the freedom of a hand drawing. You don't have that ability, as in CG, where you can go back in and find exactly what you want. What is it about the stop-motion medium that appeals to you?

Henry: Two main things. It's all real stuff: the puppets, the lights, the sets and props. There is nothing cooler than moving from one small stage to another, each containing a miniature world where a moment of the film is being created. The second, and equal, thing I like is the direct connection between animator and final on-screen performance. I sense their hands in the shot. I sense them coaxing, struggling, wrestling, as if they're invisible puppeteers. And I love that.

Bill: Is it also about the commitment involved? It's like jumping off a cliff. You summon up the requisite energy and just go with what happens.

Henry: I liken it to crossing a chasm on a tightrope. There's only one way to get to the other side—that's keep moving straight ahead. And we try to do it with style and in character.

Bill: Obviously you have digital options now. You can pretty much fix any kind of scene. But in the beginning, when you're planning something out, how detailed is your vision? You have these surreal sequences of things flying through the air, or a spider falling into its web. They defy gravity and space, and it was all done on a traditional set. Do you know every detail beforehand, or do you just figure it out as you go?

Henry: When I'm writing, I'm not only envisioning how something might look in the movie but even how we'll build it. And, because it took years for *Coraline* to get green-lit, my vision of the film was pretty evolved. Of course, when it comes time to turn your vision into a movie, there are a lot of changes and some things are more challenging than others. That spider web under the Other Mother's floor was monumental. I knew what I wanted, but it took Tom Proust, one of the art directors, to figure out where to get a solid plate of steel cut into an animatable spiral using ultra–high-pressure water. Then they had to rig it sixteen feet up in the air to give it enough travel room.

Bill: You are definitely the most complex hybrid of filmmaking styles. You have all the complexities of live action and animation.

Henry: Here's the deal with me and CG. I'm just not a person who wants to be in the dark. If you make a stop-motion film, you'd understand clearly. You're seeing the shots as you go. You're working with the sum of the parts right away. It's not wire frames, then more steps, and then it all comes together in the end. As in live action, you're seeing the world. I find that more gratifying.

Bill: What do you think will be the next advancement in stop motion?

Henry: There's an animator I've worked with, the talented Phil Beglan, who's come up with a great new way to do facial animation. I'd like to use that. And then there's always the specific challenges of a given film—that's often where innovations come from.

Bill: Do you think you could do a small film in stop motion and achieve the same success as a large feature like *Coraline*?

Henry: Yes, I do. We'd have to get more intimate. And our subject matter will need to be more powerful. Let's not remake the *Hurt Locker*, but, please, something with more weight than is usually allowed in animated features. Of course, there's always the *South Park* route, where super cheap, cute animation is combined with R-rated words and actions. It helps that the writing is brilliant on that show.

Bill: Is there something specific you look for in a story?

Henry: Having great characters, at least one, matters the most. And I suppose there's a fantasy element in everything I do. But I can imagine almost any story as an animated film. Honestly, before we made *Coraline*, most people could only imagine the book as live action. As I was writing the screenplay, it was so easy to see it as a stop-motion film.

One of the new projects I'm developing is an original story of mine about brothers; tonally, you could say it's "from the director of *Coraline*." There's another project based on a book, an epic journey over many years where one character remains constant while the world around him changes. That would be unique, something I have never seen in an animated film.

Bill: You seem to like the limitations inherent to stop motion. It must be a challenge for you.

Henry: I just don't see stop motion as being limited; there are always solutions to every problem we encounter.

Bill: You mentioned earlier that you were a musician in college. Has that experience helped in terms of selecting music and working with musicians?

Henry: Sure. During *Nightmare Before Christmas*, I wanted Danny Elfman to rework a section of the song, *Making Christmas*. He balked. So I wrote some material, recorded it on a keyboard, and cut it into his music. Upon hearing it, Danny said he, of course, could do better. And then he did. On *Coraline*, composer Bruno Coulais was a great collaborator with an easy give and take and lots of discussion. He even liked the song I wrote for the film *Sirens of the Sea* and did a nice orchestration of it.

Bill: People often generalize or even stereotype artists in our business. They say that people who animate in 2D and pencil are crazier because they have to generate so much. On the other hand, people who animate in 3D tend to be a little more reserved because they're more computer oriented. Is there some generalization about the kind of people who go into stop motion?

Henry: Stop-motion animators are more physical than the others. Remember, they're on their feet for days on end, wrestling a performance from a puppet with stiff metal joints. So they'd win in a bar fight. But they also have tender hearts and will give so much of themselves to will their puppet children to life. We're the kids who had the GI Joe clay and would spend hours sculpting and re-sculpting, pretending to bring it to life. That's something I should have mentioned when I talked about why stop motion appeals to me. There's this subconscious element that goes back to childhood. It's that moment when you had that special toy. Whether you could move it or not didn't make a difference. You *imagined* it moving. You gave it life. You connected with it.

Bill: I think that's a perfect place to stop. Thanks Henry. We truly appreciate this.

Henry: As I said in the beginning, I can waste a lot time talking about this stuff.

3

Don Bluth Interview

Don Bluth.

With some filmmakers, everything you need to know about them is on the screen. That's not the case with Don Bluth. His story is not just the films he made, but how he got them made and what that feat reveals about him.

While animators may be reclusive, directors must be expressive. Don could be described as "entrancing." From the very beginning he had a vocal eloquence and depth of commitment that made his pronouncements on the art and industry of animation seem like messages from a higher source. Don had a chance to work with the old masters at Disney and had the highest respect for their artistry. With that experience and his matchless work ethic, it is no wonder that many of the new generation of animators saw him as their mentor—and leader.

When Don left The Walt Disney Studios to start his own company, he did so for a simple reason: he wanted to make a kind of animated film that he believed was disappearing from the industry. He succeeded in making not one but ten feature films, a record unmatched by any of his contemporaries.

If there was ever a director who epitomized the glamour gulf between directing live action and animation, it is Don. Although he can work with the biggest stars, he spends more time "on the board" sitting at his animation desk than any director of his era. He really prefers the craft of shaping the movie under his pencil to roaming the departments.

Someone once said that the definition of an artist is one who cannot stop doing what he loves. Don Bluth loves to draw animated movies.

We interviewed Don by Skype from his home in Arizona.

Bill Kroyer

Bill: This book is about animation directors because I don't think people understand what an animation director does. We want to know how you came to be a director and what you eventually brought to this role. That's the essence of the book.

Don: Okay. Ask away.

Bill: When were you first aware of animation? When did you realize that you loved it?

Don: My first experience with animation was of course at a very young age. I think I was four years old when I first saw *Snow White*. So this was way back in the forties. It was frightening and at the same time absolutely gorgeous. I loved the story, the colors, the caricatured dwarves, and even the scary wicked witch. I wanted to see the picture again even after I left the theater. Those images stayed with me, and I remember wondering if I could reproduce the same thing myself at home. I began to draw the characters from memory and collected artwork from the movie. I also quickly learned the name Walt Disney. Anytime a movie came to town that said Walt Disney, I knew immediately that there was something there for me. After *Snow White* came *Pinocchio*, *Bambi*, and *Fantasia*. I became infatuated with this world of animation. I wanted to be part of making it, even as a child. But I knew my drawings didn't look as good as those on screen. I needed to improve. So from that moment up until high school I practiced over and over again. The funny thing is, I learned that you often come to hate a drawing that pleased you so much the previous day. Something happens inside your brain. Your understanding of the process increases. You go back and look at this drawing that was done twenty-four hours ago and say, "Ugh, that doesn't look good." Many artists go through the same thing. No matter how good I thought I was, there was always a way to get better. And that pushed me. I kept pushing to get to that next level.

Bill: **You put that great drawing on the fridge at the end of day. The next morning you think, "Oh, my God."**

Don: Exactly! Now, animation became an interesting thing because I didn't know how exactly they did it. But around my junior year of high school I met Judge Whitaker in Utah. He was teaching at the University (BYU) and had worked on many Disney films. That was the first time I had met someone from Disney. I learned by just watching him work. He would draw a little bit and then start flipping the paper and animating. At the moment it all came together. I remember thinking, "*Wow*! That's how they do it."

Bill: **You never saw anybody flip or even a set of pegs before that?**

Don: Nope. They weren't doing many documentaries at Disney at the time. I just saw the pictures. But at that point I knew what I had to do. So I went to various libraries and started collecting books that covered the principles of animation. Growing up on a farm, I think, limited my exposure in the beginning. I just didn't have access to information. Anyway, when I learned that The Walt Disney Studios was in Burbank, I coaxed my parents into sending me to visit my aunt, who just happened to live there. I then pushed her into getting me a tour of the studio. And I naively thought I would meet Walt Disney. As it turned out, my aunt actually knew people that worked at The Walt Disney Studios. She indeed arranged a tour. We had an appointment. I was so excited that I could hardly sleep. But my aunt wasn't good with directions or driving. We got lost. We never found the studio. She lived in Santa Monica and was just horrible with directions. But we did call again and arrange another appointment. This time we got a map and I made sure that we didn't get lost.

It was amazing. They gave me the royal treatment. There was a fellow named Bob Gibeaut (who eventually became VP of operations at the studio) and he personally took me around. I of course kept looking for "the man," but he was nowhere in sight. At the end of the tour, much to my surprise, Bob said, "I'm going to give you some things to take home." They had just finished production on *Peter Pan* and he got a whole stack of cels and put them in my hand. He said, "There you go. Now go back and dream on that." It was such an amazing experience. I couldn't sleep for several nights because it was just so thrilling. After that I only had one goal. I wanted to work there. Eventually my parents decided to sell our farm in

Utah and move to California. But when I graduated from Santa Monica High School in 1955, my parents insisted that I go to college. They sent me back to Utah, to BYU. But after one year I could hardly stand it. Finally I said, "You're wasting your money. I'm not studying and I can't think of anything else. Please, at least let me apply at Disney." This was early summer of 1956. So I called them and they told me to bring in a portfolio. Now, quite ignorantly, I actually asked what they meant by portfolio! They actually had to explain it to me, that I had to bring in a collection of my best artwork. Of course, if I had to ask, I didn't have one. I stayed up most of that night drawing as much as I could.

Bill: You had never attended any art classes?

Don: No. I had never taken any art classes. Even after that I never enrolled in any. I was completely self-taught. So I went out there the next day and …

Bill: Wait. Did you have any idea of what kinds of drawings they wanted to see?

Don: No one gave me any specific instructions. They simply said, "Just bring some of your best drawings." And I did. I remember going out there (to Disney Studios) and sitting in this room with my impromptu portfolio. Unfortunately I can't remember whom I met with that day. Actually, I think it may have been Andy Engman, the animation production manager at that time. He looked at the drawings and there was a lot of, "hmm, hmmmmm," sounds like that. He then left the room with my portfolio. Pretty soon he came back and said "I'm going to show somebody else and I'll be back." Twenty minutes went by and he came back in and said, "Okay, you're hired."

Bill: That was it?

Don: That was it. All I could say was, "When do I start?" On June 19th, 1956, I started working at Disney Studio. They put me in a room with about six other people. They called it the "bullpen." We were inbetweeners.

Ron Diamond: Did you even talk about salary or the terms of your contract?

Don: My gross salary was fifty dollars a week. My take home was thirty-six. That was the starting rate in 1956. At first they gathered clean-up drawings from *Alice in Wonderland*, *Peter Pan*, and several other pictures and told me to inbetween them. Now there was a wonderful guy at Disney Studio at the time named Johnny Bond. He had been at the studio for years. Johnny had the reputation of being able to do the most Donald Duck inbetweens, something like 60 per day. He was the champion. That was the badge he wore on his chest. And he always had a cigar, which he puffed generously in every direction. He was an institution. And he never called you by your name. He gave you a nickname that made you feel like you were part of the gang. I think I was called "Bluther." Anyway, he would come in and tell you what you were doing wrong. After three weeks of working in the bullpen and interacting with Johnny, John Lounsbery then asked if I would work with him. At the time I still lived in Santa Monica and had to carpool to work. Glen Schmidt kindly picked me up every day and drove me to the studio. He was Lounsbery's assistant animator.

Bill: Had you met any other animators? Did you interact with Frank, Ollie, or Eric?

Don: They were in D-Wing on the first floor of the animation building along with Marc Davis and Milt Kahl, and no one ever went to the D-Wing. That was the holy of holies. It was forbidden. But John came to the bullpen and said, "I want you to be my inbetweener." Now, as I said, his current assistant was Glen Schmidt. Within six months, Glen was moved out of the room adjacent to John's and I was moved in. And, that was a problem.

Bill: Carpooling, right?

Don: The carpooling stopped. I was only eighteen and a bit naive. I didn't even realize that I had offended him. About nine months later he came into my room and said, "Don, I've hated you for so long. But I have found the strength to forgive you." I didn't even know there was a problem. So I said, "Forgive me for what?" That's when he explained how he had helped me in the beginning and how I essentially took his job. At that point, I realized that I'd hurt him. I apologized. But my experience with John Lounsbery was great. He was a very emotional actor/animator and very much a great teacher. People at the studio often said, "You have no idea what a blessing it is to work with John Lounsbery." It was true. He was a very supportive teacher. John would push you to do things you thought your skills were incapable of. He wouldn't just give you the answers. Then he would come back into the room, look at your work, and say, "See. You can do it." Instilling that kind of confidence in a young artist was an extremely generous act. I worked hard for him. I remember working on *Sleeping Beauty* and learning the difference between an inbetweener and an animator's assistant. The animator gave you extremes that are very far apart. You have to figure out how to bring that action together. John would put the most amazing timing charts on his drawings. His work was so beautiful. It was never complicated. His lines were natural and free. Drawings that were lightly sketched and on model. You could easily see the figures on the paper. And they were filled with a certain emotion that made them wonderful to look at. You could understand what the character was thinking. It's a shame that so many young people today do not have the chance to see that kind of vision, a drawing on a piece of paper that inspires you. Today, the CG approach is something that reminds me of puppetry more than traditional, hand-drawn animation.

They animate a prebuilt model on a computer. They don't have the thrill of feeling that energy and creativity that emerges in your mind and spirit, which is then expressed with pencil and paper. That is what I learned from John Lounsbery. He was amazing.

Bill: How did your first year go?

Don: In 1956, we were making *Sleeping Beauty*. Walt himself was off building and fretting over Disneyland in Anaheim. It had only been open for a year, and they were fixing a lot of problems at the park. Back then the thought of replacing the nine old men was unheard of. The studio had several good animators. I think the crew was about 600 strong, including all of the animation staff, and we were still in the thrill of just creating animated motion pictures. No one was thinking of replacing them with new people. When we were making *Sleeping Beauty*, we thought we were making the greatest animated movie ever. Everything was going to be perfect: the images, the design, the acting. But the cleanup crew could only accomplish *perfect* cleanup inbetweens of Princess Aurora at an average rate of one drawing per day. So they instituted something called "the drawing count." Basically, they said, "You have to do eight girls a day or we will never get through this picture." By the time we finished making this magnificent masterpiece called *Sleeping Beauty*, the studio had spent in excess of nine million dollars. In those days nine million was a huge sum, let alone the fact that this was an animated feature. The whole process was big. Even the paper on your desk was very wide paper, to accommodate the widescreen Technirama format. And, just flipping this paper to do your drawings became very laborious. It was like flipping pan paper, two and a half fields wide. They assigned a person who came around every day and asked how many birds or squirrels you drew that day. Regardless, I was still in love with everything about the studio. Finally, the feeling that I had when I was four was coming to life. It was real. I was eighteen and in the throes of the animation business. I even began to look around at other animation studios and became very critical of their work. I was bewitched by the beautiful art we were creating at Disney. I wanted to create that feeling of being pulled into a beautiful world. Animation, for me, was like graphic music. It has a rhythm that exists in its line, its timing, colors, and emotions. Walt and his studio understood this.

Now, the downside of this story is that after just one year of this excitement, my church sent me on a mission. I'm a member of the LDS Church and was called to go to Argentina, which means that I would have to learn Spanish and move there. I had never been out of the United States. I didn't know anything about Argentina. When I looked in the encyclopedia I only saw pictures of the naked indigenous people. None of this fit in with my plans. I was really upset. Finally I went to John and said, "I'm leaving the studio because I'm going on a mission to Argentina." John was a very sweet man and would never criticize you with harsh words. Years later I remember him saying, "It was so hard for me not to slap you on the side of the head. I wanted to say that you had the whole thing in your hands. There were people who had been working at the studio for twenty years and had never been promoted. You were only there for a few months and were promoted to assistant animator. Did you know how many people didn't like you because of that? You have to be careful in life. If you go out there and you are really good, that goodness often upsets people." I remember those words because they accurately summed up my whole career. When you try to be the best, jealousy comes into the picture. People get angry with you for doing just that. I think I'm guilty of not reaching out more in the early stages of my career. I didn't help others very much. I'm trying to do that now. But at the time I was too young and too preoccupied about achieving my dream to realize that I was being selfish. Anyway, I went on the mission. I didn't draw for two and half years.

Bill: You didn't draw at all?

Don: Not really. I tried once in a while, but my brain was focused elsewhere. When I came home I decided to go back to BYU for some reason and finish my degree. I didn't even major in art. I majored in English literature.

Ron: Were you drawing at all?

Don: I started drawing again.

Bill: At BYU? And why didn't you study art?

Don: I was at BYU. And I didn't think I was going learn that much. At that point in my life, I knew a lot about music and art. I wanted to study something I knew nothing about. I say this with shame, but at that time I hadn't even read one book cover to cover. I was a farm boy. Literature was an area in which I was truly deficient. And I had a lot of catching up to do. I suddenly found myself in classes surrounded by very intelligent women who seemed to have read everything. So I read and read. In hindsight, this was one of the better decisions I'd ever made. Between my exposure to another country and culture and then studying world literature, I had finally received an education. This experience had an effect on my art. I was ready to draw something that made sense. It wasn't about duplicating other people's drawings anymore. College was great. But in the end, I needed a job. And drawing was the only thing I truly knew how to do.

Bill: Did you immediately think about Disney?

Don: That's a really good question. No, I didn't want to go immediately back to Disney. I don't think I've ever told anyone this before, but I had nightmares while working there. I kept dreaming of being trapped there. Maybe it was because of the way they administrated the artists; I don't know. I was actually somewhat afraid to go back. Instead, my brother Toby and I started a live theater in Santa Monica. We converted an old unoccupied Safeway grocery store into a theater. We produced classic musicals. Our mother made all of the costumes, hundreds of them. I would produce, design, and paint the sets, hunt down props, and play the piano. Toby would direct. We did this for about three and half years.

John and Flo Lounsbery attended a lot of the shows. During these years I met John's daughter, Andy. We started dating. Toby and I cast her as Liesl in *The Sound of Music*. At one point, she wanted to get married. I didn't. We broke up. In the end, the theater's cost outweighed its income and we shut it down. Toby went off to direct live theater with professionals at the Melodyland Theaters. Andy Lounsbery married someone else. It was at that time I decided that I would go back to animation. However, because of the Andy situation, I was too embarrassed to call John for a recommendation to get back into Disney. So, in 1968 I went to work at Filmation Studios.

Bill: **Did you apply? Or did you just walk in with a portfolio?**

Don: I just walked in with a portfolio. They hired me on the spot and gave me a great salary. In fact, from the start my boss kept giving me raises. Within a year I was making five hundred per week.

Bill: **What were you animating? Or were you directing?**

Don: At this point I was doing "layout," which, as you know, means you put in key poses of the characters and essentially design the layout. I became so efficient at it that they assigned me to work on their TV specials. My boss, Don Christensen, was giving me raises about every two to three months. He used to come in and stand over my shoulder, smoking. Now, I really don't like the smell of cigarette smoke, and he knew it. But he would come in and blow smoke over my shoulder at my drawings anyway. Clearly he did this on purpose. He would give me the raises but I didn't even know where I stood on the scale between good and not so good, or too good. I thought this might be a case of being good to the point where even Don Christensen didn't like it. He came into my office one day and said, "I cannot give you any more money. You're earning as much money as I do and I will not raise your salary beyond mine." I put my pencil down and replied, "Don, I'm not asking you to do that. I've never asked for a raise. And I don't know why I keep getting them. I don't need the money." He stormed out of the room and said, "Well, just remember … no more raises!" I stuck around for about two more years. Then I began to truly assess what we were doing. We were making commercials and TV stuff, but it just wasn't beautiful. It wasn't satisfying for me as an artist. That's when I thought about giving Disney another shot. So I finally called John Lounsbery and told him that I'd really like to come back. At first, there was this long silence. But then he invited me over for a test. They gave me paper, a room, an animation desk, and told me to animate. At the time, I equated it to like trying to spin straw into gold, with no input from anyone, just make up something. I was there for about two weeks doing these personal animation screen tests. Then one day someone came in, took all my pencil tests, and disappeared for a few hours. Finally he came back in and said, "Okay, you're going to animate. You're going on to animate on *Robin Hood*."

Bill: **To be clear, when you were at Filmation you weren't really animating, right? You were just doing layout. Then, without having animated in years, you walked into Disney and you did full animation?**

Don: Right. Honestly, I'm always a little bit behind the wagon for some reason. I didn't realize how remarkable it was to have been advanced so quickly. Usually you have to pay some dues, earn your way up, and maybe I was. But all of these doors seem to have just opened. And, I had gone through some unique experiences, which helped me, and by this time I was 33 years old. It's been a very pleasant journey for me. And, no, I had never really animated before this opportunity. My only experience on the board was when I was working on *Sleeping Beauty* as an assistant. I did observe what was going on around me. I learned from watching. And you're right. I wasn't animating at Filmation. My animation experience really amounted to those two weeks of tests. And, to my amazement, they gave me an office in the hallowed D-Wing between veteran key cleanup assistants Dale Oliver and Bud Hester, two doors away from Frank and Ollie, and down the hall from Milt Kahl. When they started to assign me scenes, I closed my door and secluded myself in my office. I would put my pencil down, close my eyes, and visualize what I was trying to put on the paper. That visualization was the guide that took me by the hand and told me what to draw. That was a learning experience for me. That's how I worked on *Robin Hood*. I especially remember the director, Woolie Reitherman. He was a fighter pilot in World War II. And Woolie was a soldier first and foremost. I don't recall ever seeing his soft side at work. When he'd call all the animators upstairs to view their scenes, I remember everyone appearing in the hall with this terrified look on their faces. We'd all go up *en masse* with our tails between our legs. And I got criticized along with the best of them up there. One time he literally said, "This is really quite disappointing. I expected that you would do much better than this." He then pointed out all the possibilities that I had overlooked. I then had to go back and try again.

Bill: **It sounds like he was your first animation instructor. Were you mentored by anybody?**

Don: Up to that point, no. But I would say that John Lounsbery was my first mentor. Everything I saw him do became very important to me. And every time I was faced with a big challenge, I would recall those moments and ask myself how John would handle things. I wanted to walk in his footsteps. With that in mind I then faced that challenge, and good things always happened. I made corrections and learned what to look for in animation. It's the entertainment, not just the drawings. Because of that early training, Milt and Woolie liked what I was doing. And if Milt Kahl complimented your work, that just gave you a warm feeling inside. On one occasion I even got to go into his office. Now, you have to understand who Milt Kahl was, and most of the young students today, or wannabe animators, haven't a clue who Milt Kahl was. Milt Kahl was the great and dreaded Milt Kahl. It was like going to see the Great Oz. And he kept his door closed all the time. He was good at everything. He was good at chess, fly-fishing. He won awards for that. And he also loved to shoot. He had a pellet gun in his room and you could hear it going off all the time, usually during break times or at lunch. He used phone books for backing the paper targets to protect the wall behind it.

Bill: He was shooting guns in his room?

Don: He had a gun in his room, yeah. Who's going to venture forth and open the door, or even knock? I remember Stan Green, who was his assistant at the time, would just go timidly to the door and lightly knock. You'd hear Milt's loud voice, "COME IN." And poor Stan would tremble, holding Milt's coffee. Milt was the man who could make the best drawings in the whole studio. A true master of his craft, his designs were flawless. And he was a great fan of Picasso. None of us understood the connection between Picasso's drawings and Milt's drawings, but he did. Anyway, one time I had a scene and had to go see Milt to get a drawing. All the veteran animators had this custom. If you couldn't get a drawing to work, go see Milt. One of his drawings would bring everything together beautifully. So I was heading to Milt to get a drawing of Robin Hood. I knocked and Milt opens the door and says, in a very friendly way, "Oh, it's you. Come on in. Come on." He was *actually* nice. But I could see the gun sitting on his table, and there were all these phonebooks that were just shredded to pieces. When I said that I was sent to get his help, he laughed and took my drawing. He said, "First of all, let's put a piece of paper over the top." Then, he began to explain what he was doing as he drew over the top of my drawing. As he made corrections, I noticed something kind of interesting about Milt at that point. You could learn by watching him draw, but it was difficult to learn by listening to him talk. He stuttered a little bit, and he would use the expression, "Well, you sort of do it like this, you know. You know what I mean? You can see it. You just do it like that." That's not a lot of help if you had no idea what he was talking about. Oddly enough, on my website I find people asking me the same question. "Well, tell me how to do it," they say. A lot of times that's not something you can communicate, because it seems to me the muses have to construct that. It's something that comes to you personally. I reflect on that experience a lot, standing behind Milt and getting that drawing. It was amazing.

Bill: At that time, was there a particular technique or point of view that was unique to Milt, something that really helped you?

Don: Yes. What Milt was doing more than anything was emphasizing a particular attitude or approach to directing. He said, "If your scene is not entertaining, then why is it in the picture? You need to think entertainment all the time. I can see a scene that you've got in the reel right now, where the sheriff is running up a stairway. I'm not at all entertained by it. I've watched people my whole life climb stairs, and you've done nothing unusual. You could have him go faster than his legs should carry him. You could have him actually hit the wall and fumble on the way, conveying that he's in a big hurry. But you didn't sit down and think about what would be entertaining." Those words of advice have echoed in my head during my entire career, at Disney and through all of our independent animated films. If it's not entertaining, why do it? A scene can convey a story point or the character's personality, but it can also be entertaining. Woolie [Reitherman] also had this saying, "Some animators, I will give bread and butter scenes. But I will never give the acting scenes to them." *Bread and butter* meant action scenes, somebody running, walking, just getting from point A to point B. But in acting scenes you must show the mind of the character at work. You must show that the character has feelings. You must show that there's a personality there, and it *must* be entertaining! It must tickle people in the audience.

I know that Walt himself, in a famous Disney interoffice memo to art instructor Don Graham back in 1935, author of that in-house Disney animation manual *Analysis of Action*, wrote, "You must caricature what we see in real life, or the audience cannot connect at all with what you're doing. You cannot just draw cartoons. The cartoon characters are symbols. They represent something common to us all, with situations and reactions similar to our own lives. We all go through this." In Cinderella there's a scene where a little mouse wakes up, yawns, and he turns around to find his little tail all in knots. He's been sleeping on it all night. So he picks it up and tries to undo the knots. Why is that so funny? Because every one of us has woken up in the morning in complete disarray, our hair all matted and twisted. So, it's a reflection of the mortal existence. Throughout my entire career the goal has been to make it funny, make it entertaining, make it fresh, and try not to duplicate what another animator has done. That's the hardest part. Because you will subconsciously hold all those images in your head and you'll wind up drawing the same thing someone else has already drawn.

Bill: **This sounds like a transitional period for you. What happened after *Robin Hood*?**

Don: My next assignment was on *Winnie the Pooh and Tigger Too*. Another door opened and I was promoted to directing animator. Thinking back to when I went back to Disney Studios, it was a very different place. This was in April of 1971. Walt died in 1966, so the new regime was there. Woolie Reitherman was now the producer/director and pretty much in charge of the animation department. And all of the management staff were trying to guess what Walt would have done. That was always the question. What would Walt have done? And in all the cupboards that you opened there was always a picture of Walt. He was ever present, even though he was no longer there physically. And Woolie … Woolie wasn't so much a "What would've Walt done?" kind of guy, because he was trying to be himself. Eventually, because they realized that everyone was growing older, they started thinking about the future of Disney animation and came up with a training program. Eric Larson was in charge of that program. And then Disney extended some financing to help California Institute of the Arts so that they could train new talent in character animation. After they graduated, some would be selected to come into the studio animation training program and get further training, starting with personal screen tests and inbetweening on actual production scenes.

I remember that Dale Baer and I were some of the first to be brought into that program. Over the next two years, Gary Goldman and John Pomeroy would enter the program. It was in 1972 that Gary and I began to question the program. I pointed out that we have a lot more to learn here than just animating. I revealed that I had an editing table and a sixteen-millimeter Moviola and several reels of Warner Bros shorts that I was studying at home. During coffee breaks, we used to talk in my office about how soon it would be when the last of the Nine Old Men would be retiring—actually it would be happening in the next 5 or 6 years; we were reminded of this often by production managers Don Duckwall and Ed Hansen. It seemed daunting to try and learn as much as we would need to know to take on something like directing and supervising other animation staff. And so, a few of the new guys would meet at my house for animation weekends, where we would do marathon viewings of the Disney feature classics, watching four or five films a day. Back in those days, you could get a sixteen-millimeter projector from the studio and check out sixteen-millimeter copies of those classic features and take them home to watch. I suggested that we start collecting more equipment, like a rostrum camera stand and a thirty-five–millimeter stop-motion camera. Then we had some small animation desks built and bought some used 12 Field animation discs. I had to have my Moviola converted to thirty-five millimeter. We even found an old Moviola projector with three attached sound heads. The shutter was mounted out in front of the lens. It looked like it could fly.

As this was going on, Woolie Reitherman called me into his office one day and said, "We've got a lot of animators who are training new animators, but we don't have anybody that's going to be a director. You're going to direct." Once again, a door opened. However, that meant one thing specifically. I had to give up animating. It also meant that you have to hold your cards close to your chest and be careful what you say to people. Woolie said, "'cause you'll either injure them, deflate their morale, or you'll elevate them and inspire them to do better." I think maybe Woolie's directorial advice affected my approach. I may have become less outgoing and even mistrustful of others. Though I did continue to help others with their animation. When I asked when this new journey would begin, he said, "Right now." Then he began to show me how he approached directing.

For instance, he explained how they built animated props. How they would spend hours working over the little model that was going to be Cruella De Vil's car. In those days we didn't have computers to build them. The props were usually constructed with illustration board. We actually built little models, painted them white, outlined them with black acrylic paint, and shot them in stop-motion photography. Then we printed out each frame onto a Photostat with registration peg holes, and the animators animated the characters to those printouts. It was a very different process. At a certain point, he pulled me off *The Rescuers* and dropped *Pete's Dragon* into my lap. He said directly, "You're going to direct the animation and I'm going to step back." That's when I started working with Ken Anderson. *Pete's Dragon* was a combination of live action and animation. Ken explained that I had to go out onto the sound stage where the live-action crew was filming the actors with the director, Don Chaffey, and make sure that when they shoot scenes where the dragon also appeared, there would be room to include the animation of Elliott the dragon in the frame. And we couldn't screw that up. So I went out to the sound stage with Ken and walked around as if I knew what I was doing. Whatever we did, it worked. The budget and the schedule was for just 10 minutes of animation. The plan for Elliott the dragon was that he would be invisible 50 percent of the time. However, when the marketing guys saw the first animated scenes, they pushed to have more footage of the dragon. It was doubled to twenty minutes, 1,800 feet. We weren't given additional funds or more time. Then the studio decided to change the date of the premiere of *Pete's Dragon* from Christmastime to Thanksgiving. That reduced our production schedule by a month and gave us only about nine months total to get all of the animation production done. We basically had to work twelve- to fourteen-hour days, seven days a week. And there was no overtime pay for off-the-clock employees, which included me and other key animation staff. This was just the job. We were also developing some green animators. Cliff Nordberg, I think, was the only real veteran animator on the picture. The process was very slow in the beginning. I found myself in a position where people were looking over my shoulder and I was correcting their drawings.

Dave Michener, Ted Berman, Ollie Johnston, Art Stevens,
Don Bluth, Frank Thomas, Woolie Reitherman on The Rescuers © Disney.

I had so many epiphanies along the way. Years before, I used to stand for hours behind cleanup supervisor Walt Stanchfield at his desk, while he corrected my drawings on *Sleeping Beauty*, and there was a moment on *Pete's Dragon* when Walt came into my room and asked me to help him with a drawing. As he stood behind me, I put his drawing on my registration pegs and placed a blank piece of paper over it—and I froze. I turned to him and said, "Walt, do you realize what's happening here? You should be sitting here, working on my drawing." He laughed, and replied, "Don't be stupid, just draw. This is why I always preach people to treat your fellow-artists nice. You never know when they might end up being your boss."

Bill: **As the animation director, how did you bring the dragon to life? How did you give him character and personality? And did you have full control over this, or did you have to consult with the live-action director?**

Don: They pretty much expected me to supervise and approve the animation, cleanup, special effects, and color for the dragon scenes, as well as deliver entertaining animation scenes, which would be combined with the live action in a special printing process. Whenever you're making an animated film, at least in my experience, you use the voice talent and the writers to help you develop who the character is. The voice talent will come in and read the words on a page, and through their experience recognize what is expected of the character and say, "Oh, I know who this guy is!" They'll add things to it that you never thought of. For *Pete's Dragon*, casting brought in an actor by the name of Charlie Callas, who was also a stand-up comedian and had been in many live-action pictures. Ken Anderson explained that we didn't want the dragon to talk, just make noises that only the boy could understand. So Charlie Callas began to make these weird sounds, and when he did his face became distorted, strange, and fun. But that wasn't Charlie, that was the dragon. The dragon is every child's friend. He's a big friendly giant who comes into a child's life and helps solve their problems. Every kid in the world is going to love that character. Charlie Callas gave that character, I think, its spirit or its life. The lesson it taught me was simply that you have to know who the character is from the inside-out. And it can also be a very fun process.

There was a moment during this time when I got an opportunity to see Woolie's softer side. He had invited me to his home for dinner. When I arrived and rang the doorbell, he opened the door and he was holding a small fox. It was domesticated and was an indoor pet. I felt like I was intruding in the very personal life of Woolie and his wife, Janie, seeing a side of him that I'd never seen before. It was somewhat disconcerting. The little fox was like a small dog, very comfortable around humans—and definitely Woolie's pet. The experience definitely gave me a different perspective on him.

Bill: **What came after *Pete's Dragon*?**

Don: After that, there was a short film called *The Small One*, adapted and pitched by Pete Young, one of only a couple of the story trainees. He was being mentored by Eric Larson and Vance Gerry. I think Eric was to produce and he was going to give the directing to Burney Mattinson, his long-time animation assistant. But Woolie stepped in and placed me in charge of the production as the producer/director, as part of his plan to groom me to replace himself. What a dilemma for me. Woolie just ignored Eric's plan and stuck me in the middle. Plus, I was aware that this would be the first religious-based film that Walt Disney Productions would create, and maybe the last. This was Joseph, Mary, and the birth of Christ. So they were trying to figure out how best to animate the story. I was stumped. We still had a very green crew. Worse still, the studio didn't give us much of a budget, nor money for anyone to write songs. We, my assistant director, Rick Rich, and I actually wrote our own. He wrote one, and I wrote two songs that went into that movie! Essentially resources were limited because it was a short. There wasn't going to be an opportunity to recoup the costs. There weren't videos or DVDs back in those days. Regardless, we finished making that picture. I remember going into a projection room with Woolie Reitherman and a lot of the other animators to watch the final product. Now that was judgment day. When the lights came up, he turned around, looked at me, and said, "I just watched Hanna-Barbera inbetweened." That was a slap in the face. It was his way of saying, that's not what we do at the Disney studio. And that was another big lesson for me, or more of a reminder: If it isn't entertaining, if it doesn't reflect real life, then it's nothing. It's just moving drawings. I put that in my cache of things I'd been taught. The next movie I direct wouldn't be like that.

Now something happened, something I think is really important. And this goes back in time a bit. In 1972, all of us in the training program knew we were being trained as animators, and thus we didn't know how to put a movie together. We didn't know how to create "texture" in a film, to place a slow sequence next to a fast one, or how you put a sad sequence next to a happy one. We could only do individual scenes. So Gary Goldman and I decided to learn how. We decided to go out into my garage and make a picture. We would stumble along and learn the process as a result. And if we don't know the answers, we'll go ask the old masters at the studio. I remember asking Frank Thomas how they

from the left, Don Bluth, John Pomeroy with his back to the camera,
1st row: John Musker, Brad Bird and Jerry Reese, 2nd row: Heidi Guedel, Linda Miller and Emily Jiuliano,
3rd: Jeff Vareb, Gary Goldman, Chuck Harvey and Bill Hajee on The Small One © Disney.

made the water in *Fantasia* so clear and real. He rolled his eyes and said, "You know, no one ever wrote that down. I don't remember. I think it had something to do with lacquer we used to make the cell paint transparent." I was just astounded. I assumed that because Disney had been pioneering animation for almost half a century that someone was keeping track. And so there were many other questions that I asked and no one remembered. That really compelled us to go out on our own and experiment. We were going to have to find a lot of answers on our own.

Bill: What was this garage project?

Don: It started with something we called *The Piper*. It was based on a poem that my brother Toby had written. We worked on it as a short for about two and half years. After we had storyboarded about twenty minutes and animated about 400 feet, we invited John and Florence Lounsbery to my house and showed them the film. It was excruciatingly painful, actually embarrassing to watch with one of the Disney animation masters sitting in my living room. It was then that we realized that the story wasn't appropriate for a short; too much information in too short of time to make sense of the story. It was like watching sports highlights. The very next weekend we decided to scrap *The Piper* and chose something simpler. I came up with a story based on a kitten that lived in our woodpile, back on my parents' farm in Payson, Utah. Toby took the first stab at a script. When we got into production, I rewrote it. The picture was a short that lasted twenty-seven minutes. It was called *Banjo the Woodpile Cat*. We thought we might get our money back, if we could just get one showing on television. Of course it took years before that happened. When John Pomeroy came aboard at Disney in February of 1973, we invited him to come see what we were doing in the garage. He was there on *The Piper* and endured the pain of starting over with us. During the next several years, we had spent a lot of money on *Banjo*. I had even taken out a second mortgage on my house to pay the orchestra for the music score. But it was so exciting, learning all these lessons. Every weekend we would get together at my house, and sometimes on weeknights. About four years into this second garage project, we wondered if we would ever recoup our investment of time and money. Then, in late 1978, we thought, what if we took it to Disney, they might agree to buy it and let us finish it there during regular work hours.

I went to the new head of the Disney Studio, Ron Miller. I said, "Ron, we're working on a side project and making numerous discoveries. Would you like to see it?" Unfortunately, he turned us down. This was also the time when the kids from CalArts started grumbling down in the bullpen. They were unhappy with the studio. They were evidently unhappy with me. In the end I went to Ron and said, "This is too hard. I don't think I'm your guy. I'm not going to be your director. I don't even want to be a directing animator. I just want to go to my office and animate." Woolie [Reitherman] was overseeing the development of *The Fox and the Hound* and *The Black Caldron*, and I'm sure I disappointed him by asking to step down and just animate. But I didn't feel like I was letting him down. I had no idea what I was doing. But by that time I knew that I was going to leave the Disney Studio.

Around this time Gary [Goldman] got a call from ex-Disney executive Jim Stewart, suggesting that he knew we were unhappy at the studio, and asked if they could finance us, would we leave Disney? Would we start a studio and produce a feature? And, if we would leave, do we have a story in mind? Strange, but just weeks before this call, Ken Anderson had brought a book to my office called *Mrs. Frisby and the Rats of NIMH*. He told me that he had brought it to Woolie's attention and got shot down. Woolie told him that they "already had a mouse—Mickey Mouse," and that they'd already made a mouse movie, *The Rescuers*. Gary told Jim we already had a company—which we incorporated for the *Banjo* property. We named it *Don Bluth Productions, Inc*. And, yes, there is a book that we would like to produce as a movie. Their company was called *Aurora Productions*, formed by three ex-Disney execs, Jim [Stewart], Rich Irvine, and Jon Lang. They had an investor, a man from Chicago, who was interested. They knew that we had experience but only as cogs in the Disney animation machine. Jim wanted to know if we had anything that we had done on our own, which would show that we could handle directing and producing a film on our own. We did have one example—*Banjo the Woodpile Cat*. It was about 90 percent animated and about 70 percent in color. They asked if they could show it to the investor. When he saw the short film, he liked it and felt that it justified investing in a film with us. He put up $5.7 million dollars. But Gary [Goldman], John [Pomeroy], and I weren't going to leave our garage comrades behind. I called a meeting for everyone who was working on *Banjo* and said, "Guys, we're taking our short and leaving. We're not asking you to leave, but you are welcome if you want to come with us." It was on my birthday, September 13th, 1979, that we went to Ed Hansen, who was the animation production manager at the time, and told him we couldn't make it happen there at the studio, that we were resigning to make our own animated feature films and were going to compete with them, and that we felt it was the only way to wake them up. He sat in his chair and laughed out loud. He said, "You haven't a clue what you're saying. You cannot make a feature film."

Animation Drawing, *Banjo the Woodpile Cat*, 1979 © Don Bluth Productions.

Bill: He actually erupted in laughter?

Don: He did. And that only made us want to succeed more. So we left. The picture we made was based on the book that Ken [Anderson] shared with us, *Mrs. Frisby and the Rats of NIMH*, which was a Newberry Award–winning novel.

Bill: What made you choose that?

Don: As I said earlier, Gary, John, and I had read the book and knew right away that Ken was right. It had potential. The story deals with basic, common issues of morality and making the right choices. It was perfect. We had scheduled it for thirty months. However, late in the production, Aurora and MGM/UA decided to move the release date up by two months, to the Fourth of July weekend. We completed it in two years and five months. It was probably the most wonderful experience of my career, and it's a picture that we never really duplicated. We never made one better, in my opinion. We poured our heart and souls into the movie. It was purely the result of our desire to create something special. We tried our best to bring back some strong story elements and production values missing from those Disney films from the early sixties and all through the mid-seventies.

Bill: Talk a bit about the difficulties of assuming the role of director, producer, and editor. That must have been challenging.

Don: Actually, it was easier than at Disney. We owned the company. My name was on the door. Just that alone gave me authority to lead—very different from being an employee director. Further, directing and running a studio is completely different from the act of animating itself—or even just directing. With artists, you'll discover that many can become very jealous or feel inferior. There's a lot of competition going on in the background. Some artists even feel like they don't count or they don't have any self-importance. You have to monitor that and make sure everyone feels like they're part of the team, that their talent is needed and appreciated. A successful project depends on that. Then you have the issue of finance. How do you keep the money flowing? You have to make sure you're on schedule and that you're spending correctly. You just can't run out of money. That takes a lot of management. There were two guys to help us oversee the finances, one at Aurora and our in-house production manager, Fred Craig. It usually came down to not creating enough inventory, or not making our footage goals, and lots of weekly meetings to discuss problems. There were many meetings that had nothing to do with animating but more about how to monitor the system or work continuity from department to department and the flow of inventory to each. It can be very frustrating.

And if you want to make good movies, you need to keep the crew happy and focused. That was a major part of my job as a director, trying to keep everyone balanced, satisfied, and working. It was tough learning how to guide an artist toward the bigger picture, to take the focus off themselves and transfer it to the project as a whole.

Bill: **When you finished *The Secret of NIMH*, how were things financially for your new studio?**

Don: When we finished *The Secret of NIMH*, we were already five months into our second film with Aurora; it was called *East of the Sun: West of the Moon*. I thought *NIMH* was going to do it for us. We're going to compete with the Disney Studio. But it was not financially a success. We were only two-thirds financed on *East of the Sun*, and the union contract was to expire on July 31, 1982.

Sketches, Don Bluth, "*THE SECRET OF N.I.M.H.*", © 1982 MGM Television Entertainment Inc. All rights reserved. Courtesy of MGM Media Licensing.

Model sheet, "Ms. Brisby", "*THE SECRET OF N.I.M.H.*", © 1982 MGM Television Entertainment Inc. All rights reserved. Courtesy of MGM Media Licensing.

Negotiations with the big studios got stalled and Local 839 voted to strike. We didn't even consider the effects of this action. We were a union house but not part of the Producer's Association. We were new at this and just waiting for the agreement. But the next week Bud Hester, our union president, arrived on our doorstep in Studio City and told all of the artists that they would have to leave the building. That meant that the editors and the camera operators would leave too, in order to respect their colleagues in 839. That left only Gary [Goldman], John [Pomeroy], our production manager, the receptionist, and me in the building. Then we received a call from Aurora telling us that the investors got cold feet and decided to not continue with the cash flow for *East of the Sun*, for two reasons: *NIMH*'s box office failure and fear of what financial damage the union demands would do to our budget. We sat there in the building for the next two months wondering how we would recover. Then, in early October we received a call from a Rick Dyer, an entrepreneur/inventor and owner of Advanced Micro Systems. He wanted to meet us and talk about a collaboration. Rick came up to our studio with another man, Jim Pierce, the co-owner of an arcade game manufacturer and distribution company. Gary, John, and I met with them in our conference room. Rick introduced Mr. Pierce, and then he said, "I just saw your *Secret of NIMH*. I'm making an arcade game called *Dragon's Lair* and you guys are the ones that should animate it." He explained that he had convinced Jim that it should be a three-way partnership, with each of the companies raising the startup money required to do their part of creating the sample of the game. Jim disclosed that Cinematronics was in Chapter 11, bankruptcy. He believed that Rick's concept would bring success. With his share of profits he could pay his debtors and get out of Chapter 11.

Now I had never even been to an arcade. I didn't know what a video game was. But it was a job, so we agreed. But when they brought in the scripts, they just weren't that good. Going back to my old lessons I could see some entertainment was missing. If you lose your money and don't win, you still want some reward. I said, "Why don't we do several kinds of death scenes that are funny, amusing, and everybody goes, 'Wow!' That way the player at least still gets entertained." The fun of making *Dragon's Lair* was seeing how many ways we could kill the little knight. That was the fun part. And this was to be done using the latest laser disc technology, which would allow us to animate the story like a movie, linear. If someone died, the game could access any death sequence on the disc; otherwise the player simply progressed forward in the story. And since we were putting the crew back to work, and since this wasn't a major feature movie, it was an opportunity to let the animators experiment once again. So they did and had fun doing it. Then, remembering that we had to find the startup money ourselves, we went into a mini-panic. I called my bother Sam, who loaned us about $35,000, which only covered us for about three weeks. So, we had to figure out a budget and schedule, and Jim Pierce needed to have a sample of the game for the upcoming March 1983 Arcade Game convention in Chicago. Gary [Goldman] came up with a budget of $300,000 for the demo. We then borrowed money from one of our attorney's friends, Ott Sorentino, of Sorentino's restaurant. By the time our attorney found a qualified investor, we had borrowed over $100,000 from family, friends, friends of friends, and, our new partners, Rick and Jim. Finally, an investor was brought in and put up the $300,000, for a 10 percent share of our profits. That investment paid back our debt and got us to the March gaming convention. Jim Pierce called from Chicago and notified us that the game was the talk of the show. Within two days it was on national television. Cinematronics had presold about $8 million worth of the game at the show. We were financed. And our part would cost a total of $1.3 million. When Rick's company finally programmed all that animation and put it in the arcade, it was a far bigger success than *NIMH*. It made a lot of money.

Ron: Did you release that?

Don: No. Cinematronics handled the distribution. You have to watch out for distributors. When the money starts rolling in, and we were told it was about $32 million dollars, the money can disappear, especially if they are in bankruptcy and do not satisfy their debt and continue to protect themselves in bankruptcy. Cinematronics used the incoming revenue to cover Rick's costs and finance us for the balance of *Dragon's Lair*, develop and produce *Space Ace*, and *Dragon's Lair II: Time Warp*. The profit

Animation drawing, *Dragon's Lair*, 1993 © Bluth Group.

Model sheet, "Dirk the Daring", *Dragon's Lair*, 1993 © Bluth Group.

money never really came back to us. And actually, in late March of 2004, they owed us production costs of around $350,000 on *Dragon's Lair II* and about $4.5 million in profits from the other two games. We had been informed that they had in excess of $12.5 million in their account. They called and told Gary that the arcade market was crashing again and they were cutting off our cash flow and shutting down the third game. We didn't even have enough money to make payroll. We called our attorney in a panic, who advised that we need to get a good bankruptcy attorney to fight the shutdown. We had an unfinished game and our two companies, Don Bluth Productions and Bluth Group, Ltd., were in bankruptcy court. It was the only way to go after Cinematronics. They had all of the partners' money but refused to distribute the funds. Then they turned over their business management to their bankruptcy attorneys and a trustee. Eventually, four and a half years later we won in court. No money was left in Cinematronics' account, but the court eventually awarded Bluth Group the three games. We were able to finally finish *Dragon's Lair II*. A company by the name of Leland Corporation had purchased Cinematronics from the bankruptcy court and called us in Ireland to inquire about us finishing the game and licensing it to them for distribution. And those games, thirty years later, are still on the shelf today. I still can't figure out how to play them. In 1984 *Dragon's Lair* went into the Smithsonian Institute along with *Pong* and *Pac-Man*. In 2010 it appeared as an app on the Apple iTunes store.

Ron: That sounds like a happy ending.

Don: Well, yes, sort of. We did end up owning the trademarks and copyrights to the three games. Their continued success, I believe, is that the animation is entertaining to watch and I'd have to credit Woolie [Reitherman], Milt [Kalh] and John [Lounsbery]. If it's not entertaining, it shouldn't be there.

Ron: How did you start the next feature film?

Don: That's a story in itself. We didn't start *An American Tail* until January of 1985. Back in the late summer of 1982, Jerry Goldsmith, who composed the music on *NIMH*, was friends with Steven Spielberg and brought the film to his attention. We got a call from Steven's office requesting our studio copy of *The Secret of NIMH* that Steven could watch in the privacy of his home. The next day they asked if they could keep the film for another day to show Kathy Kennedy and Frank Marshall. Then Steven called us up and invited us over to meet with him. We went to his office at Warner Brothers and talked about the film. Steven told us that he was amazed. He had thought the golden age of animation was over when Walt died. When he learned how much the movie cost to make, he was even more astounded. He asked if we wanted to make a movie together. Of course we said yes! We started telling him of our list of titles we'd like to produce, but he said that he would like to select the project. We left his office thrilled with the opportunity. But then the months went by with no news. We continued with the video games and it was about two years later when *An American Tail* actually surfaced. We had been in bankruptcy since the end of March and were staying alive doing small projects and commercials. Then, finally in August of '84, we were contacted by Amblin's marketing exec, Brad Globe, and producer, Kathy Kennedy, to come over to Amblin, their new offices at Universal, for a meeting. They had a script for us to read. We met in Kathy's office. We liked the title but felt the story was weak. Further, there were a few story panels done, which had the mice human-size. It reminded us of *Planet of the Apes*. Steven agreed. Once the deal was done, Amblin hired two writers from *Sesame Street*, Tony Geiss and Judy Freudberg, to come in and rewrite the existing concept. And so in January 1985, we started from scratch. Tony and Judy flew out from New York and worked in-house with us for six months. The story became about the Mousekewitz family; the little boy's name was Mousy Mousekewitz. After the first few pages of new script were delivered to Steven, he changed Mousy's name to Fievel, which was Steven's grandfather's name. It was the story of his family. A lot of things were changed to fit the new storyline. One of the two writers, Tony Geiss, wrote a song, called "Hey Mr. Man in the Moon." But Steven felt it wasn't quite right for the film. Then Steven brought in songwriters Barry Man and Cynthia Weil, who worked with James [Horner]. Finally, the three of them came up with four songs including the hit song, "Somewhere Out There."

Bill: **How did directing work, considering that you're working with a big director like Steven?**

Don: There's always somebody above you. That's just part of movie making. I remember Steven saying, "I'm going to arrange for Universal to provide you guys the money to do this. I'm going to give you some time and space to do it. I want you to be as creative as you can. I know you guys will make me a beautiful movie. But I'd like to approve the script and want your storyboards sent to me. I'll review and approve them. If there is anything I can add, I'll add it." He was extremely generous. He would send our boards back with little notes here and there. It was a pleasure. It was one of the easiest things I ever did, because they were always such positive suggestions. They made the picture better and it was easy for me to see that. Steven was as interested in creating real entertainment as I was. So once again I was being instructed by one of the best. We didn't hit a problem until we started on *The Land Before Time*.

Bill: **You have a reputation for being hands-on during the boarding and layout stage. Going back to *An American Tail*, how involved were you at that stage?**

Don: Well, yes, that's always been my flaw. But then, isn't that the director's job. And we were on a limited budget. I had done all of the storyboarding on *NIMH*, and it worked both for efficiency and budget. I believe that the more I can put into the storyboards, the more visual direction I can give. This way the entire crew can see the vision of the story. And it helps reduce the amount of time of explaining what I'm looking for in blocking or choreographing each scene. But some argue that it slights the animators' creativity. In the early years of my career we would explore the Disney animation morgue (archive) and we found the storyboards for the animation in *Song of the South*. Those storyboard panels were done by Bill Peet and Ken Anderson. Every panel reminds you of the scenes in the film. The character drawings were in great poses and on-model, and they had included background information in each story panel, creating a clear plan for the animation continuity. It helped the animators and the layout department. I could board faster and come up with more gags faster. And the faster you can conceptualize the boards, the sooner you have a road map for the entire project. That saves money. Until you have that road map, the studio is simply devouring money. As an independent studio, money was a big issue. Now the last thing I wanted was to send mediocre storyboards over to Steven Spielberg that I would have to correct later. So, yes I did get very hands-on. I did it myself. I couldn't allow us to get in trouble with the budget. And, quite frankly, we couldn't afford the additional staff. This was also easy to do with a small crew. Later, when I was working with a large room full of storyboard people, I knew that great ideas can emerge if you don't rush the process. There's a lot of creative talent to tap into. So it's a better way to work. And I would just go in and play the Steven Spielberg part at that point. I would observe and say, "Have you considered doing this?" Or, "Perhaps you might try it this way." However, it is a more expensive process.

Ron: **As you said, Steven left notes on your boards, but did you learn anything from him as a director?**

Don: Absolutely. I've always been one who learns by watching other people. I guess I'm eclectic in a way because I can just absorb things from various people and make it my own. When I was on the set and watching Steven shoot live action, I noticed that we were quite similar in our approach. Steven had a vision and he made sure that vision came to life. That's essentially how I've felt my entire career. I wanted to get hands-on because I had a vision, and I wanted that vision to come to life. I believe that's the mark of a good director. When Disney Studios was in its heyday, it was Walt Disney. He was the guy that was making everything happen. Everyone was working to build his vision, even if they couldn't see it. That's why when he was gone everyone kept asking, "What would he have done?" For years, everyone simply followed his lead. I remember one occasion, when we were making *The Land Before Time*, we were invited over to London to show the work print to Steven and George [Lucas]. When the lights came up after the screening, George, said, "Well, that scared the shit out of me!" Steven agreed. It was mainly about the *Tyrannosaurus rex*. They looked at the *T. rex* chasing the three little dinosaurs and said, "That's beautiful, and it's almost all in color. I love it. But we're going to have mothers holding their crying children in the lobbies of the theaters. That means we're going to lose ticket sales. If I cut out about a minute of that scary stuff, which you have so diligently put in there, the mothers and their kids will probably stay in their seats. And they're going to tell their friends to go see the movie. I'm ready to lose a minute." Steven was thinking a few steps ahead of the game. While you're focused entirely on the artwork, he was thinking in terms of *show business*. You're going to sell tickets, and that's going to allow you the freedom and the capability of making another picture. Or you're going to lose tickets, in which case you're going to lose popularity. That's an important issue for Steven.

Bill: **So what happened after *An American Tail*?**

Don: Let's go back twenty-two months, to December of '84. When Steven and Universal began serious discussions about *American Tail*, Universal felt that because of *NIMH*'s box office failure, a non-Disney animated film was a high risk, so they offered us just $7.5 million to do *American Tail*. This is after we showed them a budget of $11.3 million. At that time, our two companies, Don Bluth Productions and Bluth Group, Ltd., were in bankruptcy court suing our gaming partnership and game distributor for production monies and profits owed to us. We didn't feel that Universal would appreciate doing business with a company in bankruptcy. We had a business consultant working for us. He was a semi-retired mergers and acquisitions expert, Morris Sullivan, who said he would see if he could raise financing for our feature film projects. He ended up guiding Bluth Group, Ltd., through its bankruptcy. Morris offered to incorporate a company to do business with Universal, with Gary [Goldman], John [Pomeroy], and I as contracted producers and director. When we were told the maximum amount they were willing to spend, Morris immediately started inquiring about off-shore options to create an ink and paint facility with that entire operation in Ireland, with plans to move core members of the staff to that location at some time in the future.

American Tail hadn't gone into the theaters yet, and we still had all of the people on as paid staff. We needed the next project. We were in talks about picture number two—about dinosaurs, which would eventually be called *The Land Before Time*, but nothing was in writing, other than our *American Tail* contract, which gave them the rights to two films from us—the second "to be determined." We needed to keep the money flowing, so we went to Universal and explained that fact. But they clearly stated that they were not going to greenlight the picture until they were sure that *American Tail* was going to make money.

Bill: **What did you do for funds?**

Don: It was a serious issue; we didn't want to lose momentum nor have to lay off any of the talented crew. And that's the argument we submitted. Amblin came to our side, as did some of the Universal execs, but still no movement on green-lighting *Land*.

Morris [Sullivan] had closed the deal with the Industrial Development Authority in Ireland by the summer of '85. Gary had gone over and set up testing artists to train as cel painters and inkers. The company had hired 100 trainees there in Dublin, 26 of whom we tested for inbetweening and brought them to the US during *An American Tail* to train in various follow-up duties in the animation processes, from inbetweeners to Xerox and Paint Lab technicians, one even as a camera operator. They were here with us for a year. Morris' plan was working. Universal saw that we were making deadlines and meeting the budget requirements. They agreed to pay for the *Land Before Time* story and script development, character design, storyboarding, recording voice talent and rough animation, and paying the payroll for those working on *Land* with *American Tail* funds—but only on a week-to-week basis, with approval from top brass at Universal. Those funds were to be reimbursed from the approved *Land* budget, but they still did not guarantee to greenlight the film.

Ireland had specifically asked us to come to Dublin to live, work, and train Irish workers how to make animation. If we did that, they would give us money for each person we hired and trained. It was such a good deal that when Morris finally informed us one day that we're moving to Ireland. Immediately I said, "Who's we? Who's going to Ireland?" I had just remodeled my house. I was a happy guy. When it came time to move, we took eighty-seven US and Canadian animation artists and technicians, and even their families and pets, to Ireland to complete *Land Before Time*. In the summer of 1986, Gary [Goldman] and Morris went over to find a suitable building. We had to create a fully operating studio ground up. We had to round up everything that goes into a studio, including the chairs and desks, our two custom-built, multiplane rostrum cameras, the editorial equipment, the video animation tester, then build new animation desks in Ireland, and have additional custom-made 16 Field animation discs manufactured and shipped from Hollywood to Ireland! "I just wanted to draw," that's what I kept saying to everyone. They replied, "Just shut up. We're building a new facility!" So we were going take the risk, move, and start to build out a facility, as we waited for *Land Before Time* to be greenlit. But, finally near the end of August, Universal sent a letter to Morris agreeing to a "pay or play" agreement, basically agreeing to greenlight *The Land Before Time*. By the time we put Gary and the crew on a plane in mid-November 1986, we had about 25 percent of *Land* storyboarded, layouts done for about twelve minutes, and 1,000 feet of the film in rough pencil test. John and I stayed back for the *American Tail* premiere on the weekend of November 18th, and then flew out on the 21st for Dublin.

(3) - USE STRAIGHT LINES AGAINST CURVED LINES
(4) - PRACTICE - PRACTICE PRACTICE
(5) THE BODY IS AN OVAL SHAPE
(6) - STUDY HOW THE BASIC SHAPES FIT TOGETHER.
Don

Sketch, Don Bluth, *The Land Before Time*, 1988 © Don Bluth Ireland.

Bill: After the facility was built, where did you start?

Don: While we were making the transition to Ireland and getting production up and running again, Steven [Spielberg] was off making *Empire of the Sun*. It became really difficult to get ahold of him due to his schedule, and we needed his approval on our storyboards. Sometimes we had to wait up to three weeks for a response. And during that time we literally had to wait. We couldn't animate further. In the end, we decided to go ahead and animate anyway. It was the only way to keep the picture on schedule. The longer we waited, the more we drove up the budget.

Bill: Did those delays affect the overall production in any way?

Don: Well, Steven was busy. We didn't get as many suggestions. But the delays in getting his storyboard reviews caused a lot of frustration. Sometimes, to stay on schedule we had to move forward without the approvals. Then Steven's late notes would cause us to have to restage and reanimate some scenes. This really upset the animators. No one likes to have to reanimate, especially scenes that I had already approved. But making *Land Before Time* was both enjoyable and an interesting experience. One time I remember late in the production, mid-spring of '88, just a few months before the scheduled release of the film, Steven called and said that he and George thought that the story wasn't quite working. Steven was still buried in *Empire of the Sun*, and George was in London. He said that George could spare a couple of days to go through the script with us. So, John [Pomeroy], Gary [Goldman], and I flew over and met with George at Elstree Studios in Borehamwood, England. He had just released *Willow*. We took over a large conference room in the main building and used George's executive assistant to type up the new material in a copy of the previously approved script. There was restructuring or repositioning of the approved sequences and new descriptive text and dialogue added to the script to smooth out the transitions for the sequence changes. George is a really good story guy. The final product turned out to be a very big success. It did extremely well at the box office. And I think that movie spawned around twelve direct-to-video sequels.

Bill: Did you guys work on the sequel?

Don: No, we didn't. We only made the original movie. They did ask us to do the sequel to *An American Tail*, but at the same budget as the first. We had to decline. We would have had to cut the budget by 40 percent. So, after that we went right into our next movie, which was *All Dogs Go to Heaven*. Originally, I had remembered the title as a book. I had heard of it during the fourth grade. My teacher talked about it. But when I found the book, it had no story at all. It was simply an anthology of dogs. The title, however, I thought was a great title. Like a lot of people, I had many dogs growing up. And as a child you wonder what happens to them after they die. What if they do go to heaven? Maybe you'll meet them again. So we started working up a story about heaven, earth, dogs, and angels. It got horrible fast. Eventually we hired two writers from the states to come in and help us. One actually won an Oscar for his work on *Witness*. We thought he might know something about writing. But when he got off the airplane carrying his Oscar, we wondered if we'd made a mistake.

Bill: Are you kidding? He actually brought his Oscar?

Don: He brought it with him. I immediately turned to Gary and said, "We're in for trouble. Why is he carrying his Oscar?" Sure enough, we got off to a rough start. Then came an old friend from *Chinatown* …

Bill: Robert Towne.

Don: Robert Towne. Yes, very good. He called to let us know that he was in London meeting with the head of Universal Studios and was thinking of taking a trip over to Ireland with his wife and asked if he could drop by the studio. It was perfect timing because we needed his advice. We were having the hardest time with this story, and I asked him for just one hint that might help us get on track. He said, "Tell me your story in four minutes." As I quickly tried to tell the story, he stared at me for the longest time. Then, as I expected wisdom to flow from his mouth, his initial response was, "Where's the bathroom?" Okay, so he comes backs and says, "All right, you need to get rid of about half a dozen of your angels. The less heaven, the better. Just keep it on earth. Here's your story." And he lays it out in just a few sentences. It works perfectly. After we wrote it down, we still needed a writer. Fortunately, a USC film school graduate, who had won first prize for his short live-action film, sent us a script. His name was David N. Weiss. This was long before he became well known for his work on the *Rugrats*, *Shrek*, and *Smurf* movies. David would stand up and pace around the room, screaming the lines that he was writing. He'd act it out while someone wrote it down. He just couldn't sit down and write. David performed the entire movie of *All Dogs Go to Heaven* for us in my office in Ireland. Then we proceeded to make the picture.

Bill: Not all in one session, right?

Don: No, that probably took a couple of months. And afterward, of course, there's a lot of rewriting. You go back and correct your mistakes. And, as storyboarding proceeded, inspiration would come and more changes would have to be made to the script.

Bill: How did the boarding of the story change?

Don: I started out, but then added other artists that I thought were ready to storyboard, Dan Kuenster, who was one of our directing animators, and Larry Leker, the head of the layout department that wanted to show me what he could do storyboarding.

One of our big questions was about what the dog should look like. We needed some kind of connection with this dog. Now, back while making *Space Ace*, our second video game, there was a dog that came running through our parking lot with a pack of about seven dogs. Burt Reynolds had just left the building after a story meeting—strangely enough—about a junk-yard dog (and a private detective), which we were working on as a feature concept to cast Burt in. It wasn't for *All Dogs Go to Heaven*. It was going to be called *Canine Mystery*. As the dogs were running through the parking lot, suddenly this German shepherd split off from the others and came over to us. He was just covered with fleas. The dog had no collar and his ribs were showing. He looked like he'd been out on his own for some time. So we rescued him and brought him into the studio. Gary [Goldman]'s girlfriend, Cathy Carr, took the dog to a vet. She had him sheep-dipped and neutered, all in the same day. Gary brought the dog to work every day for the next 13 years. He became the studio mascot and we called him Burt, after Mr. Reynolds. He would regularly visit every person in the building.

So thinking about our studio mascot Burt, we realized there was no question at all about this dog, who is the central character in the movie. He should be a German shepherd and his name should be Burt. Obviously we changed the name later, but for *All Dogs* we did go after Burt Reynolds for the voice. And that brought in a whole new level of strangeness, fun, and craziness. Burt came in and made up a dog voice, which was not Burt Reynolds. We were expecting Burt's natural voice. He flew in on a helicopter, got off, went straight into the sound booth, and started talking in this strange voice. Now, how am I going to tell Burt Reynolds that that voice isn't what we want? I try, but Burt isn't interested in reading as himself. So then we bring in Dom DeLouise. He's not only Burt's good friend, but he had worked with us on h*NIMH*. Dom tells me flat out, "You're not going to be able to direct Burt. I can tell you that right now. Why don't you put me in the movie too. Let me be another dog, maybe his sidekick. Let me get with Burt and I'll get you the gold." That's how Dom DeLouise became Itchy the dog. When we went into the recording session he said, "Put the tape on and don't turn it off. Just roll it. Let me take care of Burt." Dom goes in, listens to Burt's dog voice, and just cuts into him. He says, "What the hell is that? You're going to look stupid." He then starts talking with Burt about pictures they've made in the past, giving him suggestions and advice. Burt got encouraged to start reading the lines just like the Burt we knew and wanted. And then they started creating their own lines, some of which we used in the final script. The session went on for about two hours. We had reels of tape. It was a gold mine. Even when it came to singing, Dom was a big help. He just told Burt that he was going to sing. It wasn't easy for him, but he did it. And he sounded great.

Bill: **That's funny since he actually made a country music album.**

Don: I know. Maybe he got inspired after that experience.

Bill: **Since you had to create this movie from scratch, did you treat the project differently? As a director, was this movie your baby?**

Don: I'd like to say yes. But I can't say that I was more partial to it. Nor was it the only movie we've created "from scratch." *An American Tail*'s story and script had to be rethought and rewritten, while I started storyboarding the pogrom sequence. *The Land Before Time* came with just Steven's brief verbal concept. Neither had a book that we might have adapted. We have brought in writers on all of our films, with the exception of *NIMH*. It had an award-winning book to work from. And *All Dogs* was the second film that we had to overlap from a previous production.

I did change the process. I would turn over the production to Gary [Goldman] once the storyboarding was done and I was happy with the quality of the animation that was being produced. Then I would start the next film's script and storyboarding process. So I jumped off *The Land Before Time* and onto *All Dogs* while Gary finished *Land*. It was apparent that I had to adjust to accommodate continuity of product. *All Dogs* was the first film that I shared directing credits. It was with Gary and Dan Kuenster. Dan had become a very good storyboard artist and could actually imitate my style of drawing. But to answer the question, I think all directors must feel that the films they direct are their babies. I've always felt very close to any movie that I was directing because it was like raising a child. You have to nurture it and provide the right kind of environment so that it grows into a wonderful movie. You're completely involved. And at the end it's always sad when you say good-bye to these characters. You create them. You truly get to know them because they have a personality and a voice. Then they're gone. It's extremely emotional to walk away. In fact, I'm not sure why, but I never go back and look at any of our pictures. I don't look back and say, "Oh, isn't that wonderful?" Nothing like that ever happens unless someone sits me down to ask technical questions about animating. The thrill of animation, for me, is putting the picture together, solving the dilemma of unifying all these little thousands of pieces so that they entertain in a visually beautiful way. I learned early on that children all over the world would watch these movies on video, over and over, memorizing the dialogue, and actually live in that fantasy world when the real world gets too hard for them. I've always felt very privileged to be able to provide that fantasy world. And if they go in and learn something from it, that just makes me even happier.

Bill: **You also had more control than ever before on *All Dogs Go to Heaven*. You were a director with a fully functional studio behind you. Did this change your approach to directing? Did you evolve in any specific way?**

Don: Well, it's not so simple, even at that level. As we moved into the next picture, the business side of the industry just seemed to take over the act of filmmaking. We conceptualized this picture called Rock-A-Doodle. In came the financier's marketing guru, "You can't show this! You can't show that!" I kept finding myself in the middle of this mass of marketing and financial people. I believe Frank Thomas used to say, "It's hard to remember when you're up to your ass in alligators that all you want to do is drain the swamp." All I wanted to do was animate. By some miracle we managed to make twelve animated films. And there were times that I really don't know how we did it. We certainly had our share of bumps in the road, outside the realm of creativity. Every time we tried to own a part of what we were creating we were held at bay. It felt like we were the goose that laid golden eggs, and all they wanted was to own us, or destroy us.

Character development, *Thumbelina*, Don Bluth Productions © 1994.

Bill: **So what brought you back to the States?**

Don: We had sold off parts of the store until there was nothing left to sell [laughs]. Actually, it was a lot more complicated than that. We no longer owned the company. In 1990, about 10 months before the completion of *Rock-A-Doodle*, our company closed a $60 million, three-picture deal with a Belgian investor. It was a great deal. However, a few months into the production of *A Troll in Central Park*, he ran into financial problems and asked if a wealthy associate could come in and take his position in the deal. Suddenly we were in a new negotiation. The negotiation went on and on until the advanced funds that we had for production started diminishing. This put our company in a weak position and with almost 490 employees between Dublin and Burbank. With no bank to bail us out, we agreed to transfer our shares in the company in exchange for the $60 million in funding from another source. Cash flow began again and then in the spring of 1993, with *A Troll in Central Park* and *Thumbelina* complete and in postproduction, and *The Pebble and the Penguin* just a few months from completion, the investor's bank came in and shut down the operation, a move that forced us into the protection of receivership or bankruptcy in Dublin. After about four months in the courts, the company was bought by a subsidiary of Star TV in China. They asked us to stay and complete the dubs of the first two films and complete production of the third film. We agreed. At least it would keep the Dublin crew employed and perhaps give us an opportunity to make more films. However, after agreeing to stay with the new company, which was using our Don Bluth namesake, they eventually reneged on the agreed contract and refused to sign it. However, what really brought us back was when I received a call from Bill Mechanic, the then-president of Walt Disney International Distribution and Worldwide Video divisions. He was being recruited to become chairman at 20th Century Fox.

Bill said he wanted to meet with me and Gary, since he would not move to Fox unless they would allow him to build a feature animation division. He knew our work but didn't know us. He had heard that we were difficult to work with and wanted to meet us in person and get to know us. He wanted us to help him build that animation division. By the end of January of 1994 we signed with Fox. And, oddly enough, we took most of the Americans, Canadians, many of our trained Irish, plus our top internationals from Spain, Brazil, and East Germany with us back home to the USA! Better still, Fox built the new studio in Phoenix, Arizona. It was so nice to be warm again. Ireland was not warm. The people were, but the weather … often misty and cold—cold to the bone. And we were very fortunate to have brought members of our trained crew back with us, 162 of them. Disney was producing animated films as fast as they could. Jeffrey Katzenberg had just left Disney, joining Spielberg and Geffen to start DreamWorks SKG; he was taking as many Disney animation staff with him as he could recruit. Between them, they hired most of the best-trained talent in LA. When it was announced that Fox had struck a deal with us, Fox was inundated with over 10,000 applicants

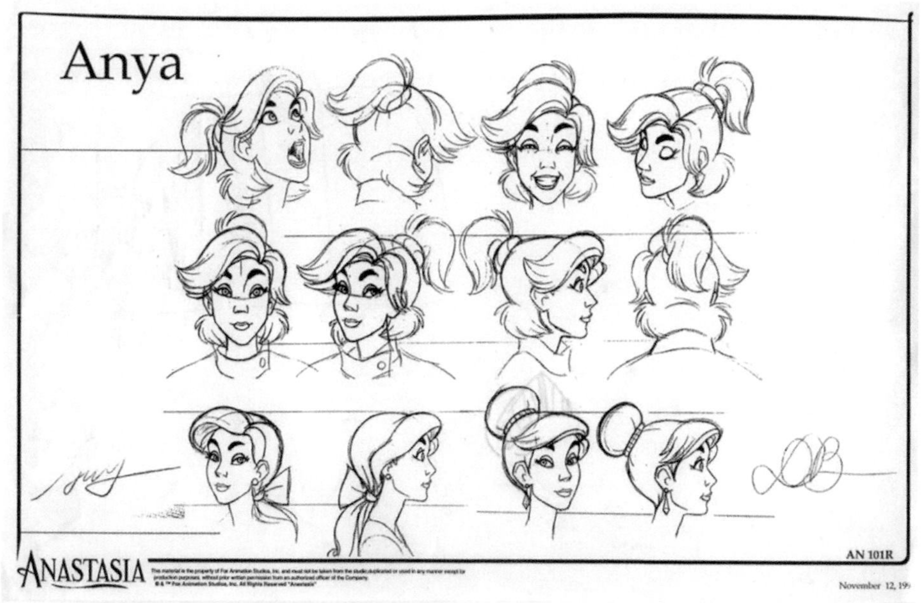

Model sheet, "Anya", *Anastasia*, 1997 © Fox.

Sketch, *Anastasia*, 1997 © Fox.

from around the world in the first month. When we finally started making *Anastasia*, we had hired animation artists from fourteen different countries, many of them from Canada, the Philippines, and local Arizona artists.

Our first film with Fox Animation, *Anastasia*, was a really fun picture to make. I had no idea that making an animated feature in widescreen had become quite so easy. You didn't have to work on wide paper anymore. There was no more Xeroxing images onto cels. In fact, we didn't use cels anymore. We just scanned the drawings in and then added color. We could add multiple levels to the animation. We could quickly do all those beautiful things that I saw Walt do in those classic animated films from the golden age of animation. You were limited only by your imagination. It was a wonderful time. Then, after *Anastasia*, Fox LA didn't have a project ready.

There was a story called *Planet Ice*, something science fiction, that was stalled and going nowhere fast. Bill Mechanic asked Gary and me if we could do anything with it. There was some recorded dialogue and something like three sequences storyboarded, which had been scanned and edited as a digital work-print, but no animation. However, there were piles of preproduction drawings for character designs and location paintings to look at. Since we hadn't been officially assigned our second project yet, money for the Phoenix animation studio was running out. Bill said candidly, "Either take this science fiction film and make it, or we have to lay everybody off." We had no choice. We took it and made what eventually became *Titan A.E.* Well, wait a minute, I almost forgot *Bartok the Magnificent*. This was a movie we came up with after *Anastasia*, in order to keep the studio crew intact, and give time to Chris [Meledandri] and his LA writers time to come up with the next feature film concept.

Storyboards, *Titan A.E.*, 2000 © Fox.

Bill: **That was your spin-off from *Anastasia*?**

Don: Yes. It was a prequel. It was never distributed theatrically as a motion picture. It went straight to video; it was planned as a direct-to-video project. However, it did keep the wolf from the door.

And as we made *Titan A.E.*, something was brewing again. There was a lot of politics going on at 20th Century Fox. Bill Mechanic had made a picture called *Fight Club*, which according to rumor, Rupert Murdoch did not like. So there was a little bit of friction there. Bill, as it turned out, was being eliminated from the studio. Since we were his baby, they chose not to promote *Titan*. That definitely hurt us. And when Bill was officially removed from Fox, the Arizona Fox Animation Studio went down too. Basically, that was the last door that opened … and slammed shut. There you have it.

Bill: What about new methods like motion capture? Did you find yourself adjusting your style as new technology was introduced?

Don: I believe the human eye is able to look at cartoons and accept them as they are. There's no problem. When you look at an animated movie that is depicting human movement, if the movement is too caricatured or too sloppy, the audience can lose the willing suspension of disbelief. And that pulls them out of the picture. I've always advocated shooting live action anytime you're trying to approach human movement. Otherwise you might miss some of the subtle nuances of the human body's rhythm. Many people don't know this, but the entire movie of *Cinderella* was shot live action, as was our *Anastasia*.

Bill: What about postproduction? How involved are you? Do you find yourself going back and making significant changes?

Don: I'm really not good in postproduction. I just don't have enough patience to sit there and go back and forth, back and forth. Gary Goldman is exceptionally good at it. I just let him have it. My attention is entirely consumed by the storyboard and preproduction. That's where you make critical decisions about characters, close-ups, long shots, lighting, *et cetera*. That's where I believe my editing strength really comes into play.

Bill: Is there anything you would like to say before we wrap up?

Don: If I had to look back on my whole career, on all the people that I had the privilege of working with, like Steven Spielberg, George Lucas, and all the actors who gave us their voices, it's almost too much to take in. It simply amazes me. I've worked with truly amazing and talented people. And that includes individuals that are not famous at all. They just worked diligently to help us put something beautiful on the screen. It's the people. That's been the joy in my career. We created unique worlds that have encouraged, inspired, and simply made people happy, whether they were having a great day or a horrible one. We gave them a sweet place in which to get lost, for just a little bit. I have no regrets. Walking away from the Disney Studio was a good thing. It forced me to cut my own path. And I always knew that

I could do that. So now I'm just trying to make sure I'm giving it all back. There are lessons that need to be passed on. We've made movies with modern technology and with antiquated technology, and I believe, second only to good storytelling (writing), drawing is still the seed and inspiration to good animation filmmaking, be it traditional hand-drawn or CG animation. Anyway, it's been great talking with you guys. Thank you for including me as one of the many animation directors you are interviewing for your book.

Ron: Thanks for taking the time to sit with us. This book wouldn't be complete without your story.

4

Pete Docter Interview

Pete Docter © Pixar.
Photo: Deborah Coleman

Pete Docter has called his life "blessed." Others might call it lucky, but most would say that it was the audience that got lucky when Pete entered animation.

He had an unlikely start, growing up in Minnesota, never a hot-bed of the industry. But strangely (or luckily), Pete stumbled onto the only animation company in the state and got some early training and encouragement. When it came time to go to school he made another fortuitous move, enrolling in the only existing character animation program in the West—CalArts. There he met some of the artists who would change the future of the business. One of them, John Lasseter, offered him a job at the only company he has ever worked for since: Pixar.

You could call Pete a towering presence, since he is (and always has been for his age) extremely tall. He has a remarkably mild, relaxed way of leading a team. His career was an example of the peculiar

Pixar culture, where a "nondirector type" is given trust and support and becomes the ultimate directorial success; a director with not just an unusual personal style but an absolutely original creative vision.

When Pete Docter accepted his Oscar for *Up*, he said, in front of that worldwide TV audience: "Never did I dream that making a flip book out of my third-grade math book would lead to this." Pete still likes flip books; he draws one every year and sends copies out as his family Christmas card. I treasure my collection. It takes talent to do a flip book. To take the time to do one when you're a world-famous director is something else again.

We interviewed Pete at the Four Seasons Hotel in Beverly Hills.

Bill Kroyer

Bill: When did you first become aware of animation and when did you first think that you might be an animator?

Pete: Well, I remember doing flip books in the corners of my math book in second grade. Even before that, I think it started for me with *Charlie Brown*. You know, there's something about those drawings, the expressivity of Schultz's work that made me think, "Wow, I gotta figure this out." But then what really hooked me was movement. Not drawing—though I always admired great drawings. You know how there's always the kid that's in your class who's the master draftsman and who's drawing dragons and horses and stuff? That was not me. My passion was making things move. That's what got me hooked.

Bill: You figured that out by yourself?

Pete: Yeah. I don't remember, maybe I saw some television special on animation or something. But I made tons—and my mom still has them of course—tons of flip books and movies.

Bill: What happened in high school? Did you somehow find a way to improve your skills in animation in high school?

Pete: There was not much going on in terms of animation or film in my high school art classes. We got to make belt buckles and linoleum prints and things, but nobody really knew anything about animation. And of course this was before the

Internet—you really had to search for information. I remember hearing about the Preston Blair animation book, and I looked almost a year for it because I didn't know it would be at the art store. I was looking at bookstores.

Bill: But you knew about it?

Pete: Yeah, I read mention of it somewhere. And then of course *The Illusion of Life* came out and when I saw that I poured over every page, trying to absorb it all. It surprised me though how much of the book's focus was on acting. This just shows you where I was. I was looking for more information on technique, like how do you get things to move nicely, with follow-through and overlap and the squash-and-stretch? Frank [Thomas] and Ollie [Johnston] covered that, but most of their focus was on the inner workings of characters and storytelling. That surprised me.

Bill: It's interesting about timing and culture. That book was so influential. There's a whole generation that found that book and managed to build a career out of it. So by the time you got to high school, had you done anything that was like a legitimate film that was actually shot with a camera?

Pete: I had made a whole bunch of really bad Super 8 silent animated films at home on my own. And then I was lucky enough to be placed in this high school program that took kids that had a passion for something and paired them with companies. Another classmate who was into artificial intelligence went over to Honeywell. I got placed at this commercial animation house called *Bajus-Jones*.

Bill: Where were you doing this?

Pete: Bajus-Jones was in Edina. I grew up in Bloomington, Minnesota.

Bill: Wasn't Bajus-Jones the only animation company in Minnesota?

Pete: So far as I knew, pretty much, yeah. So what they did was fantastic. They told me, "Well, you seem like a kid with a passion for this. Come on in, here's the paper, there's the down-shooter, use anything you want." So I just sat there all day and did my own stuff. And they said, "This will be your mentor, Bill Barder. He's working, so don't bug him too much, but if you have questions, you can go to him." Once in a while I'd go in with a scene and he'd take a look and give me pointers. So I did this film that was a really clunky sort of parody of an advertisement for the *Gifted and Talented Testing Institute*.

Bill: Commercial piece?

Pete: Yeah, it was promoting this made-up gifted and talented school, and this egghead kid comes in and they give him these tests. It barely makes sense, but that's your early stuff.

Bill: Unbelievable break. To actually live near an animation studio, and be allowed to go in while you're still in high school.

Pete: Before that I'd done my own stuff using my dad's Super 8 camera. I'd figured out looking at Super 8 film footage that each one of those little frames is slightly different. And I knew my flip books were the same principle, so I figured, "I wonder if I could film my flip books?" I tried filming as I flipped through one, and then later I tried just triggering the shutter, "Click!" once per image. Then I turned the page and "Click!" did it again, and again … and it worked! The camera took two or three frames per click, but it looked like it was moving. Eventually I wore out my dad's camera, because it was not built for that sort of thing.

Bill: Were there any good animators at Bajus-Jones who you could learn directly from?

Pete: Well, the guy that I mentioned, Bill Barder, was a great draftsman. And he was very patient with me. We stay in contact to this day. The thing, of course, working at a commercial house, you have to have this wide range of styles, because you're going from sort of RO Blechman style to Kurtz & Friends style to who knows what. So Bill was great and I got some good experience there. But it was really CalArts that took me to the next level.

Bill: So in 1986 you entered CalArts with a bit of a head start, I would think?

Pete: I was one of the only people in my class that had actually done animation before starting at school. At that time, it was hard to get access to the kind of equipment you needed to create animated films. All the other guys there had an interest in it and, of course, had drawn a lot, but, yeah, I had a head start.

Bill: How did that change your experience compared to others there? Did you end up being more productive? Do you think you got more out of it?

Pete: Well, it's funny. I remember, as I struggled to animate that first year, after five or six months there was something that just kind of clicked, and after that I could feel movement. That was the first step for me, going from just making a series of still drawings to really feeling movement. It's a difficult concept to really articulate; you just sort of feel it.

Bill: I always called it "going in the zone." You know, you're in the zone. You're not even aware of anything going on.

Pete: Yeah, absolutely. You get lost in the work when you're really going.

Bill: How long were you there? You actually graduated from CalArts, right?

Pete: I graduated after three years. I'd had credits that I transferred over from the University of Minnesota, where I'd gone for one year before attending CalArts.

Bill: How did you see yourself progressing in those three years? Other than getting that initial feeling of movement, how far do you think you came?

Pete: Well, my first-year film was called *Winter.* It was about a little kid who gets dressed up and wants to go outside, and he's all bundled up and he can't even move and he tips over. It's kind of a nothing idea, but I remember it came about as I was talking to Barry Johnson, and I was telling this story about my sister, you know, growing up in Minnesota—it's so frigid cold that you have to bundle kids up in multiple layers—and she could barely walk, and it made us all laugh. And he says, "That would be a good idea for a film." And I thought, "Hey, maybe he's right!" So I boarded it out, and it was clunky, crude drawing compared to some of the other guys. But when all the films screened, mine got big laughs. In fact it made it into *Mike and Spike's Festival of Animation*, and it was one of the biggest laughs in that show. And I realized something about films: it's really all about the idea. I initially thought it was about the quality of your drawings, good design, or how well something moved. But of course it's really all about the idea.

Joe Ranft, who was a story teacher at CalArts, used to say that making animated films is like telling a joke and waiting for three years to see if anyone laughs. It's tough to wait that long for a response, but filmmaking really is a lot like joke telling, or storytelling. And I think it's really important to be in the audience for the reaction, because that's what really teaches you.

Bill: Were there teachers or students that had a particular influence on you when you were there?

Pete: Oh yeah. Everybody! [Laughter] The first thing that shocked me was sitting down in Bob Winquist's class—he was the general director of the program—and he said, "We're going to teach you design." And I thought, "What the heck does design have to do with anything? I wanna draw cartoons!" Just shows you how ignorant I was. Bob's approach grew out of the Chouinard Art Institute, which was to teach the basic principles of abstract design: contrast, shape variation, contour continuation, all those basic concepts. And I'm surprised to this day how often I use that stuff in every single thing I do, from story, to character design, to sound design, to movement. All those basic principles apply to everything.

Winter, 1988.

Next Door, 1990.

Bill: **Why is that so important to getting the story or the character across?**

Pete: Well these fundamental principles are key to putting ideas across—for getting your ideas to read to the audience. They apply not only to design, but storytelling. When you first learn stuff, it's all very, very intellectual. But once you use them for a while, they become a natural, instinctive part of your work. They're also great tools for making things better. You'll be working on a project and you just know, "Something about this isn't working. How can I make it better?" And you step back and analyze, and it's that time that those concepts are so important.

Bill: **After CalArts you went right to Pixar, which in a way was a second job because you'd already been at Bajus-Jones.**

Pete: I'd also been an intern at Disney between my second and third year. Oh, and while I was at CalArts, Mike Giaimo—who's another huge influence—was teaching character design, and during the day at that time he was working at Bob Rogers and Company. Mike drafted a couple of us for a couple of weeks to do some story work.

Bill: **It's interesting how you were influenced so much by design, and not so much by the animation teachers there.**

Pete: Well, design and story were big for me, which I was not expecting. Chris Buck was my animation teacher. He was great, not just in being a very patient teacher, but also in adapting himself to what each student was trying to do, both with drawing and movement. "Oh, I see you're doing sort of a Canadian Film Board style," or a UPA thing or whatever. He'd support what you were doing instead of trying to change it to his style. He's an amazing animator. But even there, much of Chris' emphasis was on acting and story. So he was really great.

Bill: **So that meant you were able to kind of flow with your more natural inclination and style. Did you feel like you had a style that was different than others?**

Pete: Not really. I just kind of did what appealed to me. I love the work of Bill Watterson, which is pretty obvious in my first student film. I really relied on those "storytelling poses." I'd go from one pose to another and then just hold. And it was the pauses and funny expressions that were getting the laughs. So in a sense that first film wasn't really full animation. I remember it was Russ Edmonds, my second-year animation teacher, who pushed me to go beyond that. He said, "You can do the poppy, pose-to-pose thing. That's great. Now push further and do more full, fluid stuff."

Bill: **How did the Pixar hire come about?**

Pete: Well, I'd seen Pixar's films in the festivals. And John Lasseter had seen my films in the festivals. But I never even considered applying at Pixar because everybody knew it was just John Lasseter and a bunch of technical guys up there.

Bill: It was a tiny place in those days.

Pete: Yeah. So apparently John went to his friend Joe Ranft—my story teacher—and asked him, "Are there any good up-and-coming students that might be good hires for us?" And Joe thought of me. I remember having lunch at Tiny Naylor's with Joe Ranft and John Lasseter and thinking, "How did I get here?!"

Bill: And that was it? John just asked you to come work with him?

Pete: He said, "Could you come up?" And I didn't even ask what they were paying. I'm telling you, much of this was luck. I was born in the right year. Two years before, the only jobs out there were on *He-Man and the Masters of the Universe* and, you know, crappy stuff like that. And then right as I graduated, *The Simpsons* was starting, Disney was on the upswing, there were all kinds of opportunities. Going into school, my dream was to someday be like Frank Thomas or Ollie Johnston. "I'm gonna work at Disney and draw and animate." But instead I went to this up-and-coming computer company that hadn't really done much except short films.

Bill: So you were the tenth hire and the third animator?

Pete: Within the animation group, yeah.

Bill: Who were the other two?

Pete: John was first. And then, I think three months earlier, Andrew Stanton had been hired. So as I arrived, John said, "Well, I'm busy, so sit down and watch Andrew. Learn by watching him. He's animating his first commercial." I guess Andrew had worked on the story and some design work up until that point, so this was his first animation. I was sitting watching him, expecting to learn. And I did learn some new expletives. He couldn't get the computer to do anything!

Bill: Was it a Lifesavers thing or something?

Pete: Trident chewing gum. There was this singing mint leaf on top of a piano and an ice cube playing the piano [laughter].

Bill: Were you drawing there or did they teach you the computer right away?

Pete: It was just right into the computer. I learned key-framing and the sort of layered approach that computer animation required, which is totally different, of course, than drawing. And I remember thinking, "If I was drawing this, I'd be done in minutes.

From left to right—Pete Docter, Andrew Stanton, John Lasseter, and Joe Ranft at Pixar Animation Studios, © Pixar. Photo: Deborah Coleman.

Instead this is taking me hours!" It was really frustrating, initially. But, in the end, I learned a new way to think, and it was really valuable. Even if I were to go back to hand-drawn, what I learned from computer animation was great analysis. Plus, with computers you can try something and if you don't like it, you just revert to the last saved version and off you go.

So, first thing I did was a Listerine boxing commercial that John directed. It was funny—I thought for sure the hand of the artist came through in the drawings, and that with CG you wouldn't be able to tell my work from anyone else's. But a guy I went to school with, Donavan Cook, he had seen the commercial, and over the phone he picked out exactly which scenes I animated. Of course there's no drawing at all—computer animation is sort of like animating a puppet. And so the fact that he was able to pick out my scenes … well, I guess it was kind of bad because my stuff stood out so much. But I took it as a compliment at the time.

Bill: And what was it about your stuff that he was thinking about?

Pete: Well, my stuff was way more extreme and bouncy, and John was much more subtle with his work. But I think we kind of influenced each other. I remember him saying that he really liked how far I was pushing things. And of course his control and subtlety was something that I definitely had to learn.

Bill: So you encountered the thing that people who go from drawing to computers come up against: the need to analyze and break down and reconstruct the pieces in order to find that zone feel. Before you felt it; now all of a sudden you're confronted with this thing where you can't just feel it. And that's something that probably a lot of people end up not being able to do.

Pete: Yeah, it's true. *Toy Story* was educational for me because there were so many different artists from different backgrounds. This was the first computer-animated feature. Of course there were one or two people that had done computer animation for years up to that point, but by and large we had to train these guys. Some—like stop-motion animators—adapted pretty readily. Computer animation is closer to the way stop-motion animators think, it seems to me. Whereas for others—especially the hand-drawn guys with years of experience—the more years they'd had in another medium, the harder it was to shift their way of thinking. The key for me was thumbnailing. You know, if I could thumbnail something out and know it in my head, then I could start to break it down, and know what the torso is doing, and the upper leg, and the knee, and so on.

Bill: How long did you work on commercials and those kinds of things before you moved onto the next project?

Pete: Well, too long for me. I actually talked to John about leaving Pixar at one point. "All of my friends are down at Disney doing acting; they're doing serious feature work, and we're here making bouncy happy products. I just don't know how much longer I can wait." And I remember him saying, "Well, fine, go if you have to, but I think you'd be making a big mistake. We're just on the edge of something." Luckily I didn't leave, thank goodness.

Bill: So he didn't tell you what it was?

Pete: Well, I knew that they were trying to land this television special, because I was working on the story with him and Andrew and eventually Joe Ranft. But to be honest I doubt that John knew of anything specific at that point. He just had a general optimism and confidence in what we were doing. Of course the television special didn't work out, and it was quite a few months after that finally the Disney thing landed. It was late '91 or something in there when we started working on it.

Bill: **When that happened, what was your role in it?**

Pete: It pretty much just flowed right from the way we always worked. Every commercial we got, John, Andrew, and I would sit down and we would just brainstorm. The great thing we had with the Pixar short films ... since they had won Oscars and were so entertaining, it meant that the clients, beyond just the look of computer graphics, wanted our creative input as well. So we would take their ideas and say, "Well all right, the way they planned this spot is really kind of lousy. What are they trying to do here? Let's make our own version." And so the feature developed in the same way, where the three of us would get together and talk. What seemed great yesterday seemed crappy today, so we'd redo it and redo it again. John would rope us both in on everything. He'd say, "What do you guys think?" He's a great collaborator. We had a weird situation on that movie, because apparently John had been sought after by Disney for years, asking him to come back and work there. He'd worked at Disney years earlier but was let go. John kept telling them, "No, let us do a computer film up here for you guys." Prior to that, all animation at Disney was done in house.

Tim Burton broke that mold with *Nightmare Before Christmas*, which was produced in San Francisco with Henry Selick directing, and it worked out well enough for Disney to say, "All right, let's try it again." So John came back to Andrew and me and basically asked, "So what do you guys want to do? What should this film be about?" Of course this was exactly the opposite of everybody else in Hollywood who have their scripts they've been trying desperately to get made for 18 years. So we had this weird backwards situation. We had developed a story for this TV special, which was about a toy. Joe Ranft told John that he'd developed these great characters in the Pixar short films and felt they could be taken further. So the TV special was based around the character in the short film *Tin Toy*. And that's really where *Toy Story* started; it was built from that.

Bill: **So the small studio and informal setup allowed you to be kind of a generalist in the production, right? Rather than being pigeonholed, your first experience on a feature was a broad experience.**

Pete: Very much so. Scriptwriting, boarding, character design, everything. In fact, when students today ask me about working at Pixar, I always suggest they find a small studio to start out in. Find somewhere that you can contribute all around and really get your feet wet and can have more of an effect on the end result.

Bill: **In the production, did you focus primarily on animation?**

Pete: Story and design first, then animation. See, we were so naive, we thought: first you do the story, then that's done; and then you go on and build the characters and sets, then that's done; and then you animate and so on. So our plan was we were going to wrap up story, and then Andrew and I would go on and be co-heads of animation. And of course, the story was a lot harder to nail down than we thought, and we struggled on and on. When it got time to shift into production, the thought was that I'd lead the charge, train the animators, test models, and so on. And Andrew would come along when the story was locked. Well, story just kept getting revised, and so Andrew stayed with Joe working on story and I ended up as the sole supervising animator.

Bill: How much animation did you end up doing?

Pete: Quite a bit. I don't remember footage, but I did stuff on almost every character, and quite a bit on Woody. I can still go through that film and point out who did every scene.

Bill: You were also probably involved in software revision and making recommendations for the tools.

Pete: Well, you know the software had developed over the course of the short films and commercials. I don't recall a ton of software changes during production. It was pretty rudimentary, looking back—when we started on *Toy Story*, we didn't even have inverse kinematics. So when Woody would walk, or even stand and shift his weight, we had to work with this tool that we called *IKT*—inverse kinematics tool—which would calculate frame-by-frame what the two joints should do to make his foot lock in this place. The tool would step through and place values for the joints into the spreadsheet

Sketches, Pete Docter, *Toy Story,* © Disney/Pixar.

tool on every frame. And usually you'd hit record, and you would come back and the foot would be wobbling all over the place. You'd have to go back and hand-massage it so it would stop shuddering and just stay still. So we animators spent a lot of time doing stuff like that. I remember thinking, "Shouldn't a computer be able to figure out these calculations better than me?"

Bill: Were there dedicated riggers, or were you kind of doing that as well?

Pete: No, we animators didn't do any rigging. I would work with the riggers—we called them *modelers* at that point—to figure out where we wanted controls and stuff. I had done a little bit on commercials, both modeling and rigging, but there were separate groups of people that did that on *Toy Story*, as well as shading and lighting. We animators focused exclusively on the movement.

Bill: So on *Toy Story* you were the animation supervisor. What's next?

Pete: Well, what happened along the way—and this was a product of being so small and casual—was that Andrew and I would go everywhere with John. We'd go to recording sessions with Tom Hanks and Tim Allen, the orchestra scoring sessions, and I'd sit in on layout—all to help in any way I could. And along the way, I watched how the whole process went. So when John was out of the office, Andrew and I could fill in. We knew what he wanted, and we knew the history of what we'd already tried. But just as importantly, that really trained both of us for directing in the future. I don't think John was really thinking that far ahead—maybe he was, but I think more likely it's just that's the way he likes to work; he thrives on collaboration. I really respected the way John ran animation dailies. It was a completely open forum. Everyone would speak up with opinions on everyone else's work. I always figured he took this from his days at Disney, but apparently he learned it at ILM in the late eighties. It was an environment where everybody was free to throw out ideas. So, you know, shots would be shown and anybody from any part of the room could say, "You know, what if his eyebrow was reversed? That would be better because … blah blah blah." So you'd shout out suggestions and at the end of course John would synopsize, "All right, Mr. Animator, here are the three things I want you to do: bang bang bang." But out of this open discussion I think we really learned a lot from each other. I had a great education, watching and participating.

Bill: Are those things you continue to use in your own work?

Pete: Oh yeah, absolutely.

Bill: What an amazing thing to be able to do—because you had not really been exposed before to scoring or recording or anything like that.

Pete: No. Well, growing up I was part of a youth symphony in Minnesota, and I'd written and arranged an orchestral score for my third-year film. So I'd had very fundamental, bare bones–level exposure to music scoring, but this was at a whole new level. I learned how to talk to a composer and things like that.

Bill: What did you learn about talking to a composer that became valuable?

Pete: Well, something I learned was not to tell people how to do their job. You tell them what's necessary to inspire them. And usually that means speaking more emotionally about things—as opposed to, "I want a B-flat here," or, "take the cellos out," or whatever. Instead, you want to say, "I'm looking for the feeling of anxiety or tension here," or, "I want that sense of a beautiful spring morning and you can feel the wind in your hair." It's the same when you're communicating with animators. I don't want to tell them, "Have his hand here in frame seven and then, in five frames, move up to this." It's more productive to say, "I want him to burn his hand, and you know what that feels like when you've touched the stove and, aach, it's that searing pain." So you communicate that feeling you're after, and the animator will then kick in all these ideas, much better ideas than I would ever have. Same thing with composers. That way the film is not just the director's ideas; it's a collaboration of artists working together, plussing every stage.

Michael Giacchino and Pete Docter © Pixar. Photo: Deborah Coleman.

Bill: And how do you direct actors?

Pete: I try to do the same thing. Working with actors is especially dangerous after you've built your reels and you have a scratch track. After you watch them like 8,000 times, those scratch performances get drilled into your head. You have a certain cadence and a read that's stuck in your ear, and there's a great temptation to try to get that from the actor. You want to do a line-read: "Say it like this." But every time you do that, even if the actor asks for it, you end up with a stilted performance. I've learned instead to tune my ear to listen for believability, so that when the actor is performing the line, I just try to sense whether it feels truthful. That's what I listen for. You want to feel that they are actually in that head space, that they're going through this, whatever this scene is. I remember talking to Tom Hanks, because he was just amazing. He would do fifteen, twenty takes, and each one totally felt like he just came up with that dialog right there on the spot. Of course, it's all written on the page. So I asked him, "What's going through your head as you're acting?" and he said, "Ideally, as little as possible." He was trying not to kill the performance by overanalyzing or overthinking. Of course that doesn't really work for us as animators—you do really have to analyze everything. But that was a guide for me as to how to talk to the actors. Just get them there emotionally, and they'll do the job.

Bill: **The animator component is so much more complicated because the character is created by an entire team.**

Pete: Yeah.

Bill: **How do you discover your characters? Is there a point where you feel you're starting to know them in the design stage, or are you waiting until the actor performs?**

Pete: Well, I think the key is the word you just used, "discover." You know, I used to imagine that the way stories were created was that Walt Disney would wake up one morning and just say, "*Dumbo*!," and it would be fully formed in his head and they would just make that. And the reality is, of course, that it's this weird, organic, messy process, where you have one thing, and then you add something else, and then you take parts away. For Buzz Lightyear, for example, we had very clear ideas on what he was like when we started. At that point he was sort of a "Dudley Do-Right" type—you know, he even spoke in that sort of announcerly, superhero voice. And that's what we were looking for initially when it came to casting voice talent. But John had listened to some of Tim Allen's comedy and thought he would be great, and so he hired him. I listened to the dialog recorded at the first session and I remember Andrew and I looking at each other going, "This is a disaster. He can't do what we're looking for." You know, because we had that "Dudley Do-Right" kind of approach in mind. And he was approaching the role much more casually, or suave, like a cop.

Sketch, Pete Docter, *Toy Story*, © Disney/Pixar.

So out of desperation we started to adjust the writing to this, and in the end, because of Tim Allen's contributions and us writing to that, I think the character of Buzz is much more specific and unique than it would have been if we had just gone with the "Dudley Do-Right" guy. Since then, this process of rewriting to fit the actor is something we do routinely on almost every role.

Bill: How did *Monsters, Inc.* come about?

Pete: Well, I remember I was in the shower. I had been doing a sort of postanalysis of *Toy Story* for myself, and I was surprised how many people had confessed to me that they too believed their toys came to life when they weren't in the room. I thought, "I wonder if there are other commonly held childhood beliefs like this?" Well, I knew there were monsters that hid in my closet at night. The subject matter seemed to hold promise to me, so I put together a short pitch. The story I brought in was totally different, but I came in—there was a small group of us, just Jeff Pidgeon and Harley Jessup working in development at that time—and I pitched it to them. And over the course of weeks, months, we built on the idea, and it totally changed. Jill Culton came on shortly thereafter, and between the four of us, plus John and Andrew, this was the core group that really contributed heavily to creating the story and characters that we ended up with on *Monsters, Inc.*

Bill: So I guess the chemistry of the studio is starting to change now, right? It's growing, getting bigger.

Pete: Right.

Bill: And this is your first time as a lead on a project at Pixar. On *Monsters, Inc.*, you are really the guy.

Pete: Well, yeah, but that was sort of ill defined. Early on I was in charge of the development group. But I don't think it was really definitive that I was going to direct it. I don't remember exactly when that came along. After *Toy Story*, John Lasseter went right on into *A Bug's Life*, and then when *Toy Story 2* sort of blew up he took that on. So he was on three films, one after another, and I think he was ready to take a break. [Laughter]

Sketch, Pete Docter, *Monsters, Inc.*, © Disney/Pixar.

Bill: What was it like to have to take on that amount of work? Did you feel you had to impose a certain way of working or did it organically form around you?

Pete: Well, I remember feeling very nervous because I'm not a take-that-hill, fill-the-room kind of guy. I work well with people one on one, but I'm not the guy to put up in front to charge up the troops and give 'em an inspirational speech. Brad Bird can do that. He's just crazy good. I always feel awkward. I relate to the "shy people" Garrison Keillor talks about. So directing was uncomfortable for me at the beginning. I also had this idea that now everybody works for me, and I have this weight of responsibility. And of course what you realize very quickly is that we all work for the story. They're not working for me—we're all in the service of what's going to best communicate this story to the audience.

Bill: Did you ever feel that your reticence put you in jeopardy at Pixar?

Pete: Oh yeah. I mean, there was a time when Steve Jobs took me on a walk and said, "You know, I don't know if things are working out with you. You need to step it up. When times get hard, people need to know they can count on the leader. And I don't sense that's coming from you."

Bill: At what stage was this?

Pete: This was about halfway through—two or three years in. We were just starting production, and we were still struggling with story.

Bill: How did you react to that discussion?

Pete: Well, of course my stress level went way up. But I was the first director there who was not John, so I had to find my own way. I think in part Steve was reacting to how sort of flippant I seemed to be. My attitude was, "Let's just have fun and enjoy this." And Steve had an intensity and seriousness about him that made him who he was, and that's what everybody respected about him. But that's not who I am. And being insecure, I struggled sometimes to hear my own instincts. That inner voice is kind of quiet sometimes. Everyone has to find their own way of working. Regardless, I think the key to the whole directing thing is understanding story: how to craft a good story. That's the hard part. Because once you crack the story, you have these amazing talented people, and if you feed them the right information and steer them the right way, the film comes into focus.

Bill: Did you take anything away from that encounter with Steve Jobs? Did it affect the way you worked after that?

Pete: This sounds crass—but it made me realize the importance of salesmanship. Early on I had in my head what I wanted, but I wasn't really very good at telling other people and standing up for it. "Here's my vision, here's how it's all going to come together."

That is something that is really important, and John is just instinctively good at it. You know, anytime you sit down with somebody, it's your opportunity to get them excited about what they're working on and show them how beautiful this could be, how it will affect people, and how important what they're doing is to the story. And that goes for the team of artists but also for executives. You have to be able to refocus and see it from their perspective—how they're seeing it and what's important to them about this story.

Bill: **OK, so you're in the middle of *Monsters, Inc*. Steve has this conversation with you and the story isn't working. How did you deal with that?**

Pete: I took it very personally. You know, I had pitched this concept and everybody went, "Yeah, okay, I'm on board! *Monsters*. That sounds great!" Especially when we came up with the idea that they scare kids for a living, that's their job, they clock in, they clock out. You have all this workplace humor, juxtaposed with these big guys with fangs and slobber and horns, and everybody could see the potential in that. But the next step was finding our main character. You need to fall in love with and care about that main character, so that you as the audience want what he wants. And we just didn't have a good grasp on that until very late in production. There was this sort of vacuum, this hole in the center of the story. People were asking, "What is this guy really about?" And there again, if I could have articulated more fully my thoughts—and I had this in my head from early on—the heart of the film was the relationship between this big hulking monster and this little kid who changes him. He loves his job, but he's torn by his feelings for this kid. And the fearlessness that the kid has, and the fear that the monster has towards the kid, seemed like great potential for humor—and ultimately emotion. If I could have communicated that to people, it would have been easier. I think the thing that really turned that around was when board artist Nate Stanton—he's Andrew Stanton's brother—storyboarded this scene where Sulley is waiting for the little girl to go to the bathroom and they end up in this sort of peek-a-boo game. And people suddenly reacted to that. "Oh yeah, this is funny, this is entertaining. Okay, I see where this is going." But up until then, I wasn't able to communicate where I was placing my chips. You know, what's the audience gonna get when they go to this movie?

Bill: **So what was your role at that moment as a director?**

Pete: I was trying to find the core of the film. At that point, you do that by building the reels. We learned early on that story reels are the proof that shows whether you have a film or you don't. And so you're trying to discover the film in these little pieces. So you go, "Okay, in this scene we've proven how Mike and Sulley are going to relate to each other and how funny that's going to be. And now people can extrapolate through the rest of the film backwards and forward and see what it's going to be like."

Monsters, Inc., 2001. © 2001 Disney/Pixar.

Then you look for the next building block. Initially you're feeling around in the dark for any little toehold. Joe Ranft had these great analogies. He told me once that working on story is like driving a car with all bald tires, and you're stuck in the mud, and the more you accelerate, the more you just sink. And then you finally discover that you have one tire that has a little bit of tread on it. So you move all the sandbags over so you'll just dig in on that one tire, and it sloooowly starts to pull you out of the mud, and then you get a little more traction, and so on. And finally you're out and running.

Bill: That's fantastic!

Pete: Yeah, I know. Joe sure had a great way of looking at things. We miss him.

Bill: Every director has a different way of working with his team. You have your head of story, you have your production designer, you have your editor, all of whom are massively important. How did you find yourself relating to your team in your first big directorial effort?

Pete: I think my strength and weakness is that I'm a people pleaser—I want everybody to be happy. This instinct comes in very handy when it comes to making the film. I want the audience to be satisfied—that's what drives every decision. But it got me in trouble when I first started directing, when it came to giving feedback. I didn't want to upset anybody, so when someone came to me with an idea, I'd be like, "Yeah, that sounds great." In the back of my head I'm thinking, "That's not going to work." But I don't want to make him mad or shut him down. So this is like a disaster waiting to happen, right? You absolutely have to make decisions and close doors, and be very clear about where things should go, or you'll get nowhere. Of course since then I've discovered ways of being positive, of steering people when they come with ideas or directions that don't work with the direction I'm going. Sometimes you do just have to say flat out, "You know what, that's a great idea for a different movie, but it doesn't work here." And you try to explain clearly, "Here's what I'm trying to put across." So that's been a big lesson for me. The positive side to my trying to make everyone happy is that I do feel like I listen and that ultimately the people I work with contribute creatively to the film in big ways. It's one of the great pleasures, getting all these great new fresh ideas that wouldn't have occurred in one brain. It makes for a much stronger film.

Bill: That's a huge lesson—retaining your personal style of consideration for people without rolling over. Since at the end of the day, the film has to come first. The story and the film come first.

Pete: You have to hold to the things that make the film speak to you, and yet also invite in all the other ideas, people, and talents that you have around you.

Bill: What kind of a personal support staff did you have on *Monsters, Inc.*? Were there director's assistants or people taking notes? Being the first one after John to attempt this at Pixar, you probably had to be blazing a trail and doing something different.

Pete: I inherited the production process that had been developed on *Toy Story* and *A Bug's Life*, and we used the same kind of system on *Monsters, Inc.* The producer, Darla Anderson, had produced *A Bug's Life* with John, so at least one of us knew what was going on! We did make a few changes to the pipeline. I think the key is that you don't ever want to force a system on anybody. You're making a movie, not a process. Everybody's different, everybody responds to different things, and you tailor the system to work with the people you have. Changes were based on people and the technical needs of the show.

For example, *Monsters, Inc.* was the first film to have a simulation department, for Sulley's fur and Boo's shirt. That department didn't exist before *Monsters, Inc.* because we didn't need it until then. Also, there's a whole team of people who don't get mentioned much who are really important in making our films. The production manager is a pivotal position. He or she puts together the daily schedule in a way that allows us to focus on the right things at the right time. They tell us when we need to make certain decisions so that departments downstream have time to do their job. Then there are managers for every group—animation, story, art, lighting, et cetera—and they help us know what's going on in every department, who's available when, and so on. And then in any given meeting there's generally someone keeping track of the schedule and keeping us on time so I don't have to be constantly looking up at the clock and saying, "Oh, I only have fifteen minutes." That way, I can lose myself in the moment until somebody comes and says, "Wrap it up, we need you at the next meeting." In the end, there might be three or four hundred people working on a movie. It's like mobilizing an army, and you really have to have great lieutenants, both creatively and managerially.

Bill: Is there anything you learned on *Monsters, Inc.* that you were able to use when the time came to do *Up*?

Pete: In terms of the creative process, I learned that chaos is an essential part of the production—that you can't go in thinking, "I'm gonna have every *T* crossed and *I* dotted, and it's going to be smooth sailing." It's not going to be smooth. It's going to be a mess. And you can't take that personally. That was the big lesson for me. On *Monsters, Inc.*, I must have aged ten years in three. Because I was carrying this weight of, "I'm a failure as a person because I can't get this to go." And by the second one I realized, no, that's just the process. You don't have to know what every single shot's going to be right out of the gate. You do have to know your basics: "What is this movie about? How am I going to connect to the people watching it? What is the main character and what makes him getable and likeable?" You have to know those kind of things and be able to talk about them with your crew. Then you work your way down to the details. You have to realize that this is a long-distance run, and you have to pace yourself. Don't work weekends and nights from day one or you're gonna die before you even get halfway.

Bill: *Up* was a project that you conceived from the start. Where did the idea come from?

Pete: I spent maybe a year developing a few ideas, and there was one, a really bizarre one that I developed with Bob Peterson. It showed a lot of potential early on, but then it just got weirder. And this is where I started understanding more fully about how you need to have an emotional connection with the audience, that people go to movies to see their own life reflected up there in some way, maybe in a way that they hadn't really thought of before. The characters in this film were sort of these weird, Muppety, made-up creatures that lived on a made-up planet. Not to say you couldn't connect with characters like that, but we had so many bizarre elements to the thing. And so after pitching for a few months and not getting traction we thought, "All right, let's pull back a little bit, let's make it a grouchy human instead of a fuzzy, red, furry creature." And we talked a lot about, "Okay, what's going to make this relatable? What's going to get people emotionally hooked on it?" The bizarre, Muppety guy had lived on a floating city, this city in the sky, and that was initially very appealing to me. I started to analyze: "What is it about that idea I like, and why?" And I realized it was the isolation, the idea of just getting away from the world, which I definitely felt an empathy for. But then I realized, "Well, if he lives in a city, there are other people. So that doesn't really get to that feeling of escape and isolation. Let's make it a house instead." And then, so it's not just a house floating around magically, let's explain it a little more. How is it floating? Maybe it's held up by thousands of balloons! That's where *Up* came from. It was certainly not a "eureka" epiphany moment. It was born out of a feeling, the desire to get away from it all, this man getting away from the world in his floating house.

Sketch, Pete Docter, *Up*, © Disney/Pixar.

Bill: **Can you talk a little more about discovering that character? Did he change and evolve from what you originally thought he would be?**

Pete: I'd done a bunch of drawings. I had one of a super-grouchy guy holding a big bunch of happy colorful balloons. That kind of started the character. Then Bob Peterson and I talked about him a lot, pulling from our own observations of our grandfathers and other older folks we knew. I did a bunch of exploratory drawings, with different observations and behavior: Carl eats stewed prunes for breakfast, or he has a problem with ear hair, and all these little specific things. Bob wrote a lot of great scenes that we'd throw out for each other. And between all that, the character started developing. I think that these films are really a reflection of the people that work on them, so when you hire someone, especially someone in a key position, you really have to know what you're getting, because that person is going to influence the film in a big way. Bob Peterson has a lot of old man in him, and he is so much of what went into that character. Ronnie del Carmen was our head of story, and he had great insights into old men. He channeled his father, who apparently had some grouchy old man tendencies. A few of the story guys, like Tony Rosenast, really brought Carl to life in their boards, and of course the animators ... they all contribute to the character. And then, when you cast someone like Ed Asner ... We had listened to a bunch of different actors, but Ed really clicked. We recorded him, watched his mannerisms, looked for words he would use in his natural speech patterns, and this all affected the way we would write. We'd try to play to his strengths, you know, using clipped, short sounds and shortened sentences. We often cut out words or sentences, because Carl is a guy who doesn't want to communicate. He wants to be left alone, so he's not using as many words. Plus it was funny. We learned that from Ed.

Sketch, Pete Docter, *Up*, © Disney/Pixar.

Bill: Did you look at any other work for inspiration?

Pete: You know, probably the single biggest influence early on was a film called *The Station Agent*, written and directed by Tom McCarthy. Tom also wrote and directed a film called *The Visitor* about illegal immigrants in New York, which sounds all controversial and political, but he simplifies it down to these great relationships, very simple scenes where he's somehow able to strip out a lot of extraneous blabiddy-blah. Every word, every scene, is just what he needs, and no more. *The Station Agent* was about a man who wants to be left alone and only slowly is drawn into an odd sort of community. Very similar to our character. We learned a lot from it and eventually even hired Tom on to write for a short while.

Bill: Did you use the same kind of production system you used on *Monsters, Inc.*?

Pete: The production was pretty similar in general, but the specifics were different, because of the talents of the people involved. On *Up*, Bob Peterson was the co-writer and co-director, and his strength was story, and humor, and characters. So he was very much involved in building the reels. Once the reels were locked, I directed all other aspects by myself as Bob left the show to develop another project. I was also lucky to have Ronnie Del Carmen, who's strong in staging, and he worked with Patrick Lin, our layout supervisor, who really helped me and bolstered the cinematography. That was slightly different than *Monsters, Inc.*, where co-director Lee Unkrich commandeered editing and layout, based on his strengths.

Bill: Even though you had a solid approach and basically knew where you were going, did you have any kind of crash and burn on *Up*—somewhere in the middle when you felt, "Man, something here is just really not working?"

Pete: Really, our crash and burn was early on, when the project was on the verge of getting killed altogether. We refocused in a pretty major way. I do feel that there were enough other things going on at the studio at that time that we had a freedom that isn't always the case as we were developing the show. When we first started boarding, we were left alone for a stretch of six months, which meant that we could fail a couple of times and fix things to our liking before we had to drop our pants and show everybody else. It's a lot to ask of anybody to get it right the first time. So that gave us a leg up. Then too, thankfully Pixar has come to expect failure. By that I mean, it doesn't surprise everyone anymore when the first screening isn't perfect. Our process is, "Well, we know we're not going to get it right, let's get it wrong so we have something to fix and make it right. And we're all going to be a part of that." Anyway, that allowed us to get some pretty decent reels, so we never really had a screening where people walked away going, "Ohhhh boy," which does seem to happen in many of our films.

Concept artwork, Lou Romano and Don Shank, *Up* © Disney/Pixar.

Bill: *Up* seems like such a personal movie. Do you feel like only you could have made it?

Pete: Thanks. Yeah, I do.

Bill: What would you say most distinguishes it as your work and your style as an artist?

Pete: Well, the subject matter itself is an odd blend of deep emotional truth along with wacky talking dogs and broad physical comedy. That blend is not easy to pull off, but it's something I'm intrigued with. It's what attracted me to *Dumbo*. You have the fun of what animation can do, but hopefully it's built on a bedrock of something truthful that makes the film more than just kooky, wacky characters. Then too, in deciding on the look for the film, I got a lot of feedback from folks saying they thought we needed to go more realistic in the design. Folks felt that we needed that realism for the audience to connect with these characters and this sort of story. I felt the opposite … that if we made things more stylized, and we abstracted things a bit, people would connect more easily. It's hard for me to pinpoint what makes my films distinctly "me," because I don't think about it that way. I just make a film that I want to see. Inevitably, it's lots of little decisions that make any work unique. Other people wouldn't have made the same choices.

Bill: It must have been really satisfying to you, to have everybody be so wrong about …

Pete: [laughs] Well, you never know!

Bill: Let's face it. No studio in Hollywood would have green-lit a movie about an eighty-year-old guy. And I think everybody's reaction was, "Thank god for Pixar because they let an artist run with a vision."

Pete: Some of those articles in the *Times*, or wherever, prior to the film's release, they'd say things like, "Pixar's lost their marbles, nobody's gonna go see this, this is where they go down in flames." And truthfully, we had no idea what would happen. Having seen the audience reaction with the guys here and the folks at Disney, I was pretty sure it wouldn't be an absolute bomb. But I felt like it would be a smaller, niche film for us. So the fact that it's gone out there in the world and it was second only to *Finding Nemo* as our most profitable film … It's still kind of baffling to me.

Bill: Do merchandising considerations ever play a part in your creative decisions?

Pete: No, thank goodness. One of the big things we got lambasted for on *Up* was: "Who's gonna buy a toy of a grouchy old man?" That may have been something of a self-fulfilling prophecy, because they really didn't make much merchandise. I know that toys and tie-ins are a part of what we all do, and you just have to embrace that or figure out some way of dealing with it. Either you care about it deeply and passionately, as John does—you know, he just loves all those toys, and he wants to make them as good as he can, so he can own them too—or you just throw up your hands and say, "You know, somebody else can deal with that. I don't really want to." Thankfully we don't even think about marketing until the project is well into production. And even then, there's a consumer products group that comes in to think about what would make a good toy or whatever. They involve us filmmakers, but our first and primary job is to make as good a movie as we can.

Bill: **Speaking of toys, during your time at Pixar, you got married and had a couple of kids. Does having a family affect your creative process or have an influence on the way you work?**

Pete: Absolutely. Brad Bird says it well: "You can't create the illusion of life unless you're out there living it. You can't just live alone in a shack sitting at a computer or sketchbook. You have to have life experiences to draw from." Having a family influenced my work in a lot of ways. My son was born right at the beginning of the development of *Monsters, Inc.*, and that film became a personal story. It's a guy who really loves his work, but then this kid comes along, and the kid and his work are at odds with each other. How does he come to terms with those two things? It's a story about becoming a parent. Life not only informs the work, it is essential to the very core of the work. Also, just being a parent, and learning how to be consistent and strong and loving at the same time, this has helped me as a director. One thing that kids really need is consistency. You can't come in one day expecting this, and the next day expecting that, and the next day something else. They're going to be confused. Consistency as a director is key.

Bill: **What do you think about the two-director system? Have you ever thought it might be easier on you to do that? Or do you think you're strictly a solo director?**

Pete: Well, I'll just say that I don't think it works for the way we work at Pixar. There needs to be one final voice, the person who drives the thing. Pixar is built around the 1970s idea of "auteur" filmmaking in that sense. When it comes to production, it's probably closer to the craftsmanship and long-term investment of the Hollywood "studio system" of the 1920s to 40s. Anyway, back when I started *Monsters, Inc.*, there were certain people at Disney who felt, "Okay Pete, given your inexperience, it's not in our best interest to trust you entirely with this production. Let's give you a partner, because that's worked really well for us at Disney." And they were able to convince John of that. And right away I said, "Look, I'm not a power-hungry guy or anything, but that's not going to work." And sure enough, as we tried it out, progress was very slow because I was always checking with this other guy to make sure he liked where we were going. I'm not someone who needs to be in control. But at the end of the day there has to be one person who's telling the story. One person whose life experiences are on the screen, who makes the decisions and says, "Let's do this," and on we go. Now, having said that, at Pixar we have co-directors, which is confusing to people. But what *co-director* really means is—for example, on *Monsters, Inc.*, as I was flailing around with editing and layout, I was able to get Lee Unkrich, who worked on *Toy Story* and *A Bug's Life* with John. And besides being an amazing editor, he stages things beautifully—he knows exactly where the camera should be. And he is economical and direct, and works to reduce the number of shots, et cetera. So for incredibly complicated things, like building the door-vault sequence at the end, that was all based on storyboards and ideas that I knew I wanted, but Lee figured out how to do that, along with the layout team. So that was his area of expertise. And that's the way co-directors work at Pixar. They are in charge of one or more areas of the process, while at the same time they know that the director has the final say and that it's his vision. It's a very tough gig.

Bill: **What would you say is your favorite part and least favorite part of being a director?**

Pete: Hmmm. Probably the answer to both of those questions is: the early days of development. It's simultaneously the most stress-inducing, unsure, vague part of the process, and yet it's also the most exciting. The potential is everywhere, you can go any number of directions, and yet you create these worlds from scratch. It's why I personally am not as excited about sequels, because I feel like I already know that world and characters. I'm more interested to do something new, to explore.

Bill: **So is directing your life now, or do you see yourself maybe trying something different before moving on to your next project as a director?**

Pete: Well, every once in a while I miss animating. And I do still have fantasies of doing a hand drawn film. Maybe because Brad and Andrew went into live action, I get asked whether I'm interested in that and, once in a while, I come up with a story that feels more like a live-action story. But I can't say it's something I'm hungry to do. I really like the way animation works and what the medium brings to the party. You know that everything on the screen is entirely artificial, and yet you believe in it. It's that illusion of life that fascinates me.

Bill: **Do you have any advice or recommendations for beginning animators?**

Pete: Years ago I wrote to Frank Thomas and Ollie Johnston and asked them that same question. They were nice enough to write back, and I still have their letters. They're really charming because they obviously typed the letters themselves, with some of the letters crossed out in pen, and with mistakes and things. But Frank went through a whole list of things the aspiring student needs, which was primarily drawing ability—to draw both human and animals in movement—and a deep study of human behavior—basically to be a good actor. But then his last point was: "And luck certainly has a lot to do with it too." He's right. It does help to get good breaks. But when those good breaks come up, you also have to have the talents and ability to take advantage of them. I feel that drawing is never a bad thing, even if you're a computer animator. Watching people and drawing them … I have sketchbooks full of people. Drawing is a great tool to help you communicate when you talk with your collaborators. A lot of the time it's just quickest to whip out some paper and do a sketch. Drawing also helps you see. There's a lot of stuff I've only noticed consciously because I've drawn it.

Bill: **Aside from Frank and Ollie, is there anyone, inside or outside the industry, who you would say was an important influence? Someone who changed the way that you think or work or create?**

Pete: Frank Oz, who I got to know as a result of *Monsters, Inc.*, and his work on the *Muppets*. What an amazing performer. He does Fozzie Bear and Bert and Grover, and Miss Piggy—some of the strongest characters in history, period—regardless of the medium. I asked him once, "Where do these characters come from?" I was expecting some deep internal process that he'd worked out, or at least some tips or clues into his approach. You know what his answer was? "I have no idea." That tells you what a mystery this whole thing is, creating characters and story. It's just an intuitive thing. It's what we were talking about where you have to trust your gut, just feel these things through. Then, at some point, you step out of the pool and you analyze what you're swimming towards, and then you jump back in. It was fun getting to know Frank and talk shop. Not just because I'm so in awe of his work, but also because he has great, great insights into the process. Joe Grant was a big influence, getting to know him, and looking at his drawings and trying to see how he thinks. He did great drawings, but they were never just great drawings. They always had ideas in there that would inspire beyond the draftsmanship. Joe was a master at the "less is more" thing, where instead of detailing everything out, he alluded to it, or suggested it, in a pose, in a behavior, or just outside the frame somehow. Something Joe talked about a lot … He would say, "What are you giving the audience to take home?" I was confused by that initially, but I learned what he meant: "What is the emotional core of the story? What is the audience going to feel?" Because you can have these great intellectual ideas, but just because something is clever doesn't always mean they stick with you. The emotional connection is the thing that has long-term impact and that the audience is going to keep going back to.

Bill: **Are there any film directors, aside from Frank Oz, who have inspired you?**

Pete: Charlie Chaplin. His films are really similar to Disney's films. What I love about them is the simplicity of the story structure. He's not trying to overload it with plot. He just presents a series of great situations, where he can have fun along the way. So it's a scene of him trying to eat spaghetti or whatever, and next is a scene where he escapes from a cop, but he puts all the scenes together in a way that builds to this great thing at the end. They have wonderful structure to them, but it's simple structure—which is very hard to do. We're always struggling to do that, to simplify the story so that you can just enjoy the performance and have fun with animation, the way they did in those great films in the twenties, thirties, and forties.

Bill: **Are there any more contemporary directors?**

Pete: Jacques Tati isn't exactly current, but he pops to mind. He does things similar to Chaplin, where he'll just let scenes play. There's not the same broadly expressed poses and things; it's more like natural behavior. To me, watching Tati films are sort of like sitting in an airport and watching people. They're really fascinating that way. Miyazaki does a similar thing, where he's somehow able to capture these little truths of life. The common wisdom in Hollywood is that films are all about "what happens next," you gotta keep the audience moving and keep the plot moving. And Miyazaki proves that you don't have to have anything happening next. What's happening right now, if it's truthful, and the audience relates to it and identifies … There are great laughs and a great connection when you find those sort of things. In terms of more contemporary filmmakers, I always look forward to Tom McCarthy's work. His stories are brilliantly simple and always have great truth to them. I love all of Carol Ballard's films. And of course there are the undisputed masters like Spielberg … There's always something to learn from in all of his films.

Bill: **Aside from the terrifying Steve Jobs encounter, have there been other experiences that were particularly frightening, disappointing, or just very tough to get through?**

Pete: There's been a lot of them, mostly having to do with screenings. You know, you're working on these things, and you're so close to them that you can't really even see what you're looking at anymore. And then you show it, and stuff you thought was hilarious just dies, and stuff that you thought was emotionally true rings hollow …

Bill: **Do you always approach screenings with trepidation, or are there times where you feel like you've really got it?**

Pete: Nowadays I'd say I approach screenings with "excitement," a combination of joy and fear. I usually have things I like, that I feel good about, but I'm fearful other people won't react to it, or that I loused it up somehow. You know, in film school we all complained about audience previews and how wimpy that was, that "real filmmakers" don't change their story because of audience preview cards. I still think to some degree that's correct. But I remember talking to John Lasseter once, and he told me, "I don't think of myself as an artist, I think of myself as an entertainer." He's right. If I stand up there on the stage and tell jokes and nobody laughs, I'm a lousy comedian, regardless of what I personally think of the jokes. Our job is to reach people, to affect them and connect with them. If they don't respond, then I need to change the way I'm putting across my message so that it rings true. It might be that the subject matter isn't resonating, or maybe it's just the way I'm saying it. It may take rephrasing a joke, or twisting the sentence in such a way that the punchline is at the end, or whatever. Your job is to talk to people and say something that makes them feel.

Bill: That's a fantastic thought. I think that really addresses the whole question of why it's not sacrificing your integrity to change the ending or something to better convey the sense of the film.

Pete: Yeah. I had an experience on *Monsters, Inc.* where we did have an audience preview screening and there were a lot of areas where we could tell we had problems: people were bored, people were restless, people were too scared. Right at the beginning of the film, for example, we had this scene where the tension builds, and this monster looms up over a kid, and it's getting more and more scary, and suddenly the lights go on and some monster says, "All right, look, can you tell me what you did wrong?," and the film went on from there. But we had built up a scary mood, and there were no laughs for about fifteen minutes. And we realized, it's like that old story about *A Funny Thing Happened on the Way to the Forum.* Apparently in tryouts the show was not playing well, so they added that song *Comedy Tonight* at the beginning, basically telling you, "This is a musical. It's funny. It's a comedy! Please laugh!" And once you have that song, it sets the tone right away, and then people feel they have permission to laugh. We did the same thing on *Monsters*. We added a title sequence, which set a light-hearted, goofy tone, and we also changed the opening scene to include slapstick. Instead of just turning on the lights, the monster gets scared, reels back, slips, and does all the pratfall stuff. Right away, sitting in the audience, you can feel the relief from the tension. The kids laughed. You could feel them think, "Okay, this is gonna be a comedy." So there's a lot you can learn in watching your films with the audience. After the screening, they have all the comment cards and focus groups, and once in a while you can learn some stuff from those too, like which story points didn't communicate, or where people were confused. But most of the time you learn just by sitting and watching the film with the audience.

Bill: In contrast to the frightening experience of screenings, have you had any single moment of great elation in your career?

Pete: Well, at that same screening, one of the big notes in the discussion afterwards was that people wanted to see the little girl again. I don't know if you remember the film, but the door's been shredded, and Mike has reassembled it. Sulley puts the last piece in. The light goes on, and he goes, "Boo?" and you just hear off-screen, "Kitty!" And people in the audience said, "I want to see them hug, I want to see them get back together." And we talked about it, but there was one thing I was sure of: no matter what I came up with, I would never be able to beat what's in the audience's head. It'd never measure up. So I held firm on that, even against some pretty big pressure. So I got my ending, and at the end of the day a lot of people have told me that that they feel it's a really nice, emotional ending to the film.

Ronnie Del Carmen, Ralph Eggleston, Pete Docter and Albert Lozano, *Inside Out*, © Disney/Pixar. Photo: Deborah Coleman.

Bill: The greatest ending.

Pete: Thanks! It felt good to be right. It doesn't happen all the time.

Bill: Did inside out present any new challenges you had not faced before?

Pete: The concept itself was rather abstract—we set it inside the mind, not the brain—which was a large part of the attraction for me. It was a chance to make up a world rather than being tied to real life. But, it quickly became apparent that the design of the *Mind World* could not be whatever we wanted—nor was it really based on research. It needed to reflect the girl herself and what she was going through. The events in the human world had to have a direct, physical effect on the mind world, which would then affect Joy's journey. We were essentially telling two stories at once, and they connected through the design. That was tough. I'm sure Production Designer Ralph Eggleston felt like he aged 40 years in the 4 years he was on the film, but he was patient with us and designed some of the most amazing sets I'd ever seen.

Inside Out, 2015. © 2015 Disney/Pixar.

Bill: How does being both the writer and the director affect your process of working with other writers/storyboard artists to solve story problems?

Pete: People often mistake writing with dialog. What characters say can be entertaining, but the real writing—the stuff that makes people stay in their seats—is the ordering of the events themselves, and how characters react. In that sense, I've always been part of the writing process, from Toy Story on.

However, sitting at the keyboard to get scenes started is really one of the most difficult parts of the process. I was lucky to collaborate with several great writers on *Inside Out*. I'm glad I did, because it's always difficult to remain objective. I wouldn't recommend that first time directors try to write and direct, because it's too easy to get stuck with how you *think* it is, instead of how it really is. And really, the primary job of the director is to look at the film as an audience member.

That said, sometimes writing or drawing can bring out ideas inside you that wouldn't have come out otherwise. Then, you show them to your partners who are brave enough to tell you they stink. Then, you rewrite them again.

Bill: **Having directed three feature films, what advice you would pass on to budding film directors?**

Pete: People think directors are allowed to do whatever they want, as if their ultimate goal is self-satisfaction. A director out for self-satisfaction alone had better be prepared to get into another line of work.

On the other hand, I have no stomach for movies that are just desperate, frenetic grabs for audience attention. If you have a chance to make a movie, it damn well better say something.

One way to look at this is to imagine both of these goals at opposite ends of a see-saw. Too much weight on either side, and the thing tips over. We've all seen self-indulgent personal statements that feel like you're at the therapist's office; or the desperate loud blockbusters that try so hard to please everyone yet feel empty. A successful entertainer says something true meaningful and personal, in a way that hits right at the heart of everyone watching. And, if you're lucky enough to have that opportunity, I believe it's your responsibility to do your darnedest to add something to the human experience.

5

Chris Sanders Interview

Chris Sanders.

I first met Chris Sanders while working on *The Little Mermaid*. During the great Disney 2D musicals of the 1990s, Chris was one of the mainstays of the story department, while I would alternate between storyboarding and animation. We got to know each other well during the development periods of experimentation between big film projects. And of all things, we liked to play in the team paintball games organized by director Gary Trousdale (*Beauty and the Beast, Atlantis*). Memorable games were Disney Animation vs. Warner Bros., and Disney vs. Beverly Hills 90210. For the poster for the last event, Chris did a delightful drawing of Mickey shooting it out with a beautiful 90210 babe in a camouflage bustier.

Chris always had a wonderful personal design style. His whimsical characters look as though they are having as much fun as we are watching them. Chris has an athletic build rare among the denizens of the drawing table. As the years roll on, age and responsibility fail to diminish his youthful exuberance.

Tom Sito

Ron Diamond: Could we maybe talk a little bit about your youth and how you discovered animation?

Chris: Yeah. Absolutely. I can't say that I remember everything. Of course, I loved *The Wonderful World of Disney* and never missed an episode. Disney and Disneyland were bigger than life to me. I grew up in Colorado, and we went to California for the first time on a family vacation when I was seven. We stayed at a little motel not too far from the park. You could see it from the walkway in front of our motel room door. When I got my first glimpse of Disneyland from that walkway, I threw up. [laughs] I was that excited to see Disneyland! I couldn't believe I was there.

I remember in particular *The Three Caballeros*. That bit of animation was such pure energy and joy. That's when animation went from being something I just loved to something I paid a lot more attention to. Oddly enough, the next big turning point for me animation-wise was *The Pink Panther Show* on TV (DePatie-Freleng). One day, instead of a cartoon, they showed a little special about how they made *The Pink Panther* cartoon. As opposed to the Disney specials, where animation was always presented as somewhat magical, like the characters drew themselves, this special explained how the process actually worked. It talked about how an art director, for example, keeps the characters legible in front of the backgrounds. In contrast to that, Disney tended to keep the process of animation a lot more vague. Which is fine, unless you're a kid in Colorado that wanted to know how this whole thing worked. Oh, and Disney shows always passed by the story room and never went in. That was skipping the most important part, as it turned out. So this *Pink Panther Show* really got into the nuts and bolts of animation.

Ron: How old were you at the time?

Chris: I was probably eleven or twelve. A friend of mine also had a Super 8mm projector that could freeze-frame. We bought some Disney animation on *Super 8* and would step through it one frame at a time. My friend was actually the first one who said to me, "It's not one drawing per frame. A lot of the frames are the same drawing twice!" I didn't believe him at first.

He had to walk me through it. Some frames had only one drawing, but most had two. We ran this whole film backwards and forwards, over and over again.

Ron: **And when did you first try animation?**

Chris: Around the same time, I think. Of course I didn't have any idea how you did inbetweens and extremes. I only knew that animators worked on light tables, so I built one. Well, my grandfather built one for me. But we both had to sit down and figure it out. When it was done, I animated a scene. Then, I shot it on *Super 8*. The timing was terrible. It was atrocious. It looked weird. I was so upset and depressed that I never tried it again. I used the light table for other things. I simply didn't know what a light table was for. It wasn't until I got to CalArts that I learned that important lesson. It would have been nice to get the bit of information earlier. But when I was young I just generally imitated the process.

Fun With Father, 1984.

Ron: **Were you telling stories, or trying to do storyboards in terms of figuring out what your concept would be?**

Chris: No. I think at that point I was simply trying to make something move around. I wasn't really doing stories.

Ron: **No flip books?**

Chris: That's the other thing. I think I did just a few rudimentary flip books. Oddly enough, story really eluded me for a very, very long time. It wasn't till college that I took a story writing class. I remember being bold enough to say, "I have a stupid question. What's a story? What makes up a story?" Up to that point I could write little scenes, but they really didn't go anywhere. The teacher looked at me and said, "Story is change." That hit me hard. It was so simple. Why didn't I think of that? Now whenever I talk to kids about story, I explain that it's all about a character changing, or a character changing something around them. Why do you like that movie or television show? Most likely, it's because you are emotionally connected to the character and how he or she changes.

When I was working with Howard Ashman on *Beauty and the Beast*, we were all trying to figure out what exactly the songs were about. At one point, he kept asking, "What's the deal with Belle? Why is the town focused on her? In *The Little Mermaid* when Ariel sings 'Part of Your World', that song was originally titled 'I Want Feet'. That's what's it's really about. She just wants feet." [Laughs] That was the first time I saw someone tear off the glitter and all the fancy trimmings in order to see the bare bones. 'Part of Your World' is really about feet, and everything else is built on top of that. So, we spent a lot of time talking about what's the deal with Belle (*Beauty and the Beast*). And the best thing we came up with was that she was odd to everybody around her. To us, she would seem normal because she's just a girl who likes to read and dream, and she's a pretty stable person. Everybody around her, however, is rather small-minded. After that first day with Howard, I asked another potentially stupid question. I said, "How do you know where to put the songs?" Howard replied, "That's easy. I put them at the story turns." Once again, it seemed so clear. [Laughs]. The music guides you through the story. Ariel goes in to see the sea witch and comes out with feet. That's a turning point. I also have to say that it's incredibly tough to write a song that can drive a story through a turn, and Howard could make it look easy. Anyway, it's amazing how important the music is to moving the story along.

Story Sketch, Chris Sanders, *Beauty and the Beast*, 1991 © Disney.

So we spent a lot of time talking about what's the deal with Belle (*Beauty and the Beast*). And the best thing we came up with was that she was odd to everybody around her. To us, she would seem normal because she's just a girl who likes to read and dream, and she's a pretty stable person. Everybody around her, however, is rather small-minded. As we then started to talk more about the songs, I asked another potentially stupid question. I said, "How do you know where to put the songs?" Howard replied, "That's easy. I put them where the story turns." Once again, why didn't that occur to me before? [Laughs]. The music guides you through the story. Ariel goes in to see the sea witch and comes out with feet. That's a turning point. Thinking about that moment, I have to say it's a lot easier to write a song about suffering than it is about change. Anyway, it's amazing how important the music is to moving the story along.

Story sketches, Chris Sanders, *Beauty and the Beast*, 1991 © Disney.

Tom: That makes me think of Gilbert and Sullivan musicals, where every song introduces a character.

Chris: That's why Dean and I have a hard time with musicals sometimes. You're sitting there thinking, "Oh no! Here comes the music! It's going to be a while before anything happens."

Ron: Did you have a favorite short film? Something that stands out, and you think everybody should see?

Chris: Well, I don't really know if you would call it a short. When I was a kid I saw Buster Keaton's silent films. Those, I think, had the most influence on me, and they still do. I've collected so many of them on DVD and video. Some of them you can't even get on DVD, so I still hope to find them on VHS tapes. I actually have to keep an old VHS player alive and running so I can watch them.

Ron: Was there a particular film?

Chris: It's actually a feature film. It's a Laurel and Hardy film called *The Air Raid Wardens*. It's a film that has a special place in my heart. It has an unexpected, emotionally resonant core and a scene that is honestly one of the most true and touching things I've ever seen on film. Those early movies are masterworks of timing. The older ones have no sound or color, so everything has to be conveyed through the physical interaction between characters and objects. We often assume silent pictures are low-tech, so they must be easy to make, right? Well, I'm sure if someone tried to make one today, it would present an unexpected challenge. In fact, you would probably learn something about filmmaking by simply focusing on those basics of performance. I'm always watching *Buster Keaton* or *Charlie Chaplain*. I'm just incredibly impressed by them. As a kid I just thought they were the funniest people in the world. Their movies were magic. I couldn't believe that grown men had made these films. I remember a Keystone Cops scene where this huge hook and ladder from a fire truck was out of control and was sweeping people off sidewalks. If you had anything to do during the day, why wouldn't you want to make a film about an out-of-control fire truck?

Tom: **Now let's delve a bit into your personal technique. Let's start with where your ideas come from. How do you come up with an idea for a movie?**

Chris: The only film I ever made from an original idea was *Lilo & Stitch*. It started out as a children's book that I tried to write. That was in 1981, seventeen years before *Lilo & Stitch* was ever pitched to Disney. It was about this little monstrous, alien creature that lived in a forest. It was a mystery where he had come from. The story was all about him working out his relationship with all the other creatures in the forest.

It was a complex idea, too long for a children's book. I dropped the project, but not before I had designed the character and made a clay model of him. After I shelved the idea, I stored the model in a box. Seventeen years later, in the last days of *Mulan*, Tom Shumacher [Disney Producer] took me out for sushi and asked if I had any ideas for an upcoming feature. At first, I said no. But then, I remembered my little alien monster. It had never occurred to me to think of the story as a movie until that moment. After I pitched the story to Tom, he made one key suggestion. He said, "If this thing is an alien, being in the world of animals might not have enough contrast. However, if you move the creature into the world of humans, then you'll have that contrast." So that's where the alien in the human world idea came from.

Overall, when it comes to any idea for a film, I tend to go more toward the emotional wavelength first and then build around that. I tend to work with scenes that way as well. I follow the emotional tone. And I always think about the turning points, about how relationships would change. In terms of story, there's an emotional destination I want. With those basic concepts, I can then work out the details. I can't just say, "What if an alien landed on Earth," and then work from there in a linear fashion. I need that emotional tone and the general context of character development first. That means I start at the end and work backward toward the very beginning of the story.

Tom: A movie like *The Croods* with a caveman setting is a *tabula rasa* (clean slate) where you could interpret their Stone Age world as anything from very primitive like *Quest for Fire* (1981), to a parody of modern society like *The Flintstones*. Where do you draw your line?

Chris: This was one of the main things we had to do. The sensibilities came from the story. And we were telling a much more subtle story than if they just grunted. It was a story about families, a father and a daughter, about how families relate to new things. The cool thing about cavemen is they are not assigned to any one particular culture or nationality. When you take all this away, a dad is a dad and a daughter is a daughter.

Keeping one eye on the Flintstones, we tried very carefully to not put too many modern phrases in. When Grugg would say, "Let's put on the brakes here," we had to stop and think, no, that's too modern. He wouldn't say that.

Tom: As someone like yourself with a distinct design style, how do take that unique vision and transfer it over to a staff of 500 people? How do you maintain your vision?

Chris: You have to find somebody who knows how it works. We found two people on *Lilo & Stitch*. Sue Nichols (Mazerowski) was given the task of not only taking my style and dissecting it but also explaining it. I didn't even know I had a style until she successfully dissected it and then explained it in this booklet. It was a bit of a revelation to me. I didn't think there was anything that I was doing over and over again that could be considered a style. For example, she pointed out that a lot of my characters look like they're filled with sand, and that sand runs down to the bottom. She noticed that their extremities tend to flare out and feel heavy. She said I never use straight lines. It was amazing. With that information in hand we then found an artist that could replicate my style: Byron Howard. We gave him the task of designing our insular characters, things that I didn't have time to do. I think he did a lot better job that I would have done in that respect. You just have to find the right people.

Tom: And what about designing *The Croods*?

Chris: One of the real treats was designing cave-people. We wanted to create characters people would want to look at, but not make them look too "princessy." Eep (Emma Stone) was a good example. Making her hands and feet small gave her character a certain amount of grace. She was broad shouldered, she had a good silhouette, but not princess-pretty by any means. We tended to think of each person as an animal. Eep was a cat, Grugg her father was a gorilla, Sandy was a terrier. It worked into their mindset. Eep as a cat or panther could climb and leap. Grugg can't climb, so he was against it.

Story sketches, Chris Sanders, *The Croods*, 2013 © DreamWorks Animation LLC.

Tom: **I liked the joke of Gran (Cloris Leachman) having a tail.**

Chris: Gran was designed with a lizard in mind. One of our designers was fitting her and drew her with a lizard tail, when he decided just to give her a real lizard tail. Pointing out she was further back in the evolutionary scheme of things.

Tom: **What's your favorite part about being a director?**

Chris: I guess there'd be two things. One of them is just working with amazing artists. It sounds like such a stock answer, but it's true. A few weeks ago, I had the opportunity to talk to James Cameron. We got to sit down and ask him questions, almost one on one. That was amazing. I never would have had that opportunity if I hadn't been directing at DreamWorks. The other is just really getting to know different people at the studio, these amazing designers, background artists, and animators. They come from all over the world. Some came over from France for *Lilo & Stitch*. I guess I just love any aspect of filmmaking. I don't know if there are any other jobs in the world where you can keep trying to improve yourself. You can keep working till the last day of your life and you'll still be pushing it. And the studios want you to do the best work that you can do.

I worked with a guy named Chris Doffend, and I loved what he drew. I was always going into his room and asking, "What are you drawing today? Got anything?" Seeing his stuff and his logs was inspiring. And every year I go to Comic Con and walk away inspired. I need to keep going, do better. On top of that, if I stop and realize that I'm paid to draw, that's even a better feeling. That's the kind of thing you dream about as a kid. I never watched the Oscars when I was young. My parents did, of course. I always went downstairs and did something else. I was drawing. I didn't watch them because I really wanted to make a movie, and that was everyone who actually did. I just thought, "I'll never do that." I think it kind of hurt to watch. It was this amazing thing that I'll never get to do. But I ended up doing it, and that's still an incredible feeling. When I talk to kids about animation and directing, I always tell them it's possible. It may seem like this unapproachable world. But it is possible.

Tom: How about your least favorite thing?

Chris: The least favorite part of directing is the incessant schedule. We occasionally have to fight against it, but I understand the problem. There are a million things we have to do during the day. It's the housekeeping and scheduling that becomes very difficult. And it actually does cut into the movie occasionally. We've had a few episodes where we had to avoid some of our commitments so that we could focus on a few scenes. If it wasn't absolutely essential, it was removed from the schedule. On *How to Train Your Dragon* we were so bogged down with meetings. It was frustrating. We would be on the verge of solving a problem and then someone in production says, "Sorry, you have to move on."

Tom: How is your interaction with upper management? They often require your attention as much as the crew.

Chris: You have to learn how to interact with those above. You have to learn what might trigger a bad reaction and avoid it as long as you can, unless you absolutely have to confront it. On *Dragon* we wanted to do a few sequences with no dialogue. But you don't just pitch it like that. You wait until the sequence moves along. You work the storyboards, put some music in it, and then you present it. If you pitch something they're not necessarily well informed about, or something experimental, of course skepticism might emerge. It just might seem too risky. If you have something more substantive to show them, then you're maintaining control over your vision and what you want for the movie. As a director, you're the only person that's not allowed to panic. You're the only person that's not allowed to panic. And people panic around you. I'm kind of surprised how many times that happens. Even producers panic and get flustered easily. You can't freak out and start saying, "We'll never get this done. This will never work." Confidence and calm is everything. Your crew is depending on you. If I do need to vent, I find someone off the grid to vent my frustrations to. It's better that way, and it's healthier. I try to stay open and give each meeting my all. The last thing you want is to turn into this machine that just goes in and out of the office each day. You have to lighten up and stay personable. Don't be the guy that just walks into the room and says, "Show me your stuff," and then walks out. Making a movie is hard enough as it is. As a director, don't make it harder.

Tom: **Some directors have the entire film in their mind before production starts. Others watch it evolve during production. Where do you fall in that context?**

Chris: It's a two-part answer. I have always had the end of the story first and then work backwards. As I mentioned before, I have the emotional feel and that important turning point, but I'm usually searching for the beginning, the way into that turning point and end. I have also learned to embrace structure a lot more. The experience of making *Dragon* has especially changed my life as a filmmaker. I had always avoided structure and preferred freeform. But we only had one year to complete *Dragon*.

When we sat down with Jeffrey [Katzenberg], he said, "We usually have about three chances to make a movie like this. You guys get one. You have to get it right the first time." So, we didn't mess around. We got down to the structure right away, and within two weeks we had simplified it and began building up from there. You must have that structure down. You have to know exactly what the characters are doing and why. There will always be difficult variables and problems to solve. But if you know your character and the structure of his journey, you can avoid months, if not years, of struggling to get it right.

Working on *Mulan* was the complete opposite. I'm really surprised at how long we avoided the structure. There were so many variables concerning this Chinese girl trying to break through the limitations of her traditional society. There were so many questions concerning how she would do this. We struggled for over a year without making any progress. Worse still, after so many drafts and changes, we ended up coming full circle and settling on some of our original ideas.

Tom: Some directors will make an animator redo a scene around six times. But then they go back and choose the first one.

Chris: When Dean [DeBlois] and I started directing *Lilo & Stitch*, we felt very uncomfortable directing the animators. Animators are very talented artists. They're experts in their realm. Still, we have to go in and to a certain extent tell them what to do. Neither Dean nor I are animators. We focus on the story and boarding. So when you're talking to an artist that is clearly more talented at painting and drawing than you, there can be a little intimidation there. But you have to look at their animation and make comments. The way that works for us is to talk to them like one would to an actor. We'll talk about what the scene needs to accomplish in terms of story and conveying emotion. We never get into the finite details of timing and movement. I'm not going to suggest how to move a character's ears or shoulders. I'm more likely to say, "I think there is more tension behind this than I'm seeing."

This is why Dean and I are always in the story. That's what directing is. Ultimately it's all about story, whether you are talking about the lighting of the scene, the animation, or the design of a character. You have to make sure your animators

Visual development, Chris Sanders, *Lilo & Stitch*, 2002 © Disney.

and crew are working and creating to bring out your story. You've created a very specific tone, and the animators need to respond to that.

Tom: **Did you have any mentors or people that inspired you when you first got into story?**

Chris: Vance Gerry was such a great communicator when it came to storyboarding. His work is the very definition of a story artist. And I don't think I've ever seen anybody do it as well. But Ed Gombert was the one that could truly get into a scene. He had this innate ability to keep it fresh and original. I even recall directors taking advantage of that. Ed would nail a scene, delivering exactly what it needed. But the director would say, "Try it again. What if it was like this?" They knew he would go away and come back with exactly what they asked for. After a few more requests, they would have multiple takes on a scene. I never cared for that approach. I never wanted to do that to anybody. Besides Ed, working on *Beauty and the Beast* was a period of intense learning. I was working with Joe Ranft, Brenda Chapman, and Roger Allers. These guys were not only in tune with one another, but they were also having fun developing the story. They were bringing great characters to life. That was probably my favorite time at Disney. Every Friday we had storyboard pitches, and we were all in one big building in which we could see each other down this long hallway. You could always hear people talking and coming up with ideas. The energy was just perfect. Whenever I do a movie I still reference *Beauty and the Beast* as being the ideal experience.

Ron: **What about your crew? Do you to try replicate that same atmosphere?**

Chris: Of course, but it really comes down to the people working for you. I need people that are absolutely amazing at what they do. When it comes to finding that story and fixing the problems that arise, I always feel like we're a bunch of firefighters on the scene of an oil well fire. I don't want anybody there that does not know what they're doing. You want them to be very good, so you can put this fire out as soon as possible.

Tom: **How has it been working with Dean [DeBlois] on consecutive projects?**

Chris: One of the nice things about working together consistently is that you learn the same lessons. We were able to change things as we navigated the learning curve together. On *Lilo & Stitch* we both experienced the same frustration of stepping on a lot of Alan Silvestri's work as he created the music for certain segments of dialogue. We had to learn to let the music do the talking too, because it can do so much for your movie. The music has a very important job. We learned a lot from Alan Silvestri that we were able to put into practice on *How to Train Your Dragon*. You work hard to get the movie about halfway done, and then the music comes in and carries it across the finish line. I remember sitting with Alan and going through sequences in detail. At one point he asked us, "Where did Stitch change?" We didn't have it on screen. That moment was basically between scenes. At that moment it was a tough bit of criticism to swallow. We hadn't avoided this scene. We simply worked around it, because we couldn't figure it out. Finally Alan said, "Put it up on screen. I'll do it." So we did. We figured it out, and Alan gave it a meaningful score that captures that moment of change. I've never forgotten that. It was the music that got us to the end.

Tom: **How did you and Dean [DeBlois] collaborate creatively? Do you guys sit together over drinks at someone's house and discuss it? Or do you go off and write separately and then later compare notes?**

Chris: Well, we both create in very different ways, which I think is good for our working relationship. I'm always developing ideas using sketchbooks, and Dean goes off and makes music-driven shorts. So we're always creating and coming up with ideas. One thing we do now is meet for dinner once a week and simply talk about stories that we care about. It could be an idea for a book, a TV series, or a movie. It doesn't matter. It's about keeping the ball rolling, and it's always inventive and fun. But when it comes to the actual writing, we tend to do it together or at least in close proximity so that we can push each other. I think there were only a few days on *Dragon* that we actually wrote at different locations.

Story sketches, Chris Sanders, *How To Train Your Dragon*, 2010 © DreamWorks Animation LLC. All Rights Reserved.

Dean and I are very different people. He is a cold-weather person and I'm more of hot-weather guy. We would never bump into each other on the street. And on weekends we have our own stuff to do. But when it's time to work, we need to work together in the same room. Even if I'm boarding and he's doing

Story sketches, Chris Sanders, *How To Train Your Dragon*, 2010 © DreamWorks Animation LLC. All Rights Reserved.

Story sketches, Chris Sanders, *How To Train Your Dragon*, 2010 © DreamWorks Animation LLC. All Rights Reserved.

something else, we work in the same room. There's always moments where one of us removes our earphones and asks an important question. That's how we work together. And when it comes to the film score, we'll often listen to the same music as we write and develop sequences.

Tom: **That's fascinating, because a lot of people, regardless of creative tastes, tend to be very different when it comes to music.**

Chris: Well, when it comes to film scores, we're on the same page. And this is one of the reasons why we collaborate so well; we are making the same movie tonally. We might approach the details of a scene in different ways, but we are always writing the same movie. That makes exchanging ideas and negotiating much easier.

Ron: **Are there any film scores that you find useful in your visualization?**

Chris: When we were boarding the climactic battle between the gargantuan dragon and Hiccup, *The Dark Knight* (Hans Zimmer and James Newton Howard) score helped us create that serious energy that the moment required. That was a great one to have playing in the background. Overall, it depends on what you're writing. If it's something light and sweet, Dean often pulls out the *Cider House Rules* or *Chocolat* (Rachel Portman). If we need something exciting and energized, the Hans Zimmer catalogue is always waiting. Of course, if we want something triumphant, there is John Williams.

Tom: **Overall, how important is the role of music in your films?**

Chris: It plays a significant role. I've never boarded a sequence without music. When I know the tone for a given scene, I'll put on a piece of music that I think could possibly be the temp music for that moment. And I'll just put it on repeat. I'll let it go for hours, even days sometimes, to get this thing going. It's the most important tool I have. I even use music when I pitch the storyboard. And that music will actually stick all the way into the story reel.

Tom: **And this is temp stuff?**

Chris: It's temp stuff. The funny thing is, there were two temp tracks that I used to board a sequence which were then put in the actual story reel. When the score was written, they were remarkably close to those pieces of music that I had used.

Tom: **What sequences were they?**

Chris: There was a sequence where the Beast died and is resurrected. The music was nearly identical to this album of piano music that I was listening to when I did the scene. That sweet, tense little beat was perfect for that moment of transformation, thrill, and hope. In fact, I still wonder whether it should have been boarded differently. I originally boarded that scene where everyone stands back during the transformation. After it's over, the beast is on the ground with his back to Belle. He still looks a lot like the beast from her point of view. As he straightens up, the first changed thing you see is his hand. Only then does he turn to look at her, revealing his full transformation.

Tom: **Now that you've done a few pictures, do you feel like your personal style, as a director, has evolved?**

Chris: I've learned how to get closer with my crew and to understand their jobs better. And the technology has changed so drastically that it's a different experience from when I first started. In the beginning nobody talked about an "animation pipeline." The first time I heard that term I pictured something fairly linear. But then they unfolded this thing that was a model pipeline, and it really looked more like a city sewer system. But it didn't make any sense, because it wasn't a linear process at all. During production you'd move backwards and forwards through this pipeline. They really should rename it. Anyway, I'm trying to stay current with the technology. I want to understand it.

And that brings me back to the point of getting to know your crew personally. Your crew and this technology go hand in hand. If you know them, if you can truly talk to them, then you'll get what you want. You'll also recognize quickly what certain individuals excel at. Obviously you don't want to pigeonhole anybody. But film after film, you learn who to go to in order to solve specific problems. On *Dragon*, everyone was doing their job so incredibly well that we decided to save time by not spending a lot of time with them. I wish we could have, not because they needed it. They didn't need our input. They knew exactly what they were doing. But it would have been nice just to connect with them and to be inspired by them. I'd say we saw them twice a month, maybe three times. We didn't even have any notes to give them. That's how good they were doing.

Still, the meetings are essential. It's the moment to communicate important information to the crew, to make sure everything is moving in the right direction, and to help them with whatever they need. As directors, you're immersed in story. Any slight shift in the narrative needs to be passed on to the crew. Also, just coming together as a group is a good thing. Everyone can help each other. It's a good way of avoiding potential disasters.

Tom: **Do you ever have any happy accidents, like when an artist comes back with something completely unexpected?**

Chris: Yeah! Dean and I actually encourage it. We may have a good idea, but that doesn't mean it can't be refined and improved upon. Artists are always capable of bringing a deeper layer to a character. And sometimes you have to indulge a different vision for a given scene. It may not be the way you envisioned it, but it might add something important to the bigger picture. If it does, you go with it. And if you really want that, you have to drop in on your artists when they are in the midst of doing something. That's when you'll find something unexpected. Sure, everyone wants to have something completely finished before they show it to anybody. But that's not necessarily the best thing to do.

We had a terrific accident on *Dragon*. There was a piece of unfinished, temporary animation that was somehow cut into the reel. When we saw it we were stunned. It's when Hiccup finds this wounded dragon in the woods. The dragon had first appeared lifeless. And it isn't until he puts his boot against it that he realizes it's still alive. From Hiccup's point of view we ran the camera down the dragon's body. After you pass the wing the head is there, looking at Hiccup. But in the shot we saw the eyes closed at first. Then as the camera passes the wing the eye is now open. It was a very creepy moment, because you really think the dragon is dead. That bit of animation wasn't supposed to be in the reel, but it was so good. The scene wouldn't have been as good without it. Overall, you just have to be open. Look at your artists' work in progress. You never know what you might see.

Tom: **What do you think of drawing on Cintiq digital tablets and the mini-movies you can create on a laptop? When you started storyboarding everyone used pens and corkboards.**

Chris: It's an amazing tool, and it makes it easier to sell your ideas. I remember the difficulty of trying to explain why a certain scene was so important and engaging in my storyboard. But the drawing wasn't going to move and help me in that respect. Cintiq allows you to animate that moment. If you're skilled, you can convey subtle things much easier. It definitely helps pitching your concept. On the other hand, once you've seen the presentation, it's hard to talk about. It's over and done. You're not looking at the links in the chain of action. If you have questions concerning timing and the progression of action, you have to click backwards and forwards through it. Basically, you have to search for the issue that's bothering you.

Dean and I prefer a combination of the two methods. That may sound like a misuse of time, but you get the best presentation possible. You show the little movie made with Cintiq, and then haul out the boards. You can see the sequence of action in chunks. It's far easier to analyze it, let alone just talk about it. You can edit on the boards. You can't do that with a reel. It's a lot of work. But it's worth it.

Tom: **How have you learned to manage your time after four pictures? A lot of people in animation are more of the couch potato type. You always seem more into sports and physical activity.**

Chris: I've learned to focus more on what I'm doing. When I get to work, I work. I get it done. And if I'm truly stuck, I move onto something else. So I'm a lot better at having multiple things going on at once. When I come into the office I actually have a choice of what to work on. That's helped tremendously. Some days you just don't feel clever, and you're not. It's just not happening that day. When you have other things to do, that stops you from wandering the halls and wasting other people's time.

Realizing that has made me more efficient. It also tends to give me time for little things. If I get a board done, then I really can run down the hall and just pop in on somebody for a quick chat. Essentially I've created a flexible schedule that keeps me productive at all times. And this is completely different from the strict schedules you come across at studios. That kind of schedule can actually hinder progress. In my opinion, it's better to run a studio like a hospital. If you've got a patient that needs help, you grab the necessary specialist and get the job done. After you fix him, you move onto the next one. And when an emergency occurs, everybody gets right on it. I did that on *Dragon* and actually got in trouble for it. I was in editorial when a layout issue needed to be resolved. Instead of allowing a note taker to document my response, I got Gil on the phone and we handled it. The studio didn't like that. They wanted me to use the note taker since that was their job. I really hate that. We'll be in a meeting talking about ideas in the most general way possible, and there are three people behind you typing away on their computers. You get these giant printouts that contain everything. But all we really need is what was decided in the end.

Tom: They want to document every change.

Chris: Yeah. I don't think they really believe that you can keep a living version of the film in your head all the time. It's always being updated based on the people you talk to during the day. In a way, an animated film has its own oral history during production. But I'm very unaware of which stuff is actually written down. When we check the notes they're usually written down wrong. Worse still, we talk in film code most of the time. That doesn't help the note takers at all. Not to mention, no one speaks in slow, perfectly grammatical English. Honestly, I just prefer this oral communication aspect of animation's culture. It makes the process feel tribal.

Tom: Do you like working with your editor in post? Some directors really like this part of the job, cutting reels and bringing everything together. And do you and Dean do that together or split it up?

Chris: It's important that we are both in editorial because that's a very influential moment in making a film. I would even like to see editorial have a greater role in that respect. One of the shortcomings of animation is that we're not supplying editorial with a lot of extra footage. Their choices are limited compared to the coverage they get in live action. Regardless, those in that room have the greatest impact on the final product, so Dean and I have never divided that up, along with recording. We only divide up animation. It just wouldn't make much sense. As you're putting everything together, this is the opportunity to discuss, even argue, over what works and what doesn't. We hash it out face to face and walk away with the actual film. It's probably our favorite thing to do. Yeah, it can become grueling as you dissect your entire movie. But this is where we get to see our movie emerge. It's exciting.

Tom: So both of you work with the actors during recording sessions?

Chris: There's no question that Dean is a lot more comfortable with the actors. I don't fear them, but Dean just jumps right in and gets involved with the process. Our amount of interaction with them is pretty equal, but Dean tends to take the lead. There is clearly a certain joy that he takes from it. I tend to get really nervous. In fact, I just had a recording session yesterday with Ryan Reynolds in which I remembered that actors get a little nervous before they start. Tom Schumacher had a simple solution for this. He said, "If you ever have the opportunity, go to dinner with the person that you're going to record the night before. Or at the very least have coffee with them that morning." Taking that one or two hours to talk will have a profound effect on the recording session. Afterwards you won't be this stranger telling them to assume the role of aardvark!

Tom: Have you ever had an idea that you desperately wanted to get to the screen but either couldn't or were prevented from doing so?

Chris: *American Dog*. [laughs]

Tom: That of course was the project you started at Disney that was ultimately completed by others and renamed *Bolt*.

Chris: I'm okay with what happened. There was so much boarded that's not even in the script right now. It's one of those projects that you hope you can return to eventually. I think it's just a waiting game. But it was an interesting experience having things shift suddenly. I actually watched it (*Bolt*) for the first time about two weeks ago. I totally understand why they wanted to change directions. It wasn't their cup of tea. I actually like the changes they made. I think it would have been frustrating if the movie were essentially the same but with only slight changes. And I suppose my scenes and storylines are still sitting there on the shelf. I could actually pull them out and do them again. But it would be completely different.

Sketch, Chris Sanders, *An American Dog* (unproduced), 2007 © Disney.

Tom: Related to that, many directors have a project in mind that they'd like to do someday. For many years John Huston wanted to do *The Man Who Would Be King*. Do you have a project like that?

Chris: I have a few things I want to do. Oddly, there are several movies that frustrate me so much I just want to remake them. *Down Periscope* is a good example, the Kelsey Grammer submarine film. I just want to rewrite and recast it. And I'd love to remake the *Air Raid Wardens*. Dean and I have actually sketched out no less than twenty projects, five of which are high priority. There are even a few live-action projects in that mix, which would be great to do. After all, the industry still likes to put you in a box and say, "This is all you can do." Going from traditional animation to CG animation and then maybe live action would mean that we could just choose the right medium for the story.

Tom: I remember asking Bob Zemeckis at the premiere of *Roger Rabbit*, "Would you do another animated film?" He said, "NO! It's like watching paint dry."

Chris: But for people who love the detail it really is fun. It's very rewarding because there are endless opportunities to fiddle with things. You could start a discussion about the texture of rocks, and it might go on for months. You might even need to have a meeting solely devoted to moss. You might have to bring in a moss expert, if you really want to get into it. Seriously, though, you do have a schedule. It's a game of focusing on the things that really count. And that's why you have to let your people do their job, because they're great with the details. You have a few initial discussions and then send them on their way. It's the bigger discussions that matter. On *Lilo & Stitch* we had a large meeting to inform everyone that we wanted to use watercolor with a 1940s feel.

Tom: What about sequels? Within the last ten years, this almost seems mandatory. People, let alone the studio, want another *Shrek* or another *Ice Age*.

Chris: If it's a straight-to-TV sequel, then I wouldn't be inclined to make it. It's such an immense effort to get the first one done. Even if you are lucky enough to get it right the first time, and people want another one, it's still hard to turn around and think, "Okay, I'm going to do this again." It might be easier, since you have the designs and the style already nailed down. And there have been sequels that were frankly better than the original. But you don't expect it to be better. There is some reservation when you think about doing it all over again. Take the fourth *Shrek* as an example. You immediately think, "Is there anything left?" But I never would have expected a fourth one to be that good. Every time I see clips from another one, I just have to find out now.

So sequels have turned out to be rather cool, especially in the case of what DreamWorks has done. They're bold and have found a very original voice that has kept the studio thriving. I feel so lucky to be there because a lot of other studios have merged. DreamWorks is independent and fosters this healthy environment that embraces all kinds of ideas and voices. I'm all about that. It's like Paramount Studios back in the day. You go to the cafeteria and find gladiators sitting next to cowboys at the lunch table. And then a girl in a sailor's outfit walks by, because they just finished that big dance number. It's just a fun place to be.

Tom: Do you think your films have specific tone or style?

Chris: Yeah, I think they do. However, it's hard to describe it simply. But I think that *Mulan*, *Lilo & Stitch*, and *How to Train Your Dragon* are indicative of that style. They're all stylistically linked together. Although the stories are different, there is a consistent tone. There is always a distinct level of seriousness underwriting the lighthearted and even fun moments. I don't think I could ever do excessive slapstick or a movie with nothing but gags. There has to be something substantial about the story that I'm telling. I think that's ultimately the hook that sinks into the audience.

Tom: **Mulan and Lilo were of course 2D films, but Dragon is 3D and very much stereoscopic. Did the change in technology have any effect on your style as a director?**

Chris: I don't think it changed. I've always felt that CG films have a hard time conveying deep emotion. I don't know why that is, but I just think there is something about the look of the characters that doesn't innately convey emotion. You have to be careful what you focus on with close-ups. You don't want to start looking at eyelashes, nostrils, and pores, things that might emphasize technological artificiality. But at the same time CG offers an entirely new way for an audience to interact with an animated film.

On *Lilo & Stitch* we had less money and less time to make that movie. We had to embrace the strengths of hand-drawn animation. We chose to use watercolor because you can see the brush strokes. You see the mistakes on the backgrounds. It gave the film a look that was very similar to children's illustration, as opposed to the deep canvas stuff that was being done on movies like *Tarzan*. With CG we can render caricatured shapes, caricatured characters and environments, and bring in very realistic textures that create a suspension of disbelief that is most associated with live-action films. The audience can stop thinking of it as a cartoon and become truly immersed in it.

Tom: **What's nice about *Dragon* is that its 3D wasn't overbearing. It wasn't just about shooting something that momentarily reaches out and grabs the audience. The paddleball effect. What exactly did you have in mind when it came to employing 3D technology?**

Chris: We knew that every film going forward was going to be in 3D; 3D or not 3D wasn't something we thought about. But we did have creative choices concerning how extreme or invasive it was going to be. We insisted from the very beginning that we never wanted it to be the cart that leads the horse. We didn't want to use it in a way that removes the audience from that storytelling moment. We also didn't want it to look artificial or overly engineered. It had to accentuate the moment and add emotional intensity. When Hiccup is reaching to Toothless in that cove, for example, the CG brings you into to the moment and then backs you out slowly.

Tom: That scene is so crucial to the film. That's when they become friends. I've heard that you didn't rush into making it either. You knew that you needed that scene, but you also wanted to develop these characters first, so that you could really capture how these two would become friends. It reminds me of *The Black Stallion*, when the boy and the horse become friends.

Chris: That's exactly the kind of response we wanted! Hiccup was going to befriend the scariest dragon in the Viking world. And that was a substantial change from the original book, where both are more childlike characters. When we made that change, we actually talked about *The Black Stallion* because it has such wonderful scenes of a boy bonding with this fiercely beautiful animal. As for time, we didn't have complete freedom. There was always some kind of time constraint. That scene just seemed to get all the time it needed to develop. We also wanted to do something that we really hadn't had the luxury of doing in previous films. We wanted to create moments of character silence so we could have the score and the cinematography take you to a deeper place. It also created a bit of a problem.

It was over five minutes, which was something that had never been done before in animation. The studio jumped on that right away. Fortunately Dean and I were able to convince the studio to let it live until the testing phase. And when the movie was tested, people loved that scene. We got great feedback.

Tom: Thank you, Chris.

Chris: Sure. Any time.

6

Dean DeBlois Interview

Dean DeBlois.

I didn't know Dean DeBlois that well at first. I had known his partner Chris Sanders at Walt Disney since we worked together on *The Little Mermaid*. When Dean and Chris teamed up, I had already moved onto other projects. Dean is a big bear of a man, with a rich dark beard and piercing blue eyes, and a soft-spoken civility that is characteristic of his Canadian background. In recent years I've had the opportunity to talk film with him at the Motion Picture Academy and at the USC Film School. We found we had a lot of friends in common, from Disney story man Joe Grant to colleagues back in Canada. I've come to appreciate Dean's sharp mind and quick wit. Ron and I sat down with Dean in a room on the DreamWorks campus (the common nickname for the studio lot).

Tom Sito

Tom: So where did you get your start? What got you interested in animation?

Dean: As a kid in Quebec I was kind of raised on comic books, so I loved animation from an early age. But that was all Hollywood, and Hollywood was a place far, far away. So I learned how to draw through comic books. I would save up my allowance and buy one or two every week. That's where I learned anatomy, staging, and dynamic posing. It all came from comic books. I wanted to be an Ernie Chan. I wanted to draw for *Savage Sword of Conan* when I grew up! After high school I even had a short job at a local comic book company. But it just wasn't what I dreamed it would be. And Marvel just seemed a world away. As I was looking for jobs, I didn't want to just draw. I wanted to be involved in telling of a story. I loved writing short stories every bit as much as I loved drawing. Then I discovered a Classical Animation program at [Sheridan] college. I was selected for the summer program and learned the basic skills of animating. More importantly, I practiced telling a story through animation. This was exactly what I had been looking for. And that's when I decided that I wanted to be a part of the animation industry. After the program ended, I managed to get a job at a local TV animation studio in Canada. I worked on some Canadian TV series like *The Raccoons* for a few years.

Ron Diamond: Was there ever a short film that you found inspiring?

Dean: That would have to be *Sandman*. It came out in the early nineties by an animator named Paul Berry, who afterward was hired to work on Tim Burton's *The Nightmare Before Christmas*. I think his character design and stop motion was very important in the development of that film, which I don't think he was really credited for. It had great character designs and a certain darkness to it, like it grew out of a classic Grimm's fairy tale. I've always loved that creepy or ghostly atmosphere, things like "The Legend of Sleepy Hollow." I still don't think too many people have seen it. And I remember meeting Paul Berry on the streets of Soho. He had a *Nightmare Before Christmas* jacket on, one with a big Jack Skellington on the back. I said, "I love your short film and the influence it had on Tim's work." He was really thankful that somebody had noticed.

Dean DeBlois at Bluth.

Tom: So when did you and Chris Sanders team up?

Dean: After Canada I got hired by Don Bluth's studio in Ireland. I was there for four years. The films I worked on weren't all that great, but the experience was amazing. Toward the end I was actually Don's storyboard assistant. I learned a lot from him. I don't think Don had a knack for story, but he was an incredibly passionate filmmaker in most every other way. And he was an incredible draftsman. All he needed was a pencil and a piece of paper. He never needed any underdrawings. But since I was so interested in story, working on the board was where I wanted to be. After doing so much layout work at Don's studio, I managed to get a job at Disney as *Mulan* began production. Since there was no layout work needed, they put me in the story department with Chris Sanders and few other people. That's when Chris and I met. We had such similar sensibilities that we continued to work on stories and short stories both on and off the clock. That working relationship is what eventually brought us together on *Lilo & Stitch*.

Tom: **How did you and Chris break down your duties?**

Dean: We try to do everything together, because ours was never a forced union. We had come together on our own, and we enjoyed each other's contributions to the same overriding ideas. If I were to describe our relationship, I would say that we always have the same goal in mind, but we approach it from different angles. And when those different angles merge they actually create more texture and depth to a given scene. Consequently, we also go to animation dailies together so that our two perspectives can create a better end result. Sometimes the job demands that we split up. When that happens we tend to focus on our individual strengths. I came from a layout background, so I would spend a lot of time in the layout department. Chris, with his experience in character rotations and prop rotations at Marvel, tends to spend a lot of time with cleanup. Overall, anything that's key to the performance, like animation or art direction, we oversee together.

Tom: **You both like to work on the scripts. Is there anything while writing that you have to visualize?**

Dean: Writing-wise, the one thing that Chris and I have been pretty consistent in, ever since *Mulan*, is that we don't write with cartoon hats on. We don't write for animation. We write for movies. We want to make it feel real, even if the situation is ridiculous. The caricature comes from the story itself. It doesn't come from the way we write it. We want you to believe in the stakes. We want you to believe in the emotions. It's real peril. People can get hurt. People can die. People can fall in love and out of love. That has to feel real so that the audience is part of it, even though there's this giant suspension of disbelief based on whatever medium we're working in. If we did a stop-motion animated film, or if we did live action, which are things we plan to do one day, we would take the same approach. If we believe in the characters and we write it that way, then hopefully the audience will too.

Tom: Chris also mentioned that you two even work together with the actors during recording sessions.

Dean: Yeah, we don't leave the actor alone inside the booth. We tend to sit in there in order to read with the actor and provide constant feedback. Chris usually does the reading while I listen with earphones. Together we evaluate as we go. But we still provide creative freedom so that the actor can contribute. A lot of experimentation can occur during a recording session. Sometimes we even record multiple actors together in the room, so that they can play off of each other and even step on each other's lines. The traditional animation process avoids this method, but we love the energy of building a scene this way. When you capture actors interacting in an organic fashion, the scene ends up with a more realistic feel.

Chris Sanders and Dean DeBlois at Disney, Disney characters © Disney.

Tom: Do you cast a voice with a character in mind, or do you even create a character with a specific actor in mind?

Dean: That's a tricky question. The cast was in place on *How to Train Your Dragon* when we inherited the movie. On *Lilo & Stitch* we had character types in mind. In the case of Tia Carrere and Ving Rhames, it seemed so clear right away. Their voices just fit. But in the case of Jay Baruchel, for Hiccup, we initially thought he wasn't the right guy. Since the character was so young, he was overdoing it. The voice was very forced, nasally, and cartoony. When we met him and just had a normal conversation, that's when we heard the voice we wanted. We wanted Jay's natural voice. And he was very relieved to hear it. Jay felt like he had been pushed into performing in a range that was foreign to him.

How To Train Your Dragon, 2010 © DreamWorks Animation LLC. All Rights Reserved.

Tom: That's common for live-action actors when they first make the jump to animation. They tend to overdo it.

Dean: Yeah, they almost seem uneasy about the idea of just using their own voices. Some go even further. At the end of *Dragon*, we set up a screening for Gerard Butler and a bunch of his friends. They loved it. But Gerard came over to us and said, "I love the movie. But I want to redo all of my lines." He saw how big and imposing his character is, and he thought he didn't give him a big enough voice. I explained, "We record first and animate later." But he still insisted on trying to match the finished animation. He wanted more mass, more accent.

Ron: **Can you talk a little more about how you work with actors?**

Dean: Sure. Chris and I essentially take the same approach. Much like the crew, they are professionals at what they do. So you can't micromanage that. You have to let them do their thing. In that sense, when we write dialogue, it's always temporary. We want them to take a look at it and add their own touches. We are very much open to interpretation and ideas—as long as it doesn't lead into a tangent that takes us away from the story. Ever since *Lilo & Stitch*, we also sit down with the actors before recording begins. We like to get to know them and talk about the character and the tone of the film. That way they get a good grasp of the overall story.

When Gerard Butler first came onto the film [*How to Train Your Dragon*], we had a two-hour conversation about his character. He wanted him to have texture and be a man that the audience could relate to. He didn't want to only give speeches like Leonidas in *300*. So we quickly explained the father and son premise of the story. This is a man whose youthful heroic exploits defined him, and he wants the same thing for his son. However, his son is the complete opposite. As a parent, as a human being, he has to learn to accept that. In the beginning the two have a dysfunctional relationship. They don't honestly talk to each other. The blacksmith Gobber is the go-between, the means by which they communicate. Gerard not only quickly understood what we were going for but also began to think about how he could apply his skills as an actor to that role.

Tom: **How do you feel about using celebrities as opposed to experienced voice talent?**

Dean: You choose the voice that is right for the character, regardless of whether the actor is famous or not. The studios tend to want a name that they can market. But I think we're seeing more and more that it really doesn't reflect much in the box office. *Up* wasn't boasting huge names and it did amazingly well. Some movies that had nothing but celebrity casting did rather poorly at the box office. Still, sometimes those great actors are great for a reason. But the only thing I don't like is stunt casting. It was inappropriate for the movie. Again, it all comes back to casting the right voice for the character. That's it.

Tom: **How do you deal with the powers above? Sometimes a director has to be a salesman when it comes to studio politics in order to get your vision approved.**

Dean: In our case, Chris is very charismatic and easily interacts with the execs. I envy people like that. They can get people to buy anything, which is a fantastic ability to have when your movie hinges upon a pitch. Although I don't have that big personality in the room, I do have confidence in my ideas and my method. So when I'm pitching, I tend to invite everyone into my process. And I address both the strengths and weaknesses of the idea. I own the project, and I think that instills confidence in people.

In the beginning, my biggest concern about coming to the studio was Jeffrey [Katzenberg]'s reputation. Rumor had it that no one was really a director at DreamWorks. Everything was supposedly under Jeffrey's thumb. But that just wasn't the case. On my first day Jeffrey said, "I want three things. I want a father-and-son story, a Harry Potter tone, and a big David and Goliath ending. Give me those three things and you guys can have free reign." Later, when we invited him to view our progress, he would make a few comments and then leave. He left us to figure it out. Jeffrey wanted a few specific key things, and you had to give it to him. Other than that, you had the creative responsibility of making the movie. And although he always made astute observations, he explained that the process worked better if he wasn't in the room very much. Personalities at the top can vary greatly. Everybody wants the opportunity to color the project with their own sensibilities. As a director you have to listen to those who are paying for the movie. At the same time you still have to maintain a strong creative role. You have to know that you are making a movie that you'll be proud of. In the end, making a movie is a collaborative process that includes the execs. Jeffrey was just a great boss in that respect.

Tom: Have you ever worked with that producer who essentially wants to be another director on the film? Or have you mostly dealt with producers like Jeffrey, who sit back and oversee things from a distance?

Dean: I've been very lucky because I've worked with strong and creatively adept producers, the kind that support your vision and go to bat for you if the situation arises. Any studio has lots of demands, and there are always individuals that want to micromanage. You need a

Lilo & Stitch, 2002. © 2002 Disney.

creative buffer, somebody who can help you solve big problems and keep the studio focused on the movie's creative vision. If not, you can feel like a ping-pong ball being bounced around. We saw that happen on *Mulan*. There were too many people pulling creatively at the project, with no consistency regarding point of view. We had two directors who often didn't see eye to eye, a producer who had her own ideas about the movie, and a very driven editor with his own agenda. On top of that, at one point we had six writers pulling the story in different directions. It was quite chaotic for a while. In many ways *Lilo & Stitch* was a direct response to that. Besides directing, Chris and I took control of writing, storyboarding, and worked closely with our editor. It was the only way to maintain consistency. I really appreciate producers who don't try to be a second or third director. Their job is to balance the responsibility of the budget and the time it takes to make the movie, and to protect it from bureaucratic abuse.

Tom: **What is your favorite part of being a director?**

Dean: Well, from a selfish standpoint, it's easier to promote ideas that you strongly believe in. Those key, creative decisions are simply placed in your lap, and so you have the freedom to convey the emotions and imagery you want. When you're lower in the ranks, you have to convince a lot of people. I've been in both positions and I definitely prefer directing. From a more selfless point of view, I love being part of an experience that people look back fondly on. Even though *Mulan* was difficult, people were proud of the movie. This goal was so important when we started *Lilo & Stitch*

Dean DeBlois and Chris Sanders © Disney.

that we gathered everyone together in an assembly hall and said, "We have a smaller budget, less time, and a very ambitious movie. But we also want everybody to go home on the weekends and see their families. Let's have a good time." It was all about doing what needed to be done, yet still allowing the crew to have their lives, stay healthy, and see their loved ones.

Ron: **How did you do that? Making it possible for your crew, let alone yourself, to go home at a decent time is not always easy.**

Dean: It came down to simplifying some of the process. We couldn't afford Deep Canvas and a lot of the technology that the bigger movies had. So we simplified the character designs and did away with shadows. We ditched realism for a hand-painted watercolor look. We removed details. We removed pencil line mileage, like the prints from t-shirts and the pockets from jeans. In the end, no one really noticed. But that helped. Still, we had a tough schedule. Chris and I, as for *Dragon*, we started on the project in October 2008, and the movie had to be finished and out of animation by December 2009. We used a lot of the characters that had been rigged and the environments that had been built, but we started with the story from scratch. And we had to build new characters. It was tough on everyone, but they really believed in what they were doing. When you're running a ship that everyone is just happy to be on, it's a great feeling. It's important to me that people are proud of the movie, regardless of what the critics think.

Tom: **What's your least favorite part of being a director?**

Dean: Making concessions when you don't believe in them. It's that moment when you have to take on a note that you disagree with. It's a rare thing, actually. I wouldn't say that it happens very often. And this isn't just about disagreeing with the studio head. Chris and I have locked horns a few times, and one of us had to back down. When *Lilo & Stitch* was screened for the ratings board they didn't want to give us a G rating because of a few violent scenes. The powers that be at Disney made us go back and change sequences that worked really well. In the end we still didn't get the G rating. But then we were officially beyond the point of no return. We couldn't put things back to the way they were, the way we wanted them in the first place.

Ron: **Do you think you've grown or evolved as director?**

Dean: I think I'll be a student of story my entire life. But I've definitely learned some important lessons along the way. Telling a great story means that you have to know its elements, its overall structure and how to weave story lines together, and how to mine a scene for that gold that's just going to resonate with the audience. Embedding universal themes within a fresh, new story is important to me. I'm kind of obsessed with it. Looking back at my first experience in the story department on *Mulan*, I'm amazed that it took about five years to make. Knowing what I do now, I think we could have made it in half that time.

I think *Dragon* was a chance to prove that if you invest a lot in story, the other elements of the filmmaking process will come together quickly and smoothly. I've had a lot of time to observe other people's choices and directing styles. I've found my favorites and I've tried to emulate them. One of the things I do to keep the creative juices flowing is make music documentaries and films. It's rewarding because it has no structure. It's not about narrative. And the creative direction isn't subject to the whims of a collective body. You don't have to please others. It's all you and the band, and you're free to experiment however you wish. I love being able to grab a camera and try different lenses, different lighting effects, and different ways of editing the final product. It's truly gratifying.

Tom: **You wrote *How to Train Your Dragon 2* by yourself and directed it yourself.**

Dean: In the beginning I was nervous about it, but you are never really truly alone. I have the story team, and all the other creative heads to take suggestions from. A lot of people give a lot of good input, but you can't implement everything. You try to stay objective. Everything about the story needs to filter through you.

How To Train Your Dragon 2, 2014 © DreamWorks Animation LLC. All Rights Reserved.

Ron: **What advice would you give someone new to the industry about developing a good story?**

Dean: When Chris and I sit down to work on a project together, the first question is, "What would you pay to see? What excites you? What kind of world would grab you and take your breath away?" Once we get the ball rolling, then we talk about who the hero is and the back story that's driving him. You have to figure out what this character wants and needs, even if he can't see it himself. These are the core issues that you have to lay out in the beginning. It's something I learned from John Lasseter. He used to talk about the story minus the exact details. He simply wanted to know who this guy was, what kind of journey he's on, and what does he discover. It didn't make a difference if he was human or an animal, or if he was in the desert or the rainforest. I always tell students to read Blake Snyder's *Save the Cat* books, because they're a treasure trove of great story tools and truths. I also remember some great advice from Zack Schwartz, one of my teachers at Sheridan College. He was a background painter on *Snow White*. He said, "If it reads as a postage stamp, it will read as a billboard." I always remember that. First, see it in its most simple, strongest form. Then it will only get bolder, bigger, and better as you expand upon it.

Tom: **When you first got started, were there any artists that inspired you?**

Dean: Yeah, I was very lucky. On my very first day at Disney I was given an office that was about six doors down from Joe Grant. I met Joe on my first day, and that's when I realized he'd been there from the start. He was there the day that Walt came in and said, "I got this crazy idea. I want to make a feature length cartoon." He had this incredible wealth of knowledge and lessons to pass down. He was always evolving. Even when he left to pursue pottery and do greeting cards, he just kept developing as an artist. Joe was the guy I could go to for anything. He even took a creative interest in stuff I was doing outside of work. Any story I was developing, I always took it to him first. Any artwork that I finished, I would show him. Joe was also responsible for introducing me to Bill Pete. Bill was very inspiring. I would visit him at his home and just learn from him. One time he wanted to take me upstairs to his studio and show me a collection of his artwork. But his wife wouldn't let him, because she said it was too messy up there.

And I've had other heroes along the way. I got to meet Steven Spielberg. After he watched *Dragon*, he actually talked to us like colleagues. That was an amazing moment. James Cameron, after *Avatar*, also came over to view some of our sequences. He gave us great feedback, lots of compliments. In fact, after the Academy Awards, he grabbed us and said to his wife, "These are the guys I was telling you about." James Cameron actually went home and talked about our movie. Pretty cool.

Tom: **Do you ever feel overwhelmed by the number of decisions you have to make on a daily basis? Do you get frustrated?**

Dean: Looking back, frustration emerges when you just can't fix the thing that needs fixing. I particularly remember this early on. When I first got into story, I remember seeing well–thought-out storyboards that presented solutions to certain problems. But then they were cut apart, rearranged, and then manipulated by the director or the editors. That was frustrating. When you're the director and writer, it's in your hands. But when they seem tied, when you can't find a solution, or when you can't solve it the way you want to, that's when I feel frustrated. After all, you need to feed the machine. You're the director. It's your responsibility. And that's why you have to depend upon your team and even your producer. It's a creative brain trust, and they cannot only help you solve a problem, they can also prevent you from forcing a bad idea. It may seem great to you. You may strongly believe in it. But there's an audience out there. There are other people involved. And you have to answer to them. It's not just about you and your tastes in the end.

Tom: **Would you work again with preexisting material? Or are you only interested in developing your own stories now?**

Dean: To a certain extent, *Dragon* was based on a kids' book. We definitely brought our own interpretation to it. And we stuck to the essentials. It was a father-and-son story set in the world of Vikings and dragons. But almost every other detail went away.

How To Train Your Dragon, 2010 © DreamWorks Animation LLC. All Rights Reserved.

We also redesigned the major characters. Toothless, for example, used to be a little iguana-sized dragon. And so, even as an adaptation, it still required a lot of reinvention. Overall, getting involved in a preexisting property isn't that appealing to me. The only way I would do it is if I were allowed to put a creative spin on it, something I could believe in.

Tom: Since you're such a story guy, do you ever miss storyboarding?

Dean: I do. It's such an important stage in the creation of an animated feature. If you're writing the script and directing the picture, storyboarding is this in-between moment where somebody takes that script and does an interpretation of it. It's not always what you had in mind. And you have to be very open-minded about it, because it might be better than what you had in mind. But often that's where you can get frustrated, because the artist missed something that was so important to you and the story. So, sometimes it requires sitting down and drawing it out with the artist and letting them go from there. You can't get bogged down, because that's not your job.

Making an animated feature is a collaborative effort. It's better to have other people putting a spin on it, as long as they know what the bigger picture is. That's what you're there to remind them about. You can't let them engage in open exploration. That's a bad way to direct. Of course, everyone wanted to jump right into *How to Train Your Dragon 2*. But I had to push back. I wanted time to write a story that works before we start exploring it visually. It makes everyone's life much easier. And hopefully we avoid the frustration and wasted time allotted to designing various locations or exploring moments that aren't going to be in the movie.

Tom: Do you like the editing process? Some directors love it, because they sit down and go through sequences.

Dean: I love it! I appreciate what a good editor can bring to the process. I've worked with some really bossy ones and with some really collaborative ones. I particularly like working with Darren Holmes and John Carr. They bring in their own ideas, but they're always in tune with the overall feel and tone of the movie.

Ron: Do you also want the story finished before you bring in a composer?

Dean: Yes. I want to know that the story is locked in place before bringing the composer in. That said, I'd love to get the composer in as early as possible. They are a key part of storytelling. When Chris and I brought Alan Silvestri into the mix, he was able to pick out moments that we had either been avoiding or burying under dialogue. He added a whole new layer to the story as he removed the temporary score and inserted music that enhanced the emotions of a given scene. And when we worked with John Powell he was always experimenting. He would talk with us about music in general. He wanted to know what was on our iPods. Those conversations led to some interesting choices in the beginning. The original music was inspired by a piece of music that came from an Icelandic quartet called *Sigur Ros*. I had made a feature documentary about them. John found it to be really inspiring and rose to outdo it in the end. It captured the emotion of the scene perfectly. John's ideas added a lot to the movie.

Ron: **Now you did mention how comic books were an important inspiration early on. But was there a pivotal moment when you just knew that you were going to work in animation?**

Dean: Well, I remember being mesmerized when the Queen turned into a witch in *Snow White*, and when she is on the cliff with the lightning flashing in the background. The animation was so fluid. And that's when I started to think about the artist that actually drew that scene. The scene in *Dumbo* when his mother rocks him to sleep through the bars of the cage was also a powerful moment. However, I just didn't see the avenue by which I could pursue animation. That's why I focused on comic books. It wasn't until I stumbled upon the animation program at Sheridan College that I began to learn about the process. It was kind of funny, actually. Until that moment I didn't think you could study animation at school.

Ron: **What other movies inspired you?**

Dean: The imagery in *Pinocchio* and *Bambi* was so poetic and evocative. And as children's films, they were very bold, considering the powerful themes involved. I remember just wanting to live in those worlds. They were definitely inspirations as I moved into layout, because I wanted to draw worlds like that. In particular the European designs in *Pinocchio* fascinated me. That architecture was very romantic. It got my imagination going.

Ron: **You eventually traveled to Europe, right?**

Dean: When I went to work for Don Bluth, I found myself in Ireland. So that landscape and architecture was suddenly all around me. You didn't have to go far to find dilapidated ruins and castles. And on weekends I traveled to places like Denmark and Spain. I was always interested in the macabre, so I took the opportunity to visit the catacombs and the famous cemeteries in Paris. I also went to Scotland and visited Loch Ness. I was in my early twenties. It was a great time.

Ron: **What about live-action movies?**

Dean: I remember loving *Escape to Witch Mountain*; the theme of a younger protagonist in over his or her head in a supernatural world just resonated with me. *E.T.* was also a big influence. And, of course, there was *Star Wars*, the Indiana Jones series, and

The Black Stallion, which was such an emotionally powerful film. I think one of the most influential movies was *Blade Runner*. I actually learned to storyboard by studying Ridley Scott's directing choices. Don Bluth's studio had a conference room where I would eat dinner and watch his movies after work. I'd pause between every cut and draw the before and after frame. I really wanted to understand why certain moments in certain movies elicited such a response. For example, that scene where Rutger Hauer catches Harrison Ford from falling and then gives his death speech, that scene is so beautifully played out. I found it so poetic. People in the theater really responded to that scene. I also did the same thing with James Cameron's *The Abyss*. I drew every frame before and after cuts in key scenes. I didn't have access to anyone's boards, so I used live action to teach myself filmmaking.

Ron: **As an animation director, do you think you've evolved differently because you used live action as a reference?**

Dean: Maybe. I know that I appreciate live-action sensibilities. And I dislike that wacky, animation cliché where everything is just silly. Animation is a medium, not a genre. Yet people are still quick to categorize it as kids' stuff. It's something you give the babysitter to distract the kids with. It's much more powerful than that. There is a suspension of disbelief. If you do it right, you can transport people to places that they have never dreamed of. What James Cameron did with *Avatar* is basically what great animation does. In the case of *Dragon*, I'm currently working on the sequels, but I'm looking at it as a trilogy. It has the potential to grow and become this epic world like *The Lord of the Rings*. And the tone and themes will become more mature as the storyline grows.

Tom: **In *How to Train Your Dragon 2* you have aged Hiccup and the other characters, instead of keeping them perpetually children, like the Charlie Brown characters.**

Dean: Yes, I always saw *How to Train Your Dragon* as a trilogy showing Hiccup attaining manhood. In the first film he was fifteen and afraid of what was ahead, afraid of girls, afraid of dragons, afraid of his coming place in life. In *Dragon 2* we move up five years, so the endless playfulness of being fifteen doesn't make sense. At fifteen you already feel like an adult, but it is the last year that you are treated as a child. That is a very confusing time period. In *Dragon 2*, Hiccup is twenty. He is more confident and beginning to recognize his responsibilities. His relationship with his father has also evolved. Also in the first movie we completely played out the theme of dragons and humans mistrusting of one another. It didn't make sense to rehash that theme again.

Tom: So you are a triple threat. A writer, an animator, and a director.

Dean: I was a so-so animator. I'm a better layout guy and storyboard artist.

Ron: Do you play an instrument too?

Dean: No. I'm just fascinated by people who can. I am a serious music fan, both scores and live music. I go to a lot of concerts. Mostly I listen to alternative stuff. Sigur Ros is such an inspiring band that I felt compelled to make a documentary about them. Their music is so cinematic, so full of imagery. When I saw them at the Hollywood Bowl, they had the audience in their hands. Their music reaches out and grabs the audience in a powerful way. Great film scores do the same thing. They transcend dialogue and go right for the heart. It puts you in a unique emotional space. Whether you realize it or not, a good score is one of the reasons why you love that movie so much.

Tom: Can you talk a little bit more about what it's like to co-direct?

Dean: Sure, absolutely. Chris and I met back in 1994 on *Mulan*. He was head of the storyboard department on that film. I had just joined the studio as a layout artist, but then I quickly became part of the story team. And after Chris went off to develop a film as a director, I became head of story. There were just about ten of us then. But Chris and I had the same interests and artistic tendencies, especially for taking a fresh approach to characters and a love of quirky moments. So we were always in sync in terms of developing and writing a scene.

When it came time to do *Lilo & Stitch*, it was just a natural collaboration. Chris and I wrote well together. We direct well together. I think it's because we have different points of view, yet our artistic voice is essentially the same. Our sensibilities overlap, and that's important because we share the same goal. On the other hand, there's enough difference between us that it keeps what we do fresh. When we divide up scenes we usually gravitate towards those that we have a certain vibe for. So we don't often find ourselves wanting to write the same scene. When we're done we then read each other's work. Here, I think, is the most important moment in our process. There's a great deal of trust in each other's sensibilities, tastes, and judgment. If either of us starts pulling stuff out of those scenes, we trust that decision. No one immediately says, "You have to put that stuff back in!" If we do have a difference of opinion, we talk about it. The story is always the most important thing in the room, not our feelings. We make our decisions based on that alone. It's the way we bring together our subtle differences to make the story better that keeps our process, and our material, invigorating and fresh.

We both have that time alone to write a scene. It's a creative moment that's indicative of our individual voices. But I trust Chris to react to the best stuff in that scene. He'll usually say, "I see where you're going and I really like this. This part felt a little long. What if you do this instead?" That's when the dialogue starts. We always give each other a moment to get our ideas out on paper, so that the idea exists before you start tampering with it.

Tom: On *How to Train Your Dragon 2*, you were directing it alone (Chris Sanders moved over to direct *The Croods*). What have you learned about the process since you started?

Dean: [laughs] First, it's a lot more work! Seriously, you have to be the champion of your convictions. Three years later even the best ideas lose their freshness and people start to think they should be changed. I find myself standing up for ideas. You have to believe in what you originally saw in them.

Ron: Well, we really appreciate your taking the time to talk with us. Thanks, Dean.

Dean: It's been my pleasure.

Dean DeBlois and Chris Sanders © Disney.

7

Vicky Jenson Interview

Vicky Jenson © DreamWorks.

Vicky Jenson and I have known each other since she started working at Filmation Studios in the mid-1980s. Vicky is an effervescent woman, bubbling over with ideas and talent. She can design, paint, storyboard, art direct as well as direct, both animation as well as live action. She co-directed *Shrek*, the first animated feature film to win an Academy Award, and she worked with the likes of Robert De Niro and Martin Scorsese. She began in animation at a time when women were not expected to do more than clean up and color characters. But the word "no" had never been part of her vocabulary. Vicky kicked down barriers for women filmmakers with her fashionable suede boots, and did it all with grace and good humor. We sat down with Vicky at DreamWorks Studio to talk about her amazing career.

Tom Sito

Ron Diamond: Now let's start with a little background. When did your interest in animation begin? What was your inspiration?

Vicky: I got into the industry the way a lot of people did: nepotism! [laughs] I started painting cels for my brother-in-law at a very young age. He had a small animation studio that made commercials for things like Breck hair shampoo and Jerseymaid milk.

Ron: Was this here in LA?

Vicky: This was here in LA. I was painting cels while babysitting for him and my sister. I was about thirteen, earning a whopping five bucks per hour! Of course that five bucks also included the babysitting!

Ron: Was there a short film that influenced and inspired you?

Vicky: I remember watching *The Violinist* by Ernie Pintoff as a kid. We didn't have VCRs or DVDs then. We would rent a projector from the library and pick up a few films on 16 mm. My little brother got really good being a projectionist and even set up a little theater in his bedroom. Along with classic features my dad wanted us to see, like *Citizen Kane* and *Potemkin*, we used to watch this one short cartoon every time. It resonated with me for a couple of reasons. I did play a musical instrument when I was a kid, but mostly it was this great combination of poignancy and comedy. This man learns that life is better when it's in balance. I just thought that was a tremendous lesson. We grew up with a lot of expectation in our family to be artistic and to excel at whatever dream we wanted to pursue. That little cartoon just reminded me to keep it in balance.

Ron: Were you already considering animation as a career?

Vicky: No, I didn't think of animation as a possible career at all. I was going to be a painter or dancer. I was taking ballet and cello lessons at the time. Working in animation was just my summer job. Painting backgrounds at Hanna-Barbera was very seasonal work. I was paying my way through college at the Academy of Art in San Francisco by working each summer in LA.

When I first worked at Hanna-Barbera as a background painter on *The Smurfs* and other cartoons, I just didn't think of it as a career. But then I was hired on at Filmation and I started storyboarding and earning lots of money. Things started to change. Shows became syndicated, the work was no longer seasonal; it was much more permanent. I didn't even finish my last semester of college because there was so much work. Everyone at school kept saying, "You're already doing the work that we're trying to get into." Still, it didn't feel like my dream or the plan that I had for myself. I didn't have that feeling until I started directing.

When I started directing, I found that it embraced everything that I was interested in. You get to play with music, movement, the story, and yet you don't have to animate! I was never an animator. I was always a storyboard artist or a background painter, a designer. I just didn't have the patience for actually animating! But I just love conducting the whole thing, working with all the moving parts and telling the bigger picture.

Tom: **What was it like working at Hanna-Barbera? That must have felt like a big factory.**

Vicky: I worked upstairs in the background department. It was a bit of a boy's club. I was one of only three women painting backgrounds, but the other two, Gloria Wood and Lorraine Andrina, worked at home. I was tough, confident, and somehow I fit in. As a department we were very much our own entity. Sometimes it seemed everybody else in the building couldn't stand us because we were so noisy! We played loud music and held dart competitions, with darts we made from push-pins and tape. Worst of all, we would put a handful of pennies in a Sparkletts bottle and toss it around the concrete floor. To the departments downstairs it must have sounded like thunder and we knew it! Oh, the calls we got from the other departments!

Tom: **Who was the head of the department?**

Vicky: Al Gmuer. He was great. It was such a fun time. There was a quota system to manage how much we were expected to paint. If you painted anything for "stock," backgrounds that were used throughout the series, your painting counted double. We had to paint at least twenty fields a week, so stock was highly desired because when you reached your quota you got to go home! Another plus was getting assigned a "pan." Pans were the long paintings used for scenes where a character had to run or drive. These were super easy and so super lucrative! One of the guys even had a license plate that only background painters could understand. It said, "Repeat Pan." It's hard to explain. Nobody understands an eighty A to E pan anymore. I feel like a dinosaur.

Tom: **Artists who create backgrounds and storyboards, once established, tend to get very settled in their careers. You, on the other hand, seemed to be rather restless. When did you first start thinking about directing? What attracted you to it?**

Vicky: It wasn't really about being restless; it was about the challenge. Every time I took a job it was either to try something new or work with somebody I always wanted to work with. It was all about learning more and getting more experience. I tried animating, but like I said, I didn't have the patience for it. I liked storyboarding because it kind of included animation, in that I got to draw the characters acting. But I didn't have to stress any of the technicalities like staying on model or registration. The idea of directing didn't even come up until I was at Universal working on the *Baby Huey* series as an art director and story artist. It was a little show that aired at six in the morning, I think about eight people saw it. It was the first time I got to write an episode, storyboard it, and then direct it. I went nuts. I just put everything into it that had ever influenced me. It was so exciting and so much fun. A few months later DreamWorks formed and they were looking for people. At this point I definitely wanted to direct but I wanted to learn more about it. I put together a portfolio and applied to AFI's directing program for women. Everyone I knew was sending their resumes to DreamWorks but that was my plan B. At the time, the straightest path to directing in animation was as a story artist. I told myself if I didn't get into AFI, I'd apply to DreamWorks. And that is exactly what happened! Years later, after *Shrek*, I kind of rubbed their noses in it when they invited me to give a talk.

Baby Huey, Vicky Jenson, 1994 © DreamWorks Animation LLC.

Tom: That's kind of like when Disney once brought Charles Schulz in to talk to the crew, the first thing he said was, "This is interesting. I remember applying to Disney in 1950 before I sold *Peanuts*. I got a very nice letter back saying, 'Thank you. But we are only looking for good artists.'"

Vicky: Oh no. [laughs]

Tom: Okay, we have to get to the feminist question. Your career overlaps with the older generation, the old boys' club. Did you ever feel like you hit a glass ceiling?

Vicky: If there was, I just didn't see it. I wouldn't see it. I remember getting a comment or two when I was painting backgrounds at Hanna-Barbera, something like, "You don't paint like a girl at all!" And there was also, "You paint great for a girl." What does a girl paint like? I don't know. I just ignored that stuff. And it never intimidated me. I did my job and learned from everybody who was there. I think that attitude came from my family. My mom and dad never raised us to feel limited. We had something to contribute, and we could do that if we wanted to. On the job I just plowed ahead.

Tom: Well, even at Filmation there were always a few guys that were pretty old school about women.

Vicky: I shared a room with a chauvinist. He was afraid of birds. So I just "unknowingly" brought in birds a lot. I think the flapping scared him out of the office eventually. But it didn't make a difference that those guys were around. I didn't care if they were arrogant or felt threatened. They didn't seem to be the ones that could get in the way of me moving forward, if I needed to. This is making me sound ambitious, but it wasn't like that. I just wanted to learn how to do new things, like how to paint clouds for the *Smurfs* or *Flintstones*. And I was always fearless when it came to asking questions. I think they just kept giving me more work because I kept asking.

I was the same in the live-action world. When I was storyboarding a low-budget horror movie I kept talking about how I was in love with production design because I was taking a class at UCLA. When their original production designer decided to leave because the budget became too low, they asked me if I wanted to put my money where my mouth was and take the job. I jumped at the chance and spent nine weeks in Yugoslavia. Our budget was so low I had to wear a lot of hats on that movie. On top of being production designer and story artist, I became the set decorator and even got to be a puppeteer on the creature. None of this would've happened if I kept my mouth shut. Talking about my dreams out loud seemed to make them come true.

Tom: Unlike some of the other directors we've talked to, you came up through the Hollywood factory system. Back when everyone viewed animation as a blue-collar, day-laborer kind of job. How did you motivate yourself and refrain from getting stuck in that mentality? When you have to clock in every morning, it's easy to grow disaffected.

Vicky: I just never looked at it as a paycheck. Anything you're going to spend that much time doing each day of your life should be meaningful. For me, it wasn't a job. It was art in some way or another. It didn't matter what I was working on. I'd always find something about it that represented an artistic experience. I was going to learn something. Anything. Once, when storyboarding, I decided I wanted to learn how to draw with a brush like … oh dear, who did the comic strip *Pogo*?

Tom: Walt Kelly.

Vicky: Yes, Walt Kelly. I LOVE those drawings. So I would make these challenges for myself like: "I'm going to learn how to ink on this show." Even if I didn't care what the show is about. It was never a nine-to-five job. Every day was a lesson. Every season was a school semester. When I first started at DreamWorks, when we were making *El Dorado*, Will Finn and David Silverman would give me a sequence and say, "Just make it 'Vicky,' you know, just make it Vickyfied." I would take that sequence, give it my own personal treatment, and just keep moving forward.

Tom: You never went to film school, right?

Vicky: Right.

Tom: So most of your skills were acquired on the job and through mentoring?

Vicky: It was all on-the-job training. As I mentioned earlier, I grew up around art. I had art books and I drew all the time. But I never formally studied film or took courses in story structure or theory of cinematography. It was all a mystery until I was actually doing it on the job. For example, when I started storyboarding, we had to create a half-hour show in a month. We'd get a script and have to visualize it. Suddenly, while I'm at the movies or watching something on TV, I was aware of cuts, close-ups, and establishing shots. I couldn't look at a movie any other way again. Even when it came to live action I was learning by the seat of my pants.

Color studies, Vicky Jenson, *The Road to El Dorado*, 2000 © DreamWorks Animation LLC.

Tom: You're like Chuck Jones in that way. Chuck didn't go to college or have any formal training. He learned everything as he went along. And at the end of his life he was very much like Mark Twain. He really wanted to get under the skin of the project.

Vicky: Sometimes you can't learn anything until you actually do it. People can give you all the advice in the world, but it's just going to bounce off your forehead until you experience it. That's when you say, "Oh that's what they were talking about. Damn it! Why didn't I listen?" School is great, but I think you have to experience the gymnastics of filmmaking at the same time. I don't regret anything. If I went to film school, perhaps the theory and lessons would have limited me in some way or scared me off.

Tom: Talk a little more about your experiences in live action. How is it different in your experience? Are there any parallels?

Vicky: Yes, certainly, but there are some distinct differences. For instance there is an immediacy to live action. Obviously for both animation and live action you do as much prep as you can but in live action the thing to remember is that you're creating and gathering all the pieces that you think you will need for the editorial process after. In animation I was used to pre-editing. You're planning out what you need because in animation you don't animate coverage. When animation directors come over to live action, they often end up editing in the camera. Ivan Reitman, my producer on my first live-action feature, kept saying that to me during the dailies, "Stop editing in the camera. You're not giving yourself enough coverage. You're not giving yourself enough choices. What if your idea doesn't work?" That's very true. When we're storyboarding for animation we toss the boards away all the time and try again. In live action you don't have the opportunity to cut together a story reel. You have to plan for a lot of different possibilities. You have to give yourself some room to play with later on. That was a hard lesson for me. And that's probably the biggest difference between the two. I still love live action. I would do it again in a heartbeat. I love the interaction with the actors, watching them create that magic. In animation we are so used to hyper-controlling every edit, every audio edit, every blink. My DP kept saying, "Just count to ten before you yell 'cut,' because you don't know what the actor might do." I thought that was really good advice.

Tom: What about working with the crew? Some animation directors said they experienced a kind of passive-aggressive resistance from live-action crews, because they didn't come up through the traditional roles of a live-action set. Did you ever run into any of that?

Vicky: I don't think so. If I did, that old filter must have kicked in. I just ignored the negativity. But I've always been very inclusive. I didn't go into it assuming that everyone was out to get me. There is a really good book on directing live action called

The Working Director. It points out that everyone on set has their own issues to deal with. Your location manager isn't there to help you make a great movie. He is there to make sure he can park the trucks. Your first AD isn't necessarily there to make sure you're making a great movie either. That's YOUR job. He's thinking about airplanes flying overhead or schools nearby, the potential background noise that will make his job difficult. Everybody is fighting their own battle in some way. You're the one leading them through this whole process, and they need to feel included in the bigger picture. If you do that, they'll jump through fire for you. Not every director does this, and the movie still gets made. I wanted to create a more inclusive environment. For example, I tended to tell everybody, no matter what their position was on the movie, what the theme of my movie was all about. I wanted to talk to them about it artistically. I knew if I pulled them in they'd contribute ideas I might never think of on my own. And it worked. Everyone felt more invested. Even the prop designer on my short would come to me with little things he'd found that didn't just work, they illustrated the theme.

Tom: **When you started directing, how was the transition from working on a film to managing one?**

Vicky: It entailed a lot of personal growth. I came from a very opinionated, loud family. I was never afraid to speak out, and that got me noticed. It made me visible. But like everyone, I had to learn to balance being the boss and having empathy for my crew. As I said, everyone is fighting their own battles on set. Still, you need to make sure that everybody is making the same move. Your ego needs to be in check. I might look at a scene and want to draw it myself. But that's not my job anymore. I've surrounded myself with the best people I can find. I need to convey my vision in order to help my crew do their jobs.

Tom: **The difficulty of letting go is quite common amongst directors that used to animate or storyboard. You still want to jump in and do it yourself.**

Vicky: Well, when you don't jump in, when you back off and set someone else's mind in motion, one of the greatest benefits is being surprised. Your artist can come back with something wonderful and unexpected. You have all these incredibly talented people working with you. As you let them work, you get to watch some wonderful ideas unfold. Then suddenly you have a wealth of ideas to work with and you too get to be surprised.

Tom: **Are there any anecdotes that you'd like to share? Was there anything so unexpectedly cool that you just had to use it?**

Vicky: There are dozens. It happens all the time. We tend not to think of animation as spontaneous, but it can be. And it doesn't make a difference when that great moment or idea happens. You can use it. In live action, that can be difficult unless you have money for reshoots. Otherwise, you can't just go back and put it in. One of the cool things about animation is that you don't have to stop until the producer tells you to stop!

Ron: Did directing live action influence or change the way you direct animation?

Vicky: Yes. Live action forced me to be a stronger storyteller. You have your feet to the fire. You're working so fast, and you have to keep the story and its characters clear. The same thing goes for animation. Without a strong story and characters, you just have pretty pictures. That's certainly not a revelation. But it is a hard lesson to learn on a live-action set. In animation you have so many people there to help you. You have so many chances to change things. You get spoiled. You get to attack the story in well-defined pieces. In the storyboard process you can come up with new ideas and make the movie funnier. That was very much my experience on *Shrek*. On *Shark Tale* the story was not so clear. The original script was too violent. And we only knew where the movie started and where it ended. There was an entire process of discovery in between, and that was a great experience. But I like to start with a good story first!

Tom: On both *Shrek* and *Shark Tale* you had a lot of Hollywood stars cast in those key roles. Do you have certain actors in mind when you are creating new characters?

Vicky: No, not always. *Shrek* was simply unique that way. It was definitely a new way of approaching animation. Before that, directors didn't really let actors shape a character the way Mike Myers and Eddie Murphy did, or as Robin Williams did in *Aladdin*.

Tom: Do you like working with actors in recording studios?

Vicky: Definitely! It's really one of my favorite parts of the job. It's actually the reason why I went into live action in the first place. I loved working with actors. In animation the drawing can sometimes consume everyone's attention. Acting often gets lost. I'm just so enamored with watching the performance unfold and finding the different ways that you can work a scene. As the director you get pulled into the actors' process, the way he or she finds that character. I love being a part of that.

Tom: Most big name actors are not familiar with the animation process. How was it, directing someone like Robert De Niro or Will Smith in the recording studio?

Vicky: I made sure that it became familiar to them, so that it didn't seem so mechanical. To me, it's not voice-over. It is acting. So, I would shape a session like a rehearsal and work in ways that were familiar to them from live action. We worked in bigger story beats rather than just taking the scenes line by line and having them say it three different ways. I saw a lot of animation directors doing that at the time. Instead, we would read the whole scene together and get comfortable with it, like in a rehearsal. Then we would work on the different tactics the character might use to accomplish what he or she might be after for the whole scene. It made the performances more personal and authentic. I also never let an actor work in a vacuum during a recording session. I made sure that my actors are also good actors, so that Robert or Will had something real to react to. In fact, a lot of my direction would be to the reader because I knew that would have an effect on the actor's response. There needs to be a connection between the players in that recording studio. I wasn't so worried about making sure the line came out the way I heard it in my head; I just wanted to make sure it was honest and maybe even surprising. In preparation, I would put myself in the actor's shoes and ask a lot of questions of my characters. What do you want out of him in this scene? What do you want him to do? Are you trying to pick a fight with him? Are you trying to win him over to your side? And then I would explore what tactics one might use to do these things. The tactics are the acting choices that make the performance unique. I might pick a fight with someone differently than you do. Those are the kinds of questions going through the actors' minds. And that's how I approached it. I would get my coverage from my actors, from what they brought to the role.

Tom: **Did you ever show them storyboards? Some actors like to look at storyboards and some don't.**

Vicky: Yes. We did that a lot on *Shrek*. Not always on *Shark Tale*. By that time I was more into the whole actor process. But when we did, it was generally early in the process to get the actor excited about the role. It was a way to give them a handle on the character. But we always wanted the actor to have the freedom to play with the character anyway, no matter what we had boarded.

Tom: **Were you able to get two actors in the same room? It's often tough to schedule celebrities.**

Vicky: Yes, I did! I got Robert De Niro and Martin Scorsese together. It was also the first time I joined actors inside the recording booth. I just couldn't stay outside in the control room. I needed to be there with them like any director would when running a rehearsal. And that's how I ran the session, like a rehearsal. And it was so much fun. There were no costumes or props, just them. It was a great scene. But that shouldn't be surprising. I think while this was the eleventh movie they'd done together it was the FIRST time they were both actually acting together.

Tom: **Did you keep the tape running? You have to capture that spontaneity. In rehearsals you get all this great stuff, but then the actual take is sometimes just okay.**

Vicky: Oh yeah, we did. And you want to let them know that they're free to fail. Otherwise they won't take chances. Or I'll say, "I got this great idea. Now it might not work …" Then they really cut loose, because it's not their fault if it doesn't work. It's my fault! It's something I learned from my wonderful directing mentor Judith Weston. I cannot thank her enough for all she's taught me over the years. She was my secret weapon. Bill Damaschke [Chief Creative Officer] had

Storyboards, Vicky Jenson, *Shrek*, 2004 © DreamWorks Animation LLC.

Storyboards, Vicky Jenson, *Shrek*, 2004 © DreamWorks Animation LLC.

asked me what I was doing differently from the other directors. I guess he'd noticed a difference in the performances and I think a couple of the actors had mentioned how great the experience had been. After trying to keep her to myself I finally told him I'd been working with her. She began giving workshops to story artists and directors at DreamWorks soon after that!

Tom: **How about music? When you're working on ideas for film, do you simultaneously have music in your mind?**

Vicky: I actually do. I get a song that will, in a way, represent the tone of the movie. I'll listen to it over and over and over again. It'll be in my car, my home, even in the background while I'm drawing. That happened when I was first storyboarding on *Shrek*. One of the first sequences was rather tough. I had worked on it. Raman Hui had worked on it. Other people worked on it. But I had John Cale's "Hallelujah," his version of the Leonard Cohen song, in my head. I suggested it to my co-director Andrew Adamson and our editor Sim Evan-Jones, and they agreed they'd always liked that song, too. That song fit the moment. I sat with a junior editor and we cut out all the naughty bits of the song and storyboarded right to it.

I did the same thing on my short film. I remember listening, over and over again, to this song by Luna, "California (All the Way)." I listened all through preproduction, as I storyboarded, and it eventually became the title song. I even had it arranged as classical music and used it in the key scene at the end of the short.

Tom: **What's the difference between directing a short and a feature?**

Vicky: Well, a short can be, should be, essentially all you. It may be the closest you'll get to making something completely personal. Although you will work on it with a lot of other people, it doesn't require anyone else's approval. There's no studio involved. There's no note session. But in my case there was a producer telling me, as many producers might tell other directors on any other studio film, "We're hemorrhaging money!" Only this time the producer was also telling me "And it's your money!"

Tom: **When you're directing, do you generate artwork personally? Some people don't do any. John Musker told me he hasn't animated in years. But Richard Williams would try to draw a lot.**

Vicky: I draw a lot. I draw a lot even on a live-action set. I'm very visual when it comes to explaining myself. I was drawing a lot for my DP and my location manager. On *Shrek* and *Shark Tale*, I definitely drew a lot. I even painted on *Shrek*. I was giving a lot of work and sketches to the animators. It's a way of communicating for me, because I think visually. I'm not trying to do an animator's job. It's just that when I try verbally explaining any of my more visual ideas I can tend to get a bit frustrated with the words. Then I inevitably say, "Get me a Sharpie." That's the only phrase that'll come out. I did this pile of commercials a couple of years ago, Old Navy stuff, which was really fun and goofy. The same thing happened. There's a mannequin that takes five people to move into position. I started saying, "Head to the left. Put the arm up. You have to move … Just give me a Sharpie!" I drew it out for them.

Color studies, Vicky Jenson, *Shrek*, 2004 © DreamWorks Animation LLC.

Tom: **Do you ever have that moment when an artist takes your sketch and completely reinterprets it?**

Vicky: Yes. And if it's not interpreted in a way that works for the film or the scene, then this is where your skills as a director come into play. Some people can be really great at one thing, but not so great at another. They may try their best, but it's not working. You have to guide them. You have to direct them without barking orders. It's not so easy to do sometimes. You have to say it in the most constructive way possible, "I need you to express my vision in this case, not yours."

Tom: **You have anywhere from 5 to 500 artists, who all have big egos, and they all must act like the film is being drawn by one hand. Management skills are something that no one really teaches you. And in the end, you just can't say, "Do it because I say so."**

Vicky: If you can sit down with them and talk it through early on, even sketch out some ideas with them, that can create a connection over the concept. Now the artist has authored the idea with you. They are invested. When you leave and come back a week later, your artist isn't going to feel left out. They feel valued because they are valued.

Tom: **What's your favorite part about directing?**

Vicky: In animation, I love settling into editorial. I love it!

Tom: **A bunch of people say that.**

Vicky: I would make my tea and sit down with either Sim Evan-Jones, Nick Fletcher, or John Venzon. I even got to work with the great Sheldon Kahn [*Ghostbusters*, *Out of Africa*]! Then I just wait, like a kid in a theater, to see how they'd pulled it all together. Then we'd work in my thoughts. And I love calling a board artist in and showing them their sequence for the first time. They'll either see how something isn't working, or they'll quickly point out how something should be fixed. They are a part of the process, and you can see it their body language. They run off and start drawing. It's really fun.

Tom: **Okay, what's the worst part of the job?**

Vicky: Telling somebody something they don't want to hear. But it has to be done. Changes can be rough sometimes. But that's part of the job.

Tom: **Story artists in particular feel like they had a better idea. And you rarely meet a screenwriter who says, "That's exactly the way I saw this scene when I wrote it."**

Vicky: Well, when it's a success, then they say that. And when it's not, it's quite easy for everyone to come down hard on a director. When I first got the job, Conrad Vernon said, "Tell me what happens to you guys when you go through those big director doors, because you all come out different." I think he knows why now!

Tom: **He knows.**

Vicky: All the battles you have to fight …

Tom: **"A director is part artist, part commander, but also part salesman and diplomat." How do you deal with the inevitable politics?**

Vicky: I ran into a lot of problems initially. My nature has always been, "If I have an opinion, I'm right! Of course I'm right! How could you sa I'm not? I'm right!" Again, I grew up in an opinionated family. We argued; it was normal. But you don't argue on a film. I just had to get over that. I think I alienated a couple of producers initially, but in time I found a way to understand that people above you are there for a reason, too, just like the artists are there for a reason. They may not be drawing, but that doesn't mean they're not creative. We had a lot of them on *Shark Tale*, probably too many. But that wasn't their fault, and each brought something to the table. It was only after I let their voices and ideas be heard, just like

I did with all the artists, that I really understood and respected that position as well. If you handle it properly, it's not going to be a big speed bump for you. Some producers are actually not used to everyone getting an opinion, especially those coming over from live action. For them, it's like having the electrician or the guy holding the boom say, "I don't think that was a good take." But a great idea can come from anywhere, including your producer! I say that jokingly, but I think it's just a lot easier for artists to respect the jobs they understand. It isn't as easy for a lot of artists to understand what a producer does.

Shark Tale, 2004 © DreamWorks Animation LLC.

Tom: Some producers are very opinionated and wish to influence the creative process directly. While others just don't get involved. When I was at Warner Bros. my instructions were essentially, "Here's fifty million dollars. Go away and in a year come back, and it'd better be really good." Of course, each film presented a different situation. Do you think you have a personal style, as a director?

Vicky: I know I do. People seem to like the way I run a set. It's kind of a happy environment. It's an inclusive environment. And there's always a lot of laughter. I don't think I'm as good at creating a lot of crazy, fun games as Kelly Asbury. When I worked for him, he always came up with stuff that made Friday afternoon so much fun. He was so good at creating camaraderie.

Ron: I want to go back a little bit and talk about your parents. Can you tell us a little more about your early influences? You mentioned that they encouraged you to be artistic.

Vicky: The arts were really important to my parents, so my siblings and I were exposed to lots of things early on. There were always a lot of art books around the house. We went to museums. We took music classes. My dad would also try to expose us to what he thought were the great movies. I started watching François Truffaut films at a very early age. But I ended up with a broader range of influences than just classical art, classical music, and art films. I appreciated popular culture as well. A pop song can move you just as much as a piece of classical music. Just don't tell my mom that!

Tom: **Do you have a favorite director?**

Vicky: I watched a lot of Woody Allen. His understanding of people and relationships is so keen. I adore *Crimes and Misdemeanors*. That movie is pure genius. The films that move me aren't just funny but actually have a tremendous amount of heart in them. There's a solid exploration of a truth. There's some kind of revelation that reminds us of something we all know is true, something basically human. Look at what Chris and Dean did with *How to Train Your Dragon*. That story is strong and powerful, but at the same time it's charming and gorgeous. That's what storytelling is all about. It's bigger than the laughs.

Tom: **When *Shrek* was about to be released into theaters, did anyone have a sense of how successful that movie was going to be?**

Vicky: Nobody had a clue. It was weird. It really felt like a movie that we were sort of making in our garage. We were up north, far away from the main hub of DreamWorks. It was just this funny little building. We'd sit there, come up with an idea, and then do it. The project felt very small as a result. I don't mean that it didn't seem like a big story, just that it felt personal and even, dare I say, "indie." Now we knew it was funny. After it started to come together, laughter was an unavoidable consequence of watching some of these scenes. But we really just didn't have a clue that it was going to turn into this blockbuster. On opening weekend I remember getting a phone call from Jeffrey at six in the morning telling me the numbers were outstanding. Then he called me on the second weekend to tell me the numbers had gone up. I said, "Well, good." He then said, "No, you don't understand. That doesn't happen. Movies never go up the second week. They always drop. They don't go up." That's when it hit me. This is something big.

Tom: **How do you pace your workload? Some people say that directing is kind of like dancing on a snowball rolling downhill.**

Vicky: I remember people telling me to just ride the horse in the direction it's going. You just have to hang on. Honestly, I didn't really go with that approach. I leaned into it. If I have to stay there till nine o'clock at night, I'm there till nine. If somebody has to tell me to go home, then I'll go home. I suppose the only thing I truly pace is picking my battles. Problems tend to work themselves out better that way.

Tom: **Don't fall on the grenade over every little thing.**

Vicky: Yes. And sometimes you have to pick another day for a battle. You don't have to give up on it. There may be another way to approach it later.

Tom: Crews often respond well to directors that roll up their sleeves and do stuff. Dick Williams was like that. And he never drove you harder than he drove himself.

Vicky: I think I fall into that camp. It's not just a nine-to-five job. It's what's defining me at that moment. It's living, breathing, changing, and growing. And I'll keep going until someone says "stop."

Tom: How do you deal with moments in which you're creatively stuck or blocked? How do you solve that problem?

Vicky: You say, "I don't know." It's always okay to do that because you're going to have problems that you can't solve right away. And some things you don't have to decide right at that second. I'd rather wait than make a really bad decision. Now sometimes you have to make a decision, obviously. But that can also be the exciting part of the job, coming up with a solution on the spot. It can really happen that way on a live-action set. Your location's not available. It's starting to rain. You're going to have to shoot indoors. What do you do? You can't just say, "Let me think about it. We'll come back tomorrow." You have to do something.

Tom: What about your crew and creative partners? How do you choose them?

Vicky: Hmm. You choose them based on how they smell and how you connect over alcohol … [laughs] No, I don't know. I don't have any unique system. You look at resumes and portfolios. In the end it just comes down to talking with them. That moment of communication is key.

Tom: What's the most insane or bizarre moment that you've experienced as a director? Peter Farrelly jokes about the stiff hair scene in *There's Something About Mary*. Evidently, the prop people brought him forty examples of fake semen and said, "Pick one."

Vicky: [laughs] I did have a similar experience. I needed some on-camera cat poop for Michael Keaton to step in. The prop master brought me an entire tray of different kinds and colors of cat poo. It was a little overwhelming. The one that was made from a fudge brownie from the craft service table actually looked the best! Needless to say no one ate the fudge brownies after that. [laughs]

Tom: [laughs] That's when you've earned your money for the day.

Ron: How do you work with composers? How much control over the music do they get?

Vicky: Composers have a tremendous amount of control, but it can initially be very frustrating for them because we use temp music in our cuts and we tend to grow very attached to these clips after working with them for two to three years.

Oh, it's the composer's bane! I've had many composers complain about this, although they completely understand why it happens. And sometimes it's even their own music from another movie. Seriously, Hans Zimmer has probably heard that same little clip that everyone takes from *True Romance* countless times. It's this lovely delicate piece of music, and they'll put it in every lovely little delicate scene on every movie that he works on!

But like I said, they know it's a necessary evil. They know you need to screen the movie with music that works. They can't come in and freely compose at will. The best know how to encourage you to be open and listen to a new idea.

Ron: **Do you always bring composers in at the end of the project?**

Vicky: It can be difficult to bring them in much earlier for a variety of reasons. First, obviously, they're generally busy on other movies or not available to be part of the development process. But, most importantly, your movie just changes so much early on. The music will be in flux as much as the story is until you start to lock things down. When the themes are clearer and consistent, then it's time to underline the tone and emotions of the movie.

Tom: **Is there any job that you miss doing? It's often very difficult for an animator to stop animating once they sit in that director's chair.**

Vicky: I love painting color keys and storyboarding. But those are the two things I can still do if there's time. On every project I've done at least one key. Even if it were live action I would do at least one key and a little bit of storyboarding. As for other jobs I've held, I don't miss ink and paint and I don't miss working at McDonald's!

Tom: **What's it like working with a co-director?**

Vicky: I think in some ways it's great and I understand why it was the convention for so long in feature animation. There's so much to do on an animated film. It really helps having somebody else there. Andrew and I divided the workload. Each of us took a sequence, so we got to do everything that the director should do in leading those sequences. It also allowed us to focus and give a lot more attention to our sequences. Sometimes we'd swap sequences later, or if one of our workloads got too heavy we'd shift things around. That worked far better than dividing it by department, which we did on *Shark Tale*. And I think it was also done on *Prince of Egypt*. It just made it more difficult to keep control of the main vision and idea of the movie. As things move through various departments unexpected changes can occur.

Tom: With co-directors you can also bring together two unique skill sets. You came from a traditional animation background and Andrew excelled in digital animation.

Vicky: We were definitely a good pair in the end. Andrew was also great with story, though I didn't really recognize it when I started as a story artist on the movie. I already knew Kelly Asbury, Andrew's original co-director on the movie, and he is this completely outgoing and funny guy, very charismatic. Andrew didn't come from animation and he was a bit of an unknown to the story crew.

When I was asked by Jeffrey to direct with Andrew it initially felt like an arranged marriage, but I think we ultimately became a good team and balanced each other's strengths. His strong CG and effects background was priceless. I certainly didn't have that. I didn't even know how to work email back then! I learned so much from him. It was a perfect situation. I creatively directed the project and I learned something new in the process.

Andrew Adamson and Vicky Jenson, 2001 © DreamWorks.

Tom: Would you work with a co-director again?

Vicky: Actually no, I don't think so. I've reached a point in my life and work where I feel the value of a single artistic vision at the helm can create more unique stories. And that's what we all want, the audiences, the filmmakers, and the hopefully the studios!

Tom: It seems like in the last few years in Hollywood, and even in animation, directors have started in writing and have their idea ready to go. In the old Hollywood system you'd take a story, put a director on it, and then add a crew.

Vicky: I think that's changing. I'm glad too. You get a clearer vision. You have directors that are passionately connected to the story. It's better for a studio if the director comes in with the passion to lead, because you need that. A film is going to absorb your life for several years so it [had] better come from deep inside you. I'm writing now as well. This is my latest challenge. I think creating stories I will ultimately direct will be the closest I can get to the original thrill of making my first short. It can't get more personal or more original than that.

Tom: Did you ever experience what the industry calls "kill your children"? It's that moment when you have a great idea that's just not working. You have no choice but to let it go.

Vicky: Yes, a few actually. So many fun ideas have to be drowned. But the good ones come back in other forms, even in other movies. But I've learned to not get too attached. I think storyboarding teaches you that. You can't treat your idea as this precious object. It's going to change. That's why I storyboard now with a Sharpie. I can't get too attached. In the end it's all about the story. If it's good, it'll stick.

Tom: How do you deal with criticism and reviews?

Vicky: Every director gets them at some point. It's unavoidable. After my live-action feature I gathered together all my worst reviews and put them together on Facebook. It ends with one I actually like. Three stars by Roger Ebert! Sometimes the movie just doesn't turn out the way you hoped. You learn from that. You work harder next time. You test your ideas more. You push to see if people actually understand what you're trying to say. And in the end it really is subjective anyway. All art is subjective.

Tom: What advice would you give a first-time director?

Vicky: Have a clear idea about the story you're trying to tell. Make your own personal connection to it. See if others can connect to that as well. Test it. Is your theme universal? Do people get the message you are trying to convey? Is this idea worth all the work it is going to take to make this movie? Once you have these questions answered and start to bring artists onboard, don't feel like you have to author every idea in getting that story to the screen. It takes teamwork. And on that note, get to know everybody. Walk around and be connected. Leave your door open. As people are hired, go to all the different offices and try to get to know their names. Try to make a strong connection with them and connect them to the ideas of your story.

Ron: The studios have had huge development departments for years. All the studios have them, especially in terms of live action. That's what keeps the whole industry going. Now, many directors in animation are being asked to come and pitch movie ideas, which kind of circumvents that entire system. A director doesn't have the same support system that a development department has. Where do you find support? Where do you get the necessary training and mentoring for story development, let alone how to pitch a movie? Looking back at your movies at DreamWorks, all of them were developed and pitched by someone else.

Vicky: I haven't had a lot of experience pitching original ideas, yet. Currently I'm writing for the first time, and it's something that I'm really excited about. I'm also writing another script on spec. I think it's important to have people you can show your work to, someone you respect and whom you can bounce ideas off. I'd actually like to form a writer's group because I like creative input.

I like sitting and talking about writing with people that are immersed in the process. And I don't like working in a vacuum. That's kind of alien to me. At the moment I have an amazing creative producer and it makes all the difference in the world.

Ron: **What about mentors? Did anybody offer any guidance about developing your own projects?**

Vicky: My directing mentor, whom I mentioned before, is Judith Weston. I adore her. I've brought her a lot of scripts in the past as well as my own writing. Taking scenes into her workshop has been absolutely invaluable to me. Her insights and analysis never to surprise and inform me and affect my work.

Tom: **You've done just about everything: feature films, live action, animation, shorts, commercials. Do you have a favorite medium?**

Vicky: The one I'm in. All of them. Honestly, I've always jumped back and forth between live action and animation. Right now I'm really excited to make an animated feature again. But ultimately the medium just doesn't matter. It's the challenge that excites me. I'm excited about getting back on an animated feature because I feel like I understand how to make it work more concisely now, without as much of the searching. And it's a commitment that I appreciate. You have your vision, and you have to muscle through the day. Even when you think you don't have enough time to get it done, you do. I love that feeling. I can find that experience on any kind of set, regardless of medium.

Tom: **Since you were raised in the traditional animation pipeline, is it at all strange how everything is digital now? Even the job classifications are different now, as well as the responsibilities and duties.**

Vicky: If somebody designed a log for you in 2D, they wouldn't bring you the cylinder first. They'd actually bring you a drawing of the log. Now you see things in iterations. You receive a log that is the right volume but has no texture. How do you comment on that? That took me a while to understand. But I got to the point where I could recognize that. For instance, I just knew it was going to be too big for *Shrek* to step on. You have to recognize what stage you're at and learn what comments are appropriate. That comes with experience and time.

Tom: **Where do you see yourself in ten years?**

Vicky: Oh, I hate that question. I never see myself in ten years, so I can't answer that.

Ron: **How about in the director's book of directors who've made four feature-length, animated films?**

Vicky: Okay. Four by then? Why not. Living in Venice, maybe? Wouldn't that be cool?

Tom: Okay, last question. Did you ever have a chance to work with previsualization?

Vicky: I did. It's actually a funny story. There was this Warner Bros. project right after *Shark Tale*. It was *The Extraordinary Adventures of Alfred Kropp*. I was completely energized and was ready to jump in. I wanted to do exactly what Zack Snyder did to get *300*. So I approached about five different previsualization studios to see who would give me the best deal. I was creating a chase sequence with a Porsche and six motorcycles. Michael Cera and Clive Owen were driving. Those were the two actors I wanted to cast. And Clive Owen is a knight in our modern time. Anyway, it was this big action sequence. So I paid for a previs sequence and brought that into my pitch meeting with the head of Warner Bros. live action to prove a chick could handle action. I also brought in a huge fold-out Photoshop poster board of my thoughts for the script. It looked like a trifold science fair project. It looked like a timeline of the whole movie with clever little Photoshopped sticky notes for where the changes in the script were going to be. It also had samples of what the production design was going to look like. I wanted to convey that I've got this whole movie in my head and, better yet, it's theirs for the taking! I even had a poster designed. The head of Warner Bros. loved the pitch. But … they had already decided not to pick up the book! Nobody told me! This thing cost me around twenty-five thousand dollars. A month later I get the script for *Post Grad*. I put together a CD of some hip music and Photoshopped what an advertisement for the movie might look like on Myspace. That was it. I got the job. Cost—zero.

Tom: It's like when Mike Gabriel showed up to pitch *Pocahontas* with one card. He had made a logo for *Pocahontas* and said, "Let's do *Pocahontas*." Some other guys who pitched had eighteen paintings and other visual props and got nowhere.

Color Study, Vicky Jenson, *Shrek*, 2004 © DreamWorks Animation LLC.

Vicky: All it takes is a strong idea. If you can see the movie, even if you're just looking at a poster, and quickly get what this movie is all about, then you're most likely going to see it. Making a movie is not easy and it's very complicated. But the concept should be that simple to grasp.

Ron: I think that's a perfect note on which to end. Thanks Vicky.

Vicky: My pleasure.

8

Rob Minkoff Interview

Rob Minkoff.

To paraphrase F. Scott Fitzgerald: "Directors are different from you and me." They are artists who seem deceptively normal but have that extra something that is critically not what others have. Take Rob Minkoff, a wonderful guy, funny, considerate, easygoing, but when the chips are down he just seems to know the answer, or know the right person, or comes up with the idea that's needed.

His most famous "save" was arguably *The Lion King*, when he joined a troubled production and in a few intense days of sequestered brainstorming helped set the course for the most successful 2D film of all time. Rob knows how to connect the dots, but he has that essential skill of all great directors: he connects with people.

Rob is another guy with terrific talent as an animator that never did as much animation as we wished he would have. He did a few scenes for me on separate projects and they were always brilliant, funny, and seemingly effortless. Rob wasn't content to sit behind a drawing desk all his life. Every time I ran into him, I was amazed to find out that he had moved on to some completely different opportunity.

Very few directors have hits in 2D animation, 3D animation, and live action, but Rob has done that. He's not afraid of new challenges. I visited him on the set of his first live-action movie, *Stuart Little*, and I was amazed at how nonchalant and frank he was about what he didn't know! He got a kick out of explaining to me all the things that he needed to learn that he didn't experience as a director in animation. I think the crew loved him because they knew he wasn't a fake. In fact, he brought the critical eye of an animator to that film, and that's what made it work.

A student once asked Rob to name a director's most important asset. His answer was unique and revealing: "You have to make people believe you can do it."

We interviewed him at his hilltop home in Los Angeles.

Bill Kroyer

Bill: When did you first discover animation?

Rob: My first experience goes back to early childhood. I watched all kinds of cartoons on television. Like most kids, I would say animation fascinated me because of its magical quality. It's an illusion. Animation creates an alternate reality for the audience. I also remember an old Disney flipbook. It was a sequence of Mickey Mouse drawings. He was wearing a cowboy outfit and wielding a lasso. And my dad, who owned an audiovisual shop in Palo Alto, had a couple of Super 8 films. One was a *Mighty Mouse* cartoon and another was from *Sleeping Beauty*, where the prince fights the dragon. I watched that a lot.

Bill: Is that how you got hooked?

Rob: Pretty much. I became deeply fascinated by it, and then it became an obsession. I was constantly looking for animation everywhere. But I was mostly limited to television.

Bill: When did you start drawing your own stuff?

Rob: My cousin, Michael, actually got me started. During a family visit, my two older brothers and I watched him draw this odd character. It was this little fuzz ball with a long nose and dull eyes. It was amazing to watch this little guy come to life on a blank sheet of paper. I wanted to do that too!

Bill: When was your first experience with actually animating something?

Rob: That was in high school, in the ninth grade. I was in a children's theater production of *Snow White and the Seven Dwarfs*. It was the fortieth anniversary of the original production back in 1937. This was the Children's Theater in Palo Alto. In fact, during that production I met Kirk Wise.

Bill: Really? Kirk was in the same production?

Rob: He was. I played the Huntsman. He played the Queen's bat. And when we discovered we both liked drawing and cartoons, naturally we became friends. He had a copy of the book *Tex Avery: King of Cartoons*, and another by Andrew Loomis called *Fun with a Pencil*, which I borrowed from him for an extended period. We ended up animating a short together in high school, which I used as a portfolio piece for CalArts. The only thing I did before that was a flipbook. And a stop-motion film about an egg.

Bill: I assume you didn't have any film or animation classes in high school.

Rob: I had a film appreciation class, but it wasn't animation.

Bill: So you and Kirk just figured it out all by yourselves?

Rob: We didn't have a choice. It was the only way to do it. We read the Preston Blair animation book for the basics and ordered animation paper from Cartoon Colour.

Bill: You actually got punched paper?

Rob: We got punched paper and discs. We even built a wooden frame for it. Like I said, I was obsessed with animation! In fact, let me tell you this funny story. Around the same time I was asked to babysit these eight and ten-year-old sisters, Jenny and Emily Shapiro.

Their father was famous because he produced the movie *The Groove Tube*. So, as I'm hanging out at their house I notice this book on the coffee table. On the cover was an embossed picture of Mickey Mouse. It was the famous *Art of Walt Disney* by Christopher Finch. I began to look through it. "WHERE DID YOU GET THIS? THIS IS AMAZING!" Jenny and Emily promptly replied, "Our uncle wrote it." It turns out their uncle is Christopher Finch! Sure enough, I open the book and see their names in the dedication. When I got home, I went straight to my parents and said, "I want the *Art of Walt Disney* for my birthday!" Fortunately, on August 11, 1977, I got it. And when I got to CalArts three years later, I realized I wasn't alone. It was basically the animation bible. Everybody had their own story about when they first found that book, and what it took to get a copy.

Bill: **How did you find out about CalArts?**

Rob: Kirk told me about CalArts in high school. When he said that there was a school that teaches animation, I thought he was joking. But Kirk had the brochure to prove it. In fact, it was the only school that I applied to. My parents were so concerned that they took me to dinner specifically to ask me not to go until I had an undergraduate degree. They thought art school alone was too risky. Of course, they supported my dream. They were just trying to protect me. But the obsession still lingered. So, with a little luck, I left Kirk behind and went to CalArts in 1980. Suddenly I was meeting people like Kelly Asbury, Chris Sanders, and Chris Bailey.

Bill: **I'm sure it was refreshing to meet other people interested in animation.**

Rob: Exactly! At CalArts there were tons of people like me with similar stories. But I was fortunate to have Kirk as a friend. Back in high school we'd meet regularly after school to watch cartoons and draw. It was at that time that I started to recognize different directors, particularly Chuck Jones at Warner Bros. I would always carefully examine the credits of any cartoon to see who the director was. I liked Chuck Jones' stuff a lot. I didn't just like Bugs Bunny because of the character himself, but because of the style of a Chuck Jones' Bugs Bunny cartoon. I began to truly appreciate how a director can influence tone and style. Seriously, if you pay attention, there are several variations of Bugs Bunny. It depends on the director. I remember being in the same room as Chuck for the first time. There was a tribute to Mel Blanc at the Academy Theater and everybody from CalArts went. Chuck was one of the speakers.

Bill: **Did you meet him?**

Rob: No, I was too shy. But Jeff DeGrandis, my classmate, was not shy at all. He was wearing rabbit ears and fearlessly took the seat right behind Chuck. Jeff immediately struck up a conversation, and Chuck graciously responded. He was interested in what everyone had to say. Before I knew it, Chuck was drawing in everyone's sketchbook! But I was just too shy to approach him. A couple of weeks later Kelly Asbury grabbed me and said, "Hey, do you want to meet Chuck Jones?" Apparently, Jeff DeGrandis called Linda Jones, Chuck's daughter, who ran Chuck Jones Enterprises. Now if you can't tell, Jeff had a big personality, big enough to get invited to Chuck's house! At eighteen years old, I was just in awe of his courage. He was on the phone with Linda for forty-five minutes! What could they possibly have to talk about for that long? Lucky for us, she told Jeff to bring some friends. Since Kelly knew that Chuck was one of my favorite directors, he immediately came to me. So, on a Sunday afternoon, four of us went to visit Chuck. It was Kelly, Jeff, Chris Bailey, and I.

Bill: **The house in Corona del Mar?**

Rob: Yes, it was this beautiful house overlooking the ocean. I had never seen how an animation director lived. It was rather spectacular! I think we spent about four hours there, listening to stories about his time at Warner Brothers. Chuck was a very good storyteller. Needless to say, I was awestruck. I was eighteen years old and sitting in the house of my hero, a guy who inspired me to get into animation. Then, much to our surprise, he said, "Next time you guys come over, bring drawings." No one expected a second invite. But we weren't going to say no. About two months later we returned, with drawings. Chuck gathered us around his drawing board and began to critique and even draw for us. Chuck Jones actually gave us private drawing lessons. It was amazing!

Bill: **At this time were you thinking about becoming a director, or were you focused only on being an animator?**

Rob: I guess I was thinking about both. The thought of becoming an animator was pretty obvious for me. As I mentioned, I did a lot of children's theater. Acting was nothing new. And animating a character is essentially a form of acting. But CalArts, at the time, didn't exactly encourage you to animate. It was a big issue with the people running the program. Jack Hanna and Bob McCray insisted that we not animate too soon. The underlying assumption on their part was, "You're not ready. You can't do it." To me, that didn't make sense. I knew I could animate. I had already done it! So I was forced to animate on the sly!

Bill: **Did they ever give you any specific reasons why?**

Rob: I think that came from their experience working at Disney. The studio had a particular method for advancement. You had to come up through the ranks. You had to start as an inbetweener, then work your way up as an assistant, and then you could get a scene. And that was a long process. They openly talked about how it took years to become an animator.

At first you say, "I guess that's the system." But then you realize that it doesn't make much sense. When I finally went to Disney, this turned out to be a problem. People were getting positions based solely on their longevity, their senior status. Promotions didn't have much to do with talent or whether they were the right person for the job. This was a completely institutionalized process. Like it or not, the process of artistic assessment is subjective. You can't institutionalize that. So, that was the method at CalArts because the people who were teaching the program were ex-Disney guys. They were still mentally in that process. I think the rule of thumb was that it took ten years to become an animator at Disney!

Bill: How long did you stay at CalArts?

Rob: I was there for three years. At the end of my second year at CalArts something kind of devastating happened. Disney didn't hire anyone. That was a huge blow to the students. In my first year they hired nine people! That got us excited about our future prospects—then, suddenly, nothing. Worse still, rumor had it Disney didn't like our films. Apparently, they were too dark.

Bill: Your sophomore film?

Rob: Yeah. It was kind of a *Hansel and Gretel* story. This devious candymaker invites two kids into his store in order to turn them into candy. He literally is going to pick them up and toss them into the candy-making machine. Well, I suppose it was a little dark. But we can probably thank Tim Burton for that! In our first year they showed Tim's pencil test, and it was amazing. This little film essentially displayed every major concept that Tim is now known for. It was called *Stalk of the Celery Monster*. That film had a profound effect on us.

Bill: Did that influence your third-year film?

Rob: Well, before that, and after Disney chose not to hire anyone, Dan Jeup came in and announced that three people had been selected to do an internship. I was one of them. We got to do a summer internship with Eric Larson in the summer of 1982. This happened to coincide with the animation strike. No one was in the building because they were all out on the street picketing. That made the experience very strange. We actually had to cross a picket line to get inside the building. We weren't scabs because we weren't employed per se. We were just interns. But the nice thing was that we had Eric all to ourselves. He literally had nothing to do but teach us. At this time I also met Don Hahn, Ron Rocha, and Burny Mattinson, who wasn't picketing because he was a director. Mostly the place was empty, and that gave us an opportunity to do something we couldn't have done otherwise. We went into everybody's office and looked at their stuff. We looked at Ed Gombert's boards, Vance Gerry's boards for *The Great Mouse Detective*, which at the time was called *Basil of Baker Street*. We saw boards that Tim Burton had done for *The Black Cauldron*. One day we got very bold. We decided to march upstairs and meet Ron Miller. He had Walt Disney's old office, and we just wanted to step into that room. So we went up to Lucille … Lucille was Ron's assistant, right?

Bill: Right.

Rob: Anyway, we went in and introduced ourselves. Unfortunately, Ron was away in Europe. Hey, we tried, right? As we're leaving, Lucille says she'll tell him we stopped by. Now we didn't think anything would come of this, but sure enough Eric Larson comes in about a week later with a concerned look on his face. He says, "I just got a call from Ron Miller's office. He'd like to see you up there in fifteen minutes." We marched back up those stairs and right into Walt's old office. And it turned out to be a great moment. After all, Ron is a physically intimidating guy. He's about 6' 6" and plain huge! When he shakes your hand, yours disappears into his. But he was so nice. We sat and talked for forty-five minutes about animation and CalArts.

Bill: **Was the building that empty during your entire internship?**

Rob: It was empty the whole time. Now the next year, my third year, you asked if Disney's decision not to hire influenced my film. It did. I was working on a film that was quite ambitious. It was all in verse, kind of Dr. Seuss-ish. Ultimately, I realized that I couldn't do it. The film was just too much. Finally, in the middle of the year, I went to visit Eric Larson. I remember him saying, "Don't forget the character! That's all we care about. Just don't forget the character." Then it hit me. My film had no character! There was a ton of elaborate storytelling but no character. I had a panic attack. I really wanted to get hired. I really wanted a job! So, I scrapped the film. With about five weeks left before the show I started a new one. It was a short about a kid whose ice cream falls from the cone before he has a chance to enjoy it. He's very sad, but tries to paint a smiley face in the fallen ice cream, which kind of makes him happy again. It was an acting thing, all performance. Now I wanted to hide the fact that I was starting from scratch, but it was impossible. We were recording animation tests on video reels that everyone could look at back then. You couldn't hide it from anyone. People kept saying, "What are you doing? Don't change anything now! Finish the other film." But there was no turning back. Fortunately, I finished it and I got hired. Disney only took two of us that year.

Bill: **What was it like stepping into a fully functioning studio? As you said, it was empty during your internship.**

Rob: This was July of 1983, and *Black Cauldron* was still in production. First, we had an inbetweening test, which was a difficult skill to learn. It terrified me, actually. I also found it rather tedious.

Bill: They actually gave you an introduction to inbetweening?

Rob: Yes. First we just had to learn it. We had to get the line right. It had to be the right width. Then we had to do an actual test with Eric, which consisted of both inbetweening and a piece of animation. I did this leprechaun who dances around with his hat. I remember getting help from Chris Buck, who was working on *Roger Rabbit* at the time.

Bill: Was this the very early stages of *Roger Rabbit*?

Rob: Yeah, before Steven Spielberg and Robert Zemeckis were involved. Daryl Van Citters, Chris Buck, and Mike Giaimo had been working on it. They even shot a live-action test with Mike Gabriel as the detective. I was basically hanging out with these guys in the beginning. Joe Ranft had introduced me to them. I'd met Joe my first year at CalArts. He'd come back from Disney to give advice and critique the animation tests for some of the students. It was totally informal. Just something Joe wanted to do. We became very close after that. What an amazing talent and all-around human being he was. It was such a tragedy to lose him so young. I still think of him quite often. Anyway, I'd finally gotten a job at Disney and my first assignment was inbetweening on *The Black Cauldron* under Phil Nibbelink. It was a pretty tough job, except that Phil had all the cute girls working as his inbetweeners.

Bill: How long did that go on?

Rob: For about six months. To keep my sanity, I would take drawing breaks. I would stop inbetweening, pull out a fresh piece of paper, and draw something for fun. Then I would go back to inbetweening. After a while, I acquired a large stack of drawings, which sort of helped me later. There was a small group working on *Basil of Baker Street—The Great Mouse Detective*, that is. They were thinking about bringing in a new face for some character design work. Brian McEntee recommended me to John Musker. Eventually, John called and asked me to come to his office. He also told me to bring drawings. I reached into my desk, grabbed the stack, and walked upstairs to his office. About a week later Ed Hansen, who was running the animation department, called and said they wanted me as a character designer on the film.

Bill: So John saved you, huh?

Rob: Yes, he did. But it was only supposed to be for a limited time. Ed made it clear that as soon as I was finished it was back to inbetweening! They didn't want me to get too comfortable! I didn't care. I was just happy to get out for a while. But then the good thing was I never went back to inbetweening. Somehow I managed to stay on the movie.

Bill: What was it like, working on your first big production as a designer?

Rob: *Basil* had quite a history by the time I arrived. John and Ron had been developing the movie. It was edgy, adult, and very smart. Heavily influenced by Monty Python's absurdist humor, which I loved! This was the vision I saw when I peeked at the boards during my internship. When they pitched it to Ron Miller, he basically made them start all over again. Joe Ranft had the funniest drawing of Ron Miller at the time. It didn't look anything like him, but it was Ron as a giant blue man with blood vessels popping out of his head. The caption read, "WHERE IS THE GODDAMN WARMTH?!" So, Burny was brought in as producer, and Dave Michener also came on board as a director. We had three directors. The entire tone and feel of the movie changed. Ron Miller wanted it to be more "Disney." But if you look back at Walt's films, there was some incredibly interesting, dynamic, and scary stuff in those movies. Needless to say, everyone was frustrated. But that didn't stop me from appreciating the opportunity I had. I got to be a character designer. This was my chance to move forward. Eventually, they assigned me to work on some animation, which pushed me into the role of animator. Then someone said, "You should be an animation supervisor." I replied, "Sure. That sounds great!"

Bill: This was all on *The Great Mouse Detective*?

Rob: Yeah, it didn't take the ten years that Bob McCray and Jack Hanna said it would. But any kind of sudden advancement was met with skepticism by the senior staff. That's not an easy position for anyone to be in, but Disney was changing. There was a new generation of people that wanted something else, something better. And the frustration was often visible. I remember hearing a story about Brad Bird kicking a Sparkletts bottle down the hallway. But that's how everybody felt.

Bill: But Brad had already left Disney before you'd got there.

Rob: Yes. But soon after starting, I began hearing that Brad Bird and Jerry Rees were going to make an animated movie, based on Will Eisner's *The Spirit*, in Northern California. Brett Newton came to me and said, "Have you heard about this thing that Jerry and Brad are doing? It's gonna cause a huge revolution in animation! They're gonna hire everybody who's any good out of Disney who wants to leave and go work on a movie that's gonna break all the rules and be the salvation of animation." Of course I thought it sounded fantastic. He put me in touch with Brad and Jerry, and I soon arranged a meeting up in Northern California. Unfortunately, things weren't as bustling as Brett had claimed. It was very quiet there. It was just Brad and Jerry. They showed me the test, which I think John Musker and possibly Glen Keane had worked on. It was amazing stuff. But I didn't get the feeling that production was going to take off anytime soon. And it never did.

Eventually, I did end up working for both of them, Brad on *Family Dog* and Jerry on *The Brave Little Toaster*. I was still technically an animator at Disney, but I indulged in a little creative freelance work for them. I guess it helped with the frustration I felt at the time.

Bill: Didn't you briefly leave Disney to work with Jerry Rees?

Rob: I did. I went to see Don Hahn, who was then kind of managing the animation department at Disney. I said, "I've got this opportunity to do designs on this Jerry Rees project." Don was very gracious and understanding. I was very nervous about leaving. I had wanted to work at Disney for so long, and they took me in. But it wasn't quite the place the literature promised. Don said, "If you want to go, go. It's okay. You can come back anytime." So I took a deep breath and left Disney even though there was no guarantee I would be taken back. The door could have been closed forever.

Bill: Did you go to Taiwan?

Rob: No, I didn't. I spent about five weeks with Jerry up in Hollywood but going to Taiwan just didn't feel right. So I went back to Don, who said, "If you want to come back, it's totally fine." I immediately jumped at my chance to go back.

Bill: Is this when the takeover occurred?

Rob: It was around that time. I remember when I first heard Ron Miller was leaving. I was in John Musker's sweatbox watching some animation tests with him and Ron Clements. Steve Hulett walked in with the press release that Ron Miller had resigned. I remember being somewhat excited about the possibilities, but Ron Clements had a dour expression and said quite gravely, "It can always get worse!" And soon after, I was there when John and Ron had to pitch *The Great Mouse Detective* to the new head of Disney, Michael Eisner. I had no idea what was going to happen. They had the opportunity to kill it, if they wanted. In fact, I'd heard that they'd considered shutting down animation entirely but Roy Disney wouldn't let them.

Bill: Did the takeover affect you in any way?

Rob: Absolutely. The old Disney rules simply vanished. There was a lot of creative freedom, for better or worse. Around that time I co-wrote a song with Ron Rocha, who had been Don Hahn's assistant. Ron was an amateur composer, and Disney needed music for *Oliver & Company*. I boldly agreed, and we wrote a song for Georgette, the villain. It was called "Curiosity Killed the Cat," which we thought was very clever. But Peter Schneider and all the creative people on the movie gave us an ironic, "good effort," and "we'll get back to you." It was a classic moment. Anyway, that didn't stop us. Ron approached me a few months later and said, "Do you want to write another song?" He'd heard they were looking for something new. I said, "OK, let's try again." So we wrote another song. Shockingly, they bought it! They put it in the movie!

Bill: What was the song?

Rob: It was called "Good Company." It was just a short little ditty, a kind of nursery rhyme lullaby. They had set up a makeshift recording studio that Howard Ashman and Alan Menken were using to write the score for *The Little Mermaid*. Other people were using it too, including the Sherman Brothers. Anyway, when we recorded the demo late one night, George Scribner, Mike Gabriel, and Roger Allers overheard us. They thought it was the Sherman Brothers working on a different project. Apparently, as they were listening they said, "Hey, that would really work for us." So, we were ahead of the game when we finally presented the song.

Bill: Didn't you end up working on *Mermaid*?

Rob: Yes, I came on as a character designer, working on Ursula. John and Ron had written her as a kind of a Joan Collins-esque character, skinny with high cheekbones. I did a drawing based on Divine, John Waters's muse. She was a 300-pound diva in blue and pink makeup. Somehow it got on the board of designs, and when Howard Ashman was presented the material, he spotted my drawing and said, "Let's do that!" Of course, Ursula evolved considerably. The octopus tentacles were added, for example. I brought in my CalArts roommate, Max Kirby, who'd been an actor in the theater department, to do live-action reference. And animated the first scenes of Ursula in the movie. For a walk cycle I took footage from an undersea special featuring an octopus and used it as reference. It turned out quite well. John offered me the position of supervising animator, but at that point I really wanted to direct and was looking for opportunities to do that.

Character development, Rob Minkoff, *The Little Mermaid* © Disney.

Bill: **You wanted to create and see an entire story up on the screen.**

Rob: Yeah, that was the idea. It was also around this time that I helped push the studio to create a visual development department. I went to every artist who was important and said, "It's not right that we don't have a department where people can design and draw to influence the storytelling and creative process." It was only being done on script because that was Jeffrey Katzenberg's approach. "This is the way we do it in live action." But it didn't make sense to me, especially considering Disney's history. So I pushed. I got everybody on board and we made an appeal to Peter Schneider. We were all very happy to learn that Peter had succeeded in getting Jeffrey's approval to set it up. I think Chris Sanders was the first person that was hired for the new department. So that was how I was spending my time … making trouble.

Bill: **What about directing?**

Rob: Around that time, I started working on the *Roger Rabbit* shorts, which went into development after the feature came out. I got my own team and we put together three different shorts that we had to pitch to Steven Spielberg, Frank Marshall, Kathy Kennedy, Roy Disney, and Jeffrey.

Roller Coaster Rabbit, 1990. © 1990 Touchstone Pictures & Amblin Entertainment, Inc.

Bill: **WOW! That's a tough room.**

Rob: It sure was. But this led to my first opportunity to direct. It was a successful pitch. Roy, Peter, and Charlie Fink, the head of development, met in Charlie's office to discuss how the pitches went. Then they invited me in and said, "Rob, we want you to direct this *Roger Rabbit* ort."

Bill: **So you were happy with the finished product?**

Rob: It was released with *Honey, I Shrunk the Kids*. Overall people responded pretty well to it. Then Peter Schneider called me and asked if I would go to Florida to direct the second one, *Roller Coaster Rabbit*.

Bill: Were you a hands-on director? Did you draw boards?

Rob: I did whatever needed to be done.

Bill: Well, you can do that on small crews.

Rob: True. But I didn't do it Chuck Jones style. I didn't draw every pose and put it on an exposure sheet.

Bill: … Or like Don Bluth, who pretty much drew all the boards in the beginning. Was there a director that influenced you, somebody guiding your approach? I'm specifically referring to an animation director.

Rob: I guess that would have to be John Musker. I got to observe firsthand how he worked. But I certainly developed my own ideas about directing. And I was good at pitching a sequence. I think that was a result of my theater background. When I put together a board for a pitch, there was plenty of rehearsal involved. And like any rehearsal, it was an interactive and collaborative event. For me, a pitch was a miniproduction. At the same time, I was also influenced by live action. Billy Wilder was a favorite of mine. I'm a huge fan of *Sunset Boulevard*, which deals with a period of Hollywood history that was gone and forgotten. I related to that. Disney was that way, too, by the time I got there. It was gone.

Bill: What brought you to *The Lion King*?

Rob: It was a somewhat circuitous route. While I was in Florida, Peter Schneider called to ask if I would come in to direct *Beauty and the Beast*. They had been working with Dick Purdham but had decided to make a change. Kirk Wise and Gary Trousdale were already on it as heads of story. But Peter explained that Howard Ashman was coming aboard as the supervising creative producer. I was more interested in directing a picture from my own vision and I turned it down. It wasn't an easy decision, and one I would certainly think twice about. But I consoled myself that it was the right thing to do when I got hired to direct the sequel to *Roger Rabbit*.

Bill: How did that happen?

Rob: I had gotten exposed to live action while working with Frank Marshall on the live-action tags to the *Roger Rabbit* shorts. When my contract was up, Jeffrey sat me down and said, "We want to extend your contract. But we want you to sign you under a new deal. What do you want? What do you want to accomplish?" My response, "I'd really like the opportunity to do live action." He said, "Okay, fine. I can't promise at this very moment when that will happen. But it will. Within six years you'll have a shot at live action." I didn't have to wait long. When I got back from Florida, they offered me a five-minute short called *Mickey's Audition* about Mickey coming to Hollywood and becoming Disney's newest star. It was essentially based on the *Roger Rabbit* concept. They're not animated characters. They're toons. They exist. It was filled with cameos. It had Mel Brooks, Jonathan Winters, Angela Lansbury, Ed Begley, Jr., Carol Kane, and Joe Piscopo. Even Michael Eisner was in it. Eventually, I realized that to tell the story properly we needed to have Walt Disney in it. It would be odd to put Michael Eisner in and not have Walt. So I called Roy Disney and said, "Roy, this may sound crazy, but you look a lot like Walt Disney. Would you be willing to play Walt?" Fortunately, he agreed. It was a big success.

Bill: **What was this used for?**

Rob: It was a preshow for a ride at the MGM Studio tour. They'd bring people out of the audience and say, "Here, audition for a movie." After that, I got asked to read the script for the *Roger Rabbit* sequel. Jeffrey had always said I would direct the animation for it. But this time they wanted me to come in and pitch myself to direct the whole thing. I met with Jeffrey, Kathy Kennedy, and Frank Marshall and they ended up hiring me. But after a year of developing the script the project got shelved. It was a terrible blow. I picked myself up and took on the third *Roger Rabbit* short, *Trail Mix-Up*, but before it was finished I got a call from Tom Schumacher to come in on *The Lion King*, which was still being called *King of the Jungle*.

Bill: **Was there another director at that time?**

Rob: Yes. Roger Allers had been working with George Scribner, who had directed *Oliver & Company*. But George wasn't happy with the first couple of songs Elton John had written and left the project. I was in New York when Tom called me. It was the same week as the Academy Awards, when *Beauty and the Beast* was nominated for Best Picture. Obviously, I was feeling some regret at having passed up the chance to direct it. My first day on *The Lion King* was April 1st, 1992—I'll never forget that date. The night before, I sat down at home and read through the script. My concern was it was a bit too dry, too much like a true-life adventure. The next day I went into the office to view their ten minutes of story reel.

The Lion King, 1994. © 1994 Disney.

Bill: And?

Rob: Roger and Don came in and I asked a very straightforward question: "How much of this has to stay?" Don said, "None of it." I was happy to hear it.

Bill: Wow! You were willing to start from scratch?

Rob: Nobody loved the movie as it was. Starting over was the only option we had. Initially, Roger, Don, and I sat around and discussed how we could change the story. We had to redevelop a lot of characters. Timon and Pumbaa were originally childhood friends of Simba. And Rafiki was a kind of an advisor to Mufasa, not a shaman witchdoctor. We brought in Kirk Wise, Gary Trousdale, and Brenda Chapman and spent two days together working out a new approach. Those two days were responsible for the movie that we ended up making. When we had all the sequences up, we pitched it to Michael, Jeffrey, Roy Disney, Peter, and Tom.

Bill: Did you make any changes after that pitch?

Rob: Sure, but the structure of the movie never really changed. We maybe added one sequence to the outline. But we essentially had the movie. The big question during those two days was how to make the movie more epic. I had seen an inspiring documentary called *Lions and Hyenas: Eternal Enemies* by Dereck and Beverly Joubert. It was an incredibly powerful *story about their life and death* struggle. I just knew that if we could capture some of its power *Lion King* could be a great film. We didn't have a writer at the time, so any development had to be done on the boards. We were definitely meeting with writers, though, and we met some interesting people. We met Joss Whedon, who had worked on *Toy Story*, and we also met Billy Bob Thornton, before *Sling Blade*.

Bill: As a writer?

Rob: Yeah. He walked in wearing black leather from head to toe with metal studs and rivets. Pretty awesome. But maybe not right for our movie.

Bill: So you've reworked the story of *Lion King* …

Rob: The pitch was well received, but Michael asked if the story was based on anything. They had just made *Beauty and the Beast*, *Aladdin*, and *The Little Mermaid*, all based on famous stories. But it wasn't based on anything. Then Michael said, "Isn't this *King Lear*? Couldn't this be *King Lear*? Maybe we could turn it into *King Lear*."

Bill: Really?

Rob: Then Maureen Donnelly, who was the producer of *The Little Mermaid*, said, "No, it's not *King Lear*. It's *Hamlet*." Everyone then chimes in, "It's *Hamlet*, of course. His father is killed by the uncle." Michael promptly says, "Yes! We're doing *Hamlet*!"

Bill: *Hamlet* in Africa.

Rob: *Hamlet* with lions in Africa.

The Lion King, 1994. © 1994 Disney.

Bill: So that was the reassurance that was needed? Are we following the previously successful model?

Rob: Yeah.

Bill: Classic studio.

Rob: Obviously we knew we weren't making *Hamlet*. The question was, what do we take from *Hamlet*? We took the idea that he is a character in the throes of indecision. "To be or not to be? That is the question." That actually sounded like our pitch. Simba doesn't really stand up to his responsibility. He runs to the jungle, where he meets Timon and Pumbaa. Then Nala comes and wants him to return. But he's not sure until his father's ghost appears. Simba had to reach this point of emotional confusion and then choose to return. But we needed that critical follow-up scene with Rafiki. But conveying that moment was a creative challenge. We tried to board it several different ways but nothing seemed to work. It wasn't mystical or deep enough. Then Irene Mecchi said, as a joke, "Why doesn't Rafiki just hit him over the head with his stick?" We all laughed. But the simplicity of the idea was just so clear. We did it, and it played great.

Bill: Film is a collaborative medium.

Rob: It sure is. But, to pull it off, everyone has to be working under a unified creative vision. They need to be aware of the bigger picture. That's when you get great collaborative moments. We needed our "To be or not to be" scene, so we came together and got one.

Bill: But how did you feel about not being the sole director?

Rob: It turned out okay because Roger and I happened to work very well together. We didn't know each other all that well, but we had enough mutual respect to operate as a team. And we knew that we were working in an institutionalized system and tried to be as smart as we could about it. Also, rather than do everything together, we decided to divide up the movie. We would work together on the storyboard, agree on it, and then divide it up sequence by sequence.

Bill: Could you comment on each other's sequences?

Rob: Yes, we could, and did. But each of us had final say over our own sequences. But this process only worked if we agreed on the storyboard first. That's the stage where you truly go back and forth, show your ideas to everybody, and figure out what this movie is all about. We had to be in sync early on; otherwise it wasn't going to work. And if the pitch wasn't successful, we had to go back to the drawing board and come to an agreement all over again.

Bill: What were your disagreements like?

Rob: Honest. If you didn't like something, you had to explain why. That's part of the process. But when it came to directing the sequences, it was a little different. If Roger expressed doubt about something of mine, I still had final say. And vice versa. Overall, there was a foundation of mutual respect. We were a team, and we were emotionally invested in making a great film.

Bill: What was the hardest thing about directing *The Lion King*?

Rob: *Pocahontas* was put into production at the same time, and the whole studio was very excited about it. I remember Jeffrey saying, "*Pocahontas* is a home run! It's *Romeo and Juliet*. It's *Westside Story*. It's gonna be great! *Lion King*, on the other hand, is an experiment. But it's good to take chances. If it doesn't do well, if it only makes fifty million at the box office, that's okay." After that, all the animators wanted to work on *Pocahontas*.

Bill: What did you do?

Rob: We had to compete, and it wasn't easy. Anybody that was important got to decide which production they wanted to work on. We had some great people; don't get me wrong. But guys like Glen Keane were hard to get. On the other hand, this turned into a big opportunity for new talent at the studio. They were young and green, but super eager. We did have some experienced hands like Andreas Deja, for example, who did Scar, and Mark Henn doing young Simba. But many of the others were first timers. We were the black sheep project but that turned out to be a good thing. I don't think we could have created the same movie under any other circumstances.

Bill: That doesn't sound too bad.

Rob: When you're left alone, you have more freedom. We exploited that. We had a chance to experiment. Sometimes we went too far. For example, Elton John had written the demo for "Can You Feel the Love Tonight?" But when we got our hands on it we decided it might be more interesting if we handled it unconventionally. We decided to lampoon it a bit and have it sung by Timon and Pumbaa. We recoded Nathan Lane and Ernie Sabella and boarded it that way. We cut it together and brought it to Atlanta to show Elton.

Bill: How did that go?

Rob: Terribly. He said, What is this? There has always been a classic love song in a Disney movie. It's always been my dream to write one." Obviously, he was right and we had to take a step back and rethink it. But we ended up having Timon and Pumbaa sing the intro and outro of the song and it worked really well. We might never have done that if we hadn't experimented first.

Bill: What about "Hakuna Matata"?

Rob: Tim Rice and Elton had written a song called "He's Got It All Worked Out." It was Timon singing about Pumbaa. We had to board the whole thing and pitch it. When it finally got to Jeffrey he looked at us like, "You can do better." And we got to take another crack at it. We came up with this concept about eating bugs as a metaphor for Timon and Pumbaa's whole lifestyle. In the eyes of Simba, it's gross, weird, and just plain different. And this was supposed to be a fun song. Well, some liked that concept, others didn't. We ended up having a big meeting to hash it out. Finally, it was Tim who said, "The song needs a trademark slogan. It needs to be like "Supercalifragilisticexpialidocious" or "Bibbidi-Bobbidi-Boo." Roger and Brenda had been to Africa on the scouting trip and had come back with a few African expressions, one of which was *hakuna matata*. Tim said, "That's got some potential. I can work with that."

Bill: I don't think I've heard that story before.

Rob: So, Tim and Elton wrote the song. But at first it was more of slow song with a long introductory verse. The hardest thing to do in a musical is to get the characters singing so that the audience goes along with them. The transition has to be natural and smooth. You don't want the movie to stop so that the singing can begin. Unfortunately, Tim and Elton weren't around, it was just Roger and I. But I did have something of a musical background. At any rate, we had to make the call. We decided to cut the verse and start with the chorus, just jump straight into "Hakuna Matata" and its philosophy. We boarded it and it worked. But when we pitched it to Chris Montan, the music supervisor at Disney, he said, "You can't start with the chorus." I said, "Why not? The Beatles did it," and sang, "Can't Buy Me Love!" I knew Chris was a Beatles fan. He agreed. So that's the way we did it.

Bill: That's a great example of your skills as a director. It's not always easy to convince somebody on the spot that your idea is the better one.

Rob: Like I said before, pitching was something I was good at.

Bill: Okay, *The Lion King* debuts, and suddenly you're the director of the biggest movie ever, right?

Rob: Just before the movie opened I got a call from one of my agents, who asked if I'd be willing to talk to one of his other clients. Turns out it was Francis Coppola. "Are you kidding?," I was thinking. Apparently, he wanted to ask me about how we storyboarded *The Lion King*. He was working on his own version of *Pinocchio*. I got home one day and found a message on my answering machine from Francis asking, "for a little advice." I was so excited, I called my mom and played her the message. Later that summer, I got invited to his winery in Northern California. I had lunch with his long-time production designer Dean Tavoularis, who had done *The Godfather* AND *Star Wars*. I mean, come on! Also, Francis' mother, Italia, joined us. Francis stood in the kitchen wearing shorts and a T-shirt and made pasta. I was in movie heaven.

Bill: So your deal was over? How did *Stuart Little* come to you?

Rob: I spent about two years after leaving Disney trying to get a live-action movie off the ground. I worked with Bob Zemeckis briefly on a movie he was producing for Universal. I also worked on a version of *Mr. Popper's Penguins*, where I met the producers Craig Zadan and Neil Meron. After that I worked with them on a live-action version of *Into the Woods*. Obviously working with Stephen Sondheim was one of the highlights of my career. But getting these films off the ground proved frustrating. I started to lose hope when I got a call from Jason Clark, who I'd met while working on *Into The Woods*. He was brought onto that film to help bring the budget down from around eighty million to somewhere south of sixty. He was very close with the head of production at Columbia Pictures, and they were looking for a director for *Stuart Little*. Jason got me pumped up to meet with them about it. I read the script, which was written by M. Night Shyamalan, who hadn't yet become famous from *The Sixth Sense*. In fact, he had just sold that script and had to leave us to start prepping the picture. We needed other writers and brought on Lowell Ganz and Babaloo Mandel, who I'd met on *Into The Woods*. Jason came on as a producer and we got underway sometime in '97–'98.

Bill: Do you think your skills and experience gave you an advantage on a project like *Stuart Little*?

Rob: Doing that first movie was a trial by fire. I hadn't come up through the live-action process so I wasn't familiar with all the requirements. When we started filming, I wasn't doing any coverage. I was just shooting what I needed to cut the film together as I imagined it. After all, that's what you do in animation. After the second week, the studio stopped me outright and said, "You have to shoot the coverage, too." So it was a learning experience.

Bill: You're directing a movie, but you have an animation director, Henry Anderson, working under you. How did that differ from working with a co-director like Roger?

Rob: In Henry's case I treated him like he was the supervising animator. He would work directly with the animation team and then at various stages I would go over the shots with him and give direction. Then he'd relay that back to the team.

Roger, on the other hand, was a full partner in the creative process. But Henry's contribution developing the character of Stuart for the film was immeasurable. But as far as the live actors' performances or the overall storytelling of the film, that was my responsibility.

Rob Minkoff and Jonathan Lipnicki, *Stuart Little 2*, © Sony.

Bill: **When you were directing the live actors in scenes with Stuart, were you subconsciously visualizing Stuart's performance as an animator would?**

Rob: We tried when possible to storyboard. Unfortunately, the script kept changing prior to principle photography and it became impossible to keep up with it. When we got to the stage we had to start from scratch with blocking and staging. Fortunately, I had Guillermo Navarro as my cinematographer. He was an amazing collaborator and gave me confidence to work things out in rehearsal. We would figure it out and then plan the shot list and just start building the sequence. We always had an actor off camera performing Stuart Little's lines. Jim Doughan, who I'd met originally as an actor in the *Groundlings*, was always around and gave us a sense of what Stuart was up to. That way if there was any improvisation going on we could include Stuart. What was tough was playing every scene without seeing the main actor's performance. We had a little Stuart doll that we referred to as the "stuffy" to stand in for Stuart, but it wasn't very emotive. Now, as an animator, I could imagine what Stuart might be doing and that helped me see if the actor's performances were believable.

Bill: **So you were steering their performances based on what you sensed was coming in animation?**

Rob: Well, I wasn't thinking Stuart's performance was already a fixed thing. Good acting is sometimes reacting and you can't know exactly what's going to happen with the actors until it happens. It's good to know what you want but be open to what happens in the moment. I knew that no matter what the actors were giving, Stuart would be right there with them giving back. I had faith in the animators and knew they'd be able to go toe-to-toe with Geena Davis or Hugh Laurie or any of the other "live" actors. That's one of the challenges of animation, to make it appear spontaneous. Getting that requires a willingness to improvise and go with the flow.

Stuart Little, 1999 © Sony.

Bill: **I remember you saying you had trouble with eye lines and came up with an interesting solution.**

Rob: It became apparent very quickly that getting the actors to look in the right place was going to be a challenge, especially if Stuart was moving around at all. If the actors didn't look like they were looking at Stuart, it ruined the whole illusion. We would make marks with tape whenever that was appropriate, but sometimes even when the actors had exactly the same mark it would appear they were looking in different places. So we even resorted to using different marks for different actors in the same scene. What became really challenging was getting the cats to look in the right place. The animal trainers were unbelievable. They managed to get the cats to walk on cue and stop on their marks, but getting them to look at Stuart when he wasn't there was impossible. Someone from the camera crew came up with a brilliant solution. He brought in a laser pointer that he had synchronized with the camera shutter so you'd see the red dot but it wouldn't show up on film. It would turn off when the shutter was open. This turned out to work not only for the cats but for the humans as well.

Bill: **That last sequence with all the cats in the tree—was that literally like herding cats?**

Rob: There's an old saying in Hollywood, "never work with animals or children." I've made a career doing both. The cats turned out to be amazing performers. But it was the animal trainers that were the true magicians. They could get the animals to do ridiculous things. But they were very particular about how the animals were treated. I remember one situation where we weren't getting the shot. I needed the cat playing Monty to laugh at Stuart. I imagined him throwing his head back in a hearty guffaw. We tried getting the cat to do it with traditional methods but nothing worked. Finally, I asked the trainer if I could pick up the cat. He let me and I very gently picked him up under his arms and used him like a puppet. On cue I rolled him off camera and he surprised me by opening his mouth in what appeared to be a giant laugh. It worked great. When the clock is ticking you do what you have to do.

Bill: **Stuart was another big hit for you, and you decided to do the sequel. Easy decision? Easier picture to make?**

Rob: Well, at first I really didn't want to do it. I had barely gotten through the first one and was surprised and gratified it became a hit. But when I finally made up my mind to do the sequel, I was determined to make it better than the first one. I thought that would be reason enough to do it. One of the things that frustrated me about the first one was Stuart didn't get to move around as much as I would've liked. That was mostly due to late changing script pages and having to pull it together on the set. We couldn't have elaborate shots because that would take time to plan. And if you don't have the script until right before shooting there's no time. But on the sequel I wanted to move the camera a lot more and we got to do that. So in many ways *Stuart Little 2* is a superior film to the first one. That fact was mentioned in many critics' reviews and that was nice to see.

Bill: **How did *The Forbidden Kingdom* come your way? Did your animation background help you with a martial arts picture?**

Rob: I think having an animation background is good for any kind of filmmaking. Animation is the ultimate storytelling medium. You have to imagine everything in advance. Being able to visualize things is the key. And what happens on a martial arts film is the ultimate in filmmaking. We had the master marital arts choreographer Yuen Wo Ping handling the action. He was the only guy that both Jackie Chan and Jet Li would listen to. Jackie had made his first hits under Wo Ping's direction. But he hadn't worked with him in almost thirty years. Jet had worked with him a number of times on his recent pictures.

Bill: **So what was it that attracted you to it?**

Rob: I had read the script, which was called *The Monkey King* at that time. It wasn't a traditional retelling of the Chinese classic. It was a mash-up of all sorts of characters and storylines from Chinese films and mythology. It was very clever and I'd been thinking about doing a film in China since I'd first visited there in 1997. I met with Casey Silver, the producer, many times before he finally chose me to direct the picture. There was a sizable amount of visual effects in the film and I was comfortable with that. But I think it was the fact that I already owned an apartment in Beijing. I'd bought it in 2005 after my future mother-in-law suggested it would make a good investment. Turns out she was right. But it showed my commitment to China and that I understood the culture and knew my way around.

Bill: You're one of the few guys who has had success in both animation and live action. You had the most successful 2D animated film with *The Lion King*, and now you've done a fully CG animated film with *Mr. Peabody & Sherman*. Why did you decide to go back into full CG?

Rob: It's interesting. It wasn't really a decision to go back, because I actually had the first conversation about making this movie in 2002. It was twelve years ago, when I was working on *Stuart Little*. I didn't really imagine at the time that it would take this long to get the movie out, so it wasn't really a decision just to go back. I brought the project to DreamWorks in 2005, and it took them almost six years before they were ready to green-light the movie. Then it took three years to make.

Mr. Peabody & Sherman, 2014 © DreamWorks Animation LLC.

Bill: Wow. That's Hollywood, isn't it?

Rob: Very much so. In fact, it's interesting, because in the interim, between the time that I pitched it and the time that they green-lit it, I think DreamWorks were already committed to making CGI movies, but then the whole idea of making all of them in 3D was something that was more recent, and so that became part of the production as well.

Bill: **With so much directing experience behind you now in both mediums, how did you approach this movie? Did you approach it in a way different from other things you've done in the past?**

Rob: Well, the truth is that this is the first time I'd actually done a 100-percent CGI movie, so a lot of it was new to me. I found the production process really a cross between an animated movie and a live-action movie, because now, with everything in 3D, you think about it in terms of a live-action movie more so than an animated movie. Because the camera is a virtual camera and it can function like a regular camera, you think about it or set up shots that you might set up in a live-action movie.

Bill: **At DreamWorks, don't you block with mocap, so you have almost a live-action step there?**

Rob: I think on other productions, they do. We didn't. We went from storyboards to previs. There was a little bit of animation done, a threadbare, bare-bones animation by the previs department. The previs is the equivalent of layout, so it was a layout step. But we never did mocap. What we did do, interestingly, was that the animators actually acted out their own scenes and recorded them, and then we would play them as part of the launch and approval process. We would go through the storyboard phase, edit it into the story reel, then go through the layout process. Then we would launch each shot deliberately, one at a time. The animators would go away, and rather than showing thumbnails, they would actually just act out the shots, and we would look at them and review them and give them notes and suggestions—critiques or whatever. Then they would go away, and either they would begin their animation process—in which case we might see something that amounted to a pose-test—or, if necessary, they would go back and do another physical performance before getting it right.

Bill: **Would every animator do that? Was it a policy you tried to put in?**

Rob: It was a policy. It was actually not my idea. It was Jason Schleifer's idea—Jason was our head of animation—and I think he'd used that technique before. Jason comes from an acting background. He's been a performer, so he was very comfortable with it and I was comfortable with the idea of it, having a similar background. In fact, we both grew up in the same hometown—many years apart. And both acted at the Palo Alto Children's Theater. Anyway, that was something he suggested. The idea of animators performing or acting out their shots made sense to me as an animator, but it was never something that we would show or be critiqued on by the director in my experience as an animator, but it seemed like a reasonable way of going about it. Even though the animators themselves weren't necessarily trained actors, they were getting across the idea of their shots in a performance, and you could at least work with them on what they were doing—and sometimes the performance was pretty good. Either way, there was going to be another step of animation to approve or not. It wasn't really that we were locking ourselves into the performance, and since it wasn't a mocap performance, they were just using it as a rough guide anyway.

Bill: **Interesting. I had never heard of anybody approaching it with the acting like that. Individual animators will go into a room and film themselves on their iPhones or something, but making it a policy where you actually review it is a new thing. Do you think you would want to do that every time?**

Rob: I would say it worked very well. Part of the challenge of making the movie was that I was based in Glendale, while most of the studio was actually up in Redwood City at PDI. So for the most part, we would have to do everything via teleconference, which turned out to work surprisingly well. Again, it was an adjustment to get there, but if you had a good system of how you handled approvals and reviews, you could overcome that limitation.

One of the things Jason would do was isolate the individual animators. There would be a room of animators for any launch or any review, but when it came to a specific animator's shots, that animator would actually go and sit in the middle of the room, sitting next to Jason. They were isolated and you could obviously see them very well and you knew who you were talking to and could focus. Also, I think it made reviews very concentrated. You'd have to boil down what it was you were thinking or wanting to express in a way that could be communicated on the video teleconference (VTC). It became, I would say, pretty efficient.

Bill: **After working in live action, was it unusual for you to go back, to not have a cinematographer that would help you block things out? Nothing really like that exists in that system, right?**

Rob: It was a guy named Kent Seki. He was really the DP of the movie. Early on in the production, we did hire a consultant, Guillermo Navarro, who I'd already worked with on Stuart Little, and who had done a lot of work at DreamWorks Animation. It was interesting. I was feeling a little bit like that piece of manpower was missing, so we brought Guillermo in.

He went through a couple of sequences—which, of course, were early on—so they changed pretty dramatically through the course of the production. But it was good to experience it that way, and then Ken was able to step up into that role.

We managed to do most of the film after Guillermo was involved, but it was a good test case for how different it is when you have a DP involved.

Bill: **Did you find yourself doing anything different as a director? Having done so many things now, did you feel more at ease? Did you feel that you anticipated things better?**

Rob: Because I've had to do a little bit of everything, it was just a matter of getting to better understand the unique process of doing a CGI movie, and then working with the particular individuals. That's another thing that can change from one movie to another, and you never really know until you get there how someone is going to work or think. You have to apply yourself as a director to understand how to communicate best with your team. There's a gradual, getting-to-know-everyone process, which I think also works both ways, because the team, obviously, has worked with a variety of directors, and every director comes at it differently. My tendency is to be very collaborative, pretty much for the simple reason that I can remember my experiences as an animator and the way I would always want the directors to work with me. As an animator, I wanted to make a contribution to the film, so I encourage that from the team.

Bill: **Did you ever pick up a pencil and do thumbnails for anybody?**

Rob: Yes, but rarely. We had a Cintiq in the VTC room that you could use if you needed to draw a pose to clarify something. Occasionally, I would or could do that, but I found, again, that it was not necessarily the most efficient. When it comes to that kind of thing, I like the animators to take responsibility for their work.

Bill: **I know there's a point, when you become a director, that you feel like you're intruding on their turf.**

Rob: I want them to bring their best selves to the project, and their commitment, and a sense that they are participating and can have some ownership over what they've done. That's the kind of creative environment that I like, and I think the feedback I got from people is that they really appreciated that and felt more rewarded through the process. It's hard if you're working with a director who basically forces you to do it exactly a certain way. It's pretty limiting in terms of the creative satisfaction. For me, again, it was the idea that my job as a director was to make sure that the ideas were expressed clearly. I look at it like there's an infinite number of ways of approaching any particular idea to communicate it, and it can be very specific to the individual, but there's no one way of doing anything. There certainly is my way of doing it, which is not the same way as your way or any other individual animator. The most important thing is that they were communicating the thing that needed to be communicated and that I, as the director, felt was the important idea, the important thing to communicate.

If they were accomplishing that, if they were expressing the idea as I saw was necessary for the story and for the film, then I was okay with the form. Occasionally, if I didn't like the way the animation was done or anything, I would give them notes and suggestions and criticisms, but I would express it in a way that they understood it and could go and do it. Typically it was like, "The idea is not being expressed clearly enough," or even sometimes, "The animation is not good. This is not good animation." But I would hopefully think of it as a benchmark or a touchstone that they would understand, or at least maybe Jason would understand, that it's mechanically not good; it should be improved, or the idea's not clear and it's not being communicated properly.

Bill: But you want each animator to bring his own unique feel to it.

Rob: Exactly. It's like when you're working with a human actor. You cast your human actor because they're bringing something to the role; it's not because they're a puppet. I want the animators to feel like they're the actors of the movie and that they have a responsibility for the performance. We have a series of supervising animators, so you can rely on them to govern the style. You make sure the best animators are obviously leading the charge and the younger or less-experienced animators have something to work towards, so you get a unified look in everything.

Bill: You don't want to give them visual line readings.

Rob: That's exactly right. You do if you have to. Sometimes you'll resort to that. It's a last resort. You want them to get it themselves, but if they can't get it themselves, then if you have to hold their hand, you do. But I would prefer that they can do it, and generally, you get better work from people, and certainly more enthusiasm.

Bill: You had the original idea for this project years ago and finally got it up. Then when it gets going, of course, the industry—especially different studios—have different ideas of who the audiences are that they're targeting. Did the project morph and change in ways, as you went along with it, different from how you originally conceived it?

Rob: "Yes" is the simple answer. When we first brought it to DreamWorks, we had an entirely different pitch on what the story would be. We then hired a writer, developed the first draft of the screenplay, and the studio didn't like it—not to put too fine of a point on ... They felt it was too dark, too satirical, too edgy. So we took a step back and said, "Okay, how are we going to change the direction of the storytelling?" I understood it, because the movie that I pitched and started was probably not necessarily for their core audience, which is families. I understood who they are as a company and what they're trying to do, and the fact that they feel like they have a brand and a style.

I would say even within that, they were pretty flexible. I think the way the movie turned out wasn't so much a typical DreamWorks movie, so there was certainly some room to make the film unique. But like I said, we were in development for six years, so we went through—I don't even know—a half a dozen approaches before the studio was happy with the one that they green-lit.

Bill: **I take it you were happy with the final approach, or is there a previous version that you preferred?**

Rob: I was very happy with it. But that doesn't mean I liked it better than some of the earlier versions. The first one, for instance, really appealed to my sense of humor, which can be a little darker and more subversive than what we landed on for the final version. But I'm very pleased with how it turned out. It's still a little highbrow, which I'm proud of.

Bill: **I especially enjoyed the historical jokes. Of course, it's a history-based thing, but it was pretty funny how you hit some of those figures in history and how you portrayed them. I really enjoyed that. You've been directing now for twenty years. How is the business different for a director? Have you seen a change?**

Rob: There are more animated movies being made, which may be the biggest difference. But how is it different for a director? It doesn't seem different for me particularly. Obviously, the tools and techniques have changed—that's the biggest difference—but as far as working with the studio, it's not that much different.

Bill: **It all depends on, I guess, the project and the studio person you're working with, right?**

Rob: Right. And I think every director has a different relationship with the studio. Obviously, because I go back with Jeffrey such a long way—I've been through it all, up and down, with him—that familiarity becomes comfortable on both sides, which allows more freedom, which is good.

Bill: **But he has that kind of Socratic method, right? He doesn't tell you how to fix it. He just says, "I feel there's something missing here."**

Rob: There was a little bit of both, but your job is to go away and figure it out. His notes are generally pretty straightforward—"This isn't funny. The pacing is slow. This idea …" He can get specific. If he doesn't feel like the idea is coming across or if the character is not working or if the emotional moment isn't there, he'll give you his opinion, and then it's your job to go figure out … First of all, it's to agree or not. But because it's a collaborative situation, you've got a producer involved, or in our case two, Jason Clark and Alex Schwartz, there was Bill Damaschke—who was head of creative at DreamWorks—you have an editor, a head of story, a writer. Those are all people that are going to weigh in on how it's going. Before we'd screen for Jeffrey, of course, we're going to screen for ourselves. Hopefully, we'll be able to screen it a week ahead, because we'll look at it and we'll have our own set of notes. Then we'll discuss amongst ourselves what works and what doesn't work and what needs to be improved and how to improve it, and then we'll take a week to do what we can to fix the problems that we see before we go show it to the studio. But then when the studio sees it, they'll have their notes. Sometimes you feel like you've achieved a certain amount and you've missed the mark on a certain amount. It just keeps the process moving forward. I think it's a healthy process to constantly review the work and to get an outside opinion about it.

Certainly, at Disney, that was the way it was done, and I think it's still done that way. It's interesting. You hear a lot about the films at Pixar and Disney, because of Ed Catmull and John [Lasseter], being "director driven." And yet, when you examine what they do, they have a very similar process. They will always review the material. They show the material to their creative brain trust. Certainly John sees it and gives notes and opinions and feedback and says, "This works. This doesn't work. You need to fix this, and go do that." Then the team, led by the director, will go ahead and do that and, again, come back several months later with another screening and review.

Bill: **There are obviously differences between directing a live picture and an animated picture. Now you've done everything—2D, live, 3D—are there things you prefer about one of those directing experiences or things that you are glad to not have to do in one of those directing experiences?**

Rob: It's funny. Directing a movie is a mixture of joy and pain. I haven't found it different on any movie. It's like when things are working, it's great, and when things are not working, it's painful. And you're always having to engage in it. But I have to say that I feel very fortunate to be able to do it, because it's a lot of fun. It's a lot of fun even when it's not fun.

Bill: **Since this book is about directors of animated films, you're one who is in a good position to compare the difference in skill sets and challenges between directing live action vs. animation. How do they compare?**

Rob: First off, animation is a lot quieter than live action. The pressure can be intense when you're on set shooting a live-action picture, especially if things aren't pulling together. Animation is so much more deliberate. You plan everything out. Hans Zimmer once pointed out there are no mistakes in an animated film. Everything is put there for a reason. "There are no cigarette butts lying about." You storyboard, build your reels, record your voices, design the characters and the world, plan the layouts, and supervise the animators. But it's generally handled one artist at a time. In live action, you've got the entire cast and crew working simultaneously to create something. The whole orchestra is playing at the same time. But when you break it down, animation and live action probably have more similarities than differences. Both are mediums for telling stories. Both require writers, actors, musicians, costume designers, set designers, et cetera, et cetera.

Bill: **What do you still find challenging about directing?**

Rob: I still feel like I'm learning how to do it. Every movie is different, so there's always a new challenge. And since I've always gravitated towards doing things I haven't done before, my life is an ongoing learning process.

Bill: **Is that what keeps you going?**

Rob: Probably, since I would never want to do something I've already done. It wouldn't be as challenging.

Bill: **Among the films you've directed, is there a favorite?**

Rob: *The Lion King* is clearly the most successful, and perhaps the best loved. But if I have to choose a favorite, I hope it's my next film.

Bill: **I think that sentiment accurately describes you as a director.**

9

Jennifer Yuh Nelson Interview

Jennifer Yuh Nelson.

When I first became an animator in the 1970s, the image I formed of animation directors was of silver-haired lions like Woolie Reitherman and Chuck Jones. Larger-than-life, cigar-chomping, scotch-swilling leaders of men.

What is delightful about Jennifer Yuh Nelson is that her career runs roughshod over all those stereotypes of what an animation director should be. A slim, almost waifish, soft-spoken, Asian-American woman, she just happens to like making kick-ass action movies and comedies and is one of the best storyboard artists the medium has seen in our time.

She perfected her technique doing storyboards on Todd McFarlane's moody noir series *Spawn*. At DreamWorks she excelled at creating storyboards for *Spirit: Stallion of the Cimarron*, *Sinbad: Legend of the Seven Seas*, *Madagascar*, and *Kung Fu Panda*. DreamWorks quickly recognized her ability and made her director of the *Kung Fu Panda* franchise.

Her directorial debut, *Kung Fu Panda 2*, for a time was the highest-grossing film ever made by a woman ($665 million), until surpassed by Jennifer Lee's *Frozen*. In 2016, Jennifer Yuh Nelson was named to the Board of Governors of the Motion Picture Academy of Arts and Sciences for Short Films and Feature Animation. That same year she began developing her first live-action film project.

Her career is a testament to the idea that regardless of gender or background, anybody can do anything if they have the talent and the will to use it.

We interviewed Jennifer in her office at DreamWorks Animation.

Tom Sito

Ron: Back in the day, when we first started this whole thing, the idea was to interview leading directors who've had a chance to direct at least two movies. Because there's one thing about making one movie, where you're kind of finding a way, you're beaten up by everybody in the process. The second time you're kind of a little more knowledgeable about what you're doing and hopefully have learned through scar tissue.

Jen: [smiles] "It never gets easier." Each one's just equally as hard, no matter what.

Ron: But you learn in the process, you have experience working with crew, and with all of that.

Jen: Wasn't it like some forms of torture, though? There's the torture like if something bad is going to happen to you when you walk in, but there's the form of torture that tells you exactly what to expect and—

Ron: That's Hitchcock's philosophy of filmmaking.

Jen: [laughs]

Ron: So, Tom's going to lead the questions and I'll maybe pop in occasionally … though I actually would like to start off with one quick question. And that has to do with whether you've seen something early in your career, something before you became an animator. Was there any animated short film, that made you go, "that's it."

Jen: Do *Looney Tunes* qualify?

Ron: **Yes. Absolutely!**

Jen: I used to watch those all the time, because when I was a little kid, and first came here to the States, I didn't know a lick of English. And my mom would plop me down in front of the TV for a couple hours and I'd watch *Looney Tunes*. That's how I learned English … [smiles] It made me talk really weird.

There's *Looney Tunes*, *Merrie Melodies*, all [that] stuff that's playing in the afternoons. When you're a kid, you just watch these things on rotation all the time … *Tom and Jerry* cartoons ….

Ron: **And those had an impact on you?**

Jen: Because some of them were just visually amazing and beautiful. There were some that were simpler in appearance, but some of them were, I mean, they were meant for the theater. And they were meant for adults—that was the big difference. They're meant for adults … they didn't censor them back then either. 'Cause after a couple years they said, "Oh! There are all sorts of un-PC things!" And they'd snip them all up, but they left them alone on the first broadcast and, so you see them [in their] unaltered glory, and they were beautiful.

What [was] that … *Peace on Earth* (MGM 1939). That one was so beautiful … I was, like, watching that, like, that's insane, it didn't even have any words in it really … so I could actually get it. It was so beautiful.

Tom: **That movie used to run during wartime, like *You're a Sap, Mr. Jap* and *Bugs Bunny Nips the Nips*.**

Jen: Yeah, it was all very not PC at all. But then you know, I was Korean, so you know, I was used to seeing all sorts of anti-Japanese propaganda as a kid.

Tom: **So let's start with a little bit of your background and how you got into animation. You must have had a very interesting path.**

Jen: When I was a kid, I drew a lot. My sisters drew, we all drew together, and all of us were illustration majors in college. We all went to CalState Long Beach. And I had always assumed I'd do book illustration, magazine illustration, editorial art, comic books … that kind of thing. I didn't really like illustration very much, but it was what was available to us. No storyboard classes, no animation classes, nothing like that at the time at our school.

But strangely enough, a lot of the CalArts teachers would also teach at CalState Long Beach's illustration department. And there I learned about what storyboards were because David Lowery, who did a lot of Steven Spielberg movies back then, came in to do one of those guest speaker things. He showed his boards, and I was just amazed at how beautiful they were! I realized that there was something called *storyboarding*. That I was doing storyboarding before I knew what storyboarding was. I would be drawing stories, I would be doing little film reels of what all these scenes could be, and I wanted to do that so badly I actually thought I would go into live-action storyboards. But when I graduated, I saw all the jobs were in animation. Everybody was hiring for animation, everybody thought that it's the big moneymaker, so all these studios were popping up everywhere. So there were a lot of opportunities for kids straight out of school.

Tom: What year was that?

Jen: I graduated in 1994. I was actually in my final semester and, you know, final semesters are always that rattling time, where you kind of have stuff to do, but you kind of don't. I was working on [my] thesis, and my sister called me up and she was working at an animation studio at the time. She said, "We need a PA [production assistant]! So why don't you come be a PA while you're finishing your classes as a part-time job? Now it was in Woodland Hills, so I drove my mom's car. It was a Hyundai Excel, and it was 8 years old and barely making it. So I would drive from Long Beach up to Woodland Hills after class in the worst traffic ever, and the air conditioning didn't exist. And the engine would overheat—it would barely go over the hill.

Illustration by Jennifer Yuh Nelson.

Tom: Those early Hyundais ...

Jen: The first Hyundai Excel. It had a putt-putt engine. I'd have to turn on the car's heater just to make it over the overpasses. Otherwise the engine would overheat.

Ron: What was going on at the studio at the time?

Jen: They were doing these little direct-to-video stories.

One of the producers there was walking by, and he saw that I was doing sketches and he saw that I could draw, so he put me to work. It was such a tiny hole-in-the-wall company; everybody had five jobs. I was doing cleanup and character design, in addition to photo copying and making model packs. But I was only there for about four or five months, then I moved to Hanna-Barbera.

Ron: Did you observe anything there that stuck with you?

Jen: It was my first "office job," where you go in and actually park your car in an underground parking garage. To actually see an office building, see the kitchen and how they make coffee. How people work their business and what a producer does, and what a director does, and what everybody's jobs are. What was really useful was, because it was such a small place, you could see everything. It wasn't like the departments were over there and separated; you can't walk in. Everybody had five different jobs. So you'd look and see what everybody's doing, everybody's desks were right next to each other. So just learning what it was to work in a professional environment, showing up in the morning at a certain time of the day, breaking for lunch, that kind of stuff.

Tom: What was Hanna-Barbera like? Because they were really old school. And I can't think of a single storyboard artist who's a woman.

Jen: There were very few.

Tom: Yeah, yeah. So with a lot of those old guys like Bob Goe, Bob Taylor, and Alex Lovy, who had been there for decades.

Jen: Not only was it rare for woman to be doing storyboards, but I was a little kid.

Ron: And you were hired to do storyboards initially?

Jen: I wasn't. I was actually hired to do character cleanup. And there was already a character designer for Johnny Quest. So I was taking those rough sketches, and doing the clean line version, and going blind using a technical pencil, making a perfect line.

Tom: Back then the quality of the line was important.

Jen: Yeah, there was line quality 'cause they had to make cels out of it. So I was doing that, but within just a couple months, they had these one-minute openings that was separate from the Johnny Quest show itself. I had always made a lot of noise about "I wish I could someday do storyboards." So one of the producers said … just on a whim, he says, "Here—here's a one-page cold open. Just try it. Not for production, just to try it. Just to train yourself." And I grabbed it and ran to my office, came back within two hours, and I had done it, two hours … and I said "here!" He sat and looked at it, then he and the other producer looked at it. Then they just took the rest of the script and handed it to me. And that's how I got my first storyboard job.

Tom: Cool.

Jen: Yeah. I wanted it so badly.

Ron: Had you been practicing storyboarding at all? Or did you do comics or anything that would lead you to do storyboards before that?

Jen: I had been doing storyboards since I was five, when I didn't know what it was. I had so many pages and pages of stories in my head. My sisters and I would come up with stories together, and I would literally [story] board entire films without knowing what it was. Because that was the only way I could output the films in my head, 'cause I didn't have a camera. You didn't have access to cameraphones back then. So at that age, I was doing storyboards

Storyboards, Jennifer Yuh Nelson.

and what I had to learn, actually, was interesting. It was not how to think of film; it was how to limit what I was doing so it was animatable. Because I hadn't been trained in animation, I didn't know animation camera, which is actually a very specific thing. Like there's pan, push, fade—that's all you get. You don't get rotation, you don't get like a lot of parallax, you don't get any of that for TV animation. So what I had to learn was what not to do.

Tom: Yeah, Hanna-Barbera was good for that. When I worked on Saturday morning TV stuff, you learned how to economize, but you made the most out of what you had.

Jen: Yeah, you have to really, really economize, and that was a great training ground for that. 'Cause you can't do everything that you can do in live action. And the other thing that was really confusing to me was I was a huge watcher of anime, and anime breaks all the laws of what we can do here. They do rotating camera, they do bi-pack, they do all that stuff on TV shows, and we just couldn't do it here.

Tom: The first time I ever saw your work, I think you were working on *Spawn*. In storyboards there are comedy people, and there are action-adventure people. You always struck me as being more the action-adventure kind. It's like, what attracted you to that more than—I mean without, without stereotyping, it seems a lot of young Korean girls that I know prefer the *Hello Kitty* kind of design.

Jen: I know. I don't understand that. I just don't get it. I've never liked *Hello Kitty*. I've never understood that sort of 2D design sensibility. I mean it's a very specific thing: you either think of design or think of motion and space. Design and space just don't go together. And I'd always thought spatially. I'd always been interested in more action-adventure stuff, because I was raised on anime. And I remember when I was first starting out at Hanna-Barbera, anime was barely getting over here.

Tom: It was just starting to catch on in the US.

Jen: *Akira*, *Ghost in the Shell* was around and people were like, "Oh." And that's what I wanted to do. That's what appealed to me. What I thought was cool.

Tom: One old-timer said that anime was all "nine-year-old kids in SS uniforms blowing up robots." [laughs]

Jen: And that. That's cool. Why not? I remember just, you know, talk about being in an old-school environment, and then you're trying to get this anime sensibility in some of the stuff and it was not necessarily understood. [laughs] But that's what I want to do. I want to do, like, hardcore action anime stuff. And, not just with the design sensibility or storytelling sensibility; they do stuff with camera and cutting, the editing style which they just did not do in American animation. And it was not more labor-intensive—it was just a sensibility. And that's what I was raised on, wanted to do, was interested in just coming in and seeing all that.

Ron: You said—you said that in live action, though, didn't you? In some of the movies you were watching? What kind of movies stood out to you as kind of really important cinematically?

Jen: Of course, things like *Blade Runner* and you know, *Terminator* and all that stuff was happening when I was growing up. And in the 80s they did movies that didn't really dwell on seriousness, and it was just all about how cool something could be. You could tell probably everyone just got high on coke and made something. And had that crazy over-the-top sensibility, and that's what I thought was really fun to watch about them. They didn't take themselves too seriously, and they were just fun to watch.

Tom: I didn't realize until I had seen some very early Japanese anime ... how focused they were on graphic frame composition in films. While American 1940s cartoons, like Hanna-Barbera's *Tom & Jerry* and *Bugs Bunny*, were all studying Buster Keaton and focused on performance.

Jen: Central ... character in a space.

Tom: Buster Keaton and Chaplin came from the English musical hall and vaudeville, where you stood on stage and did your routine.

Jen: Right. Exactly, it was very theater stage-based. And I remember when I was first learning about the process, because again I wasn't trained in animation, I knew nothing about it. I came in cold and people were trying to tell me, explain to me what "crossing the line" was. And I was sitting there and I could not understand what they meant by "crossing the line." Because in my mind, it's what the camera sees and how you naturally would—I don't think "crossing the line," I just think what feels right. And they're trying to explain to me what "crossing the line" was and I realize that is based on stage terminology. I had no experience in that.

But the thing that's different about anime vs. American animation, is it's all focused on the subject matter, and American animation is about character. And what is a character going to do—it's that sort of stage philosophy, whereas in [the] Asian sensibility, a lot of it was environmental. It was about, "What is the space that the character is in?" *Akira* was about, "What is the feeling of nighttime?" When the motorcycle's going through the streets. And the feeling of the streaks of light behind a character. It has nothing to do with the character. It's an emotion, viscerally what the character is experiencing. So much more emotion-based rather than theatrically based.

Tom: Hollywood animation since the 1930s, you know, the star system, the focus was on the performing actor, the person. And the stuff around him was negligible. While with anime, it's about the complete whole composition.

Storyboards, Jennifer Yuh Nelson, *Madagascar*, 2005 © DreamWorks Animation LLC.

Jen: So, things like the whole composition, the environment, how the motion goes across cuts, no one did that in American animation at the time, TV animation. They [didn't] bother; it wasn't something that was noticed or cared about as much. And multicuts of action, you know, people would not do that because it was expensive to do multicuts, whereas things like that are so common nowadays. People expect to see that action shot, to see perfect hookups of action across a multicut moment.

Tom: Did you ever run into stereotyping? You know, you'd get an old-school producer who would take one look at you and say, "Oh, you probably want to do *Care Bear* stuff, right?"

Jen: Every single day. Every single day.

Tom: Yeah, I was wondering how you dealt with that.

Jen: Well, the fact is I would be terrible on those shows. I think there's a choice where people make assumptions about you and then you can either agree with those assumptions and bend to them, or you can say, "No, the way I can be the most useful to you is like this." I think that it just makes business sense and creative sense—if a producer sees that they can make use of

Storyboard panel, Jennifer Yuh Nelson, *Madagascar*, 2005 © DreamWorks Animation LLC.

Storyboard panel, Jennifer Yuh Nelson, *Madagascar*, 2005 © DreamWorks Animation LLC.

Storyboard panel, Jennifer Yuh Nelson, *Madagascar*, 2005 © DreamWorks Animation LLC.

you in a certain way, they're not going to push you out of that. They go, "This widget is useful doing this. Why put it over there when I can see I can use it for this? Didn't expect that to do that but it works." So, that's—that's been my career. Every single time I meet someone new. It's not like something I ever said; it's just very much understood.

Look at me, and you assume something, and I understand that. I didn't spend my life deciding, okay, I'm going to try to make people understand by looking at me that I am a certain way. I could just go out and get a crazy haircut, tattoos all over my face, wear leather all the time, pull up on a motorcycle. You know, I could do that, but honestly, I don't think that would be very good. [laughs] I understand that the natural response will be a certain thing, and then what I usually do is I nod when they say, "Well, how about this project?" I nod, and then I say, "Well, how about this?", and I show them what I do. And then usually the conversation changes pretty quickly.

Tom: **People who can do really good action-adventure, really good action cutting, are rare in Hollywood, especially in TV. Many are frustrated comic book artists who think they can do storyboards, but it's not the same. It's not a comic book.**

Jen: It's motion. It's time. And print comics are often about composition of beautiful poses in a page layout ... What I love is dealing with the percussive cutting, the speed of action. And I always like approaching action scenes like a deeply emotional scene, because there's nothing as emotional as a life and death action. Characters going through massive dynamic ranges of emotion. That's what makes me excited to do action scenes—because you feel so much more. Everything is hyper-real, and everything's moving quickly, and you experience it that much more.

Tom: **What's cool about your stuff is, when some people board action, it's like video game, first-person shooter action. It's bang! bang! ... but your stuff is cerebral. It's more like you can tell what the characters are thinking, while they're going through everything, rather than some avatar mindlessly moving from A to B.**

Jen: I think it's the most important thing, really. Because you either have an action [scene] for [action's] sake—that's where you can literally interchange any moment in any [other]—or you can have an action scene that's all about what is the character trying to achieve, and then you know what the stakes are. And then, it's like watching ... a sporting event or something ... you know, "Okay, the team has this—the points are like this, and then if they get this particular goal then it's going to go over overtime, or not, and maybe they'll make the playoffs." I don't know anything about sports, so I'm making all this crap up, so I don't know. But unless you know what it means to the players, the game doesn't mean anything—then it's a technicality. And action scenes, a lot of the time they think the reason why people don't respect action scenes as much as I think they deserve to be respected, is because they don't necessarily address that emotion of that action scene. Because they're really hard to do, but they don't get the respect of, like, you know, [a] touching emotional scene with two people crying in a room, which is also an incredible feat of acting but is not necessarily an incredible feat of filmmaking.

Ron: **When did you first become aware [that] you wanted to do action scenes? When did you start thinking about art direction, lighting, and even camera work in regards to your action scenes? Because those are all important components of building a scene.**

Jen: Very important and I think that, well, people have asked me that before, and I have a very un-useful answer to that … unfortunately. In that, I'm one of all those weird fishes where I think of an action scene finished in its entirety in my head before I ever start, so that includes lighting, sound, cutting, acting, everything, every single detail. So, I can't think of an action scene without those things. I don't think of those as separate things. Everything is helpful to progress the narrative of the action scene. So, I've always thought of it that way. Even when I think back on those action scenes I was thinking of when I was five or six years old, they had lighting on them, they had mood in them, they had all that part of the storytelling narrative. So, later on it was just a process of understanding what each department covered, but I didn't think of them as being separate things.

Tom: **When we were mentioning mentors before, like David Lowery, did you have any other sort of major people in your [life] who showed you the ropes?**

Jen: Yeah, my sisters did that a lot. Because coming from a family of artists was a big advantage. I think that a lot of people are just weird mutations in their family, and they're the only artist and everybody thinks they're weird … that's kind of what happens. But my family was weird in that all of us were artists. And so growing up 'cause I was the youngest, I could see two and a half years in the future in my middle sister, and two and a half years in the future from her from my older sister—as far as ability, progress, classes she took, you know, what she'd do with her job, all that. I could see five years into the future at all times.

Tom: **Mention your sisters' names so we spell them right.**

Jen: Oh, Gloria Yuh Jenkins, she's the oldest. And Catherine Yuh Rader, she's the middle sister and she also works at DreamWorks. She's been on all the *Panda* movies too, and she worked on all the *Shrek* movies … She's the reason I got onto

Spirit: Stallion of the Cimarron, because I was at *Spawn*, HBO and she heard about *Spirit* and she said, "Hey! They need people who can draw horses. It was hard to find people drawing horses.

Tom: People either like to draw horses or they don't. You could draw a rabbit a hundred different ways, and it still looks like a rabbit. If you don't draw a horse perfect, it looks like a dog or …

Jen: … a donkey. It's not a horse. And it's got to be a beautiful horse, like an acting, beautiful, emoting horse. I drew horses all the time, and so my sister said, "Send in your portfolio." And I said, "Okay." So I sent in my book, and I got hired. And I ended up working with you.

Tom: I always remember one of the things that impressed me the most [that] you did back on *Spirit: Stallion of the Cimarron* was you storyboarded a sequence of one of the ways that they used to train wild horses. Horses that refused to be ridden, they would blindfold them. They'd cover their eyes and then you'd get on the horse's back and the horse would be intimidated because he couldn't see. And you actually did a storyboard sequence of Spirit in the first person being blindfolded, sensing the rider was getting on his back, and another man is about to open the corral gate, and Spirit still manages to throw him anyway. But you did it from the point of view of Spirit, while he's blindfolded. I was like, holy shit!

Jen: And it wasn't a black screen. [laughs]

Tom: But it was so damn good, and the directors went, "Meh."

Jen: Yeah, it got thrown out. But you know, it was an interesting experiment, and it was that whole thing of thinking [of] things a different way, finding a different way of telling a story. That particular idea, it was based off those martial arts movies where the character is either blinded and they have to use sound. And you could see the way they turn their head, and you can experientially tell the story of what that character has to do, in order to win the fight. But it's told through the emotion and the experience of that character. That's from watching all those action movies where you go, "Oh my gosh, the guy's been blinded by acid and he's still going to take care of that guy." It's so much more nail biting. But it's solved with the slight tilt of the head, and the showing the sounds of what the character's hearing and putting it together. Seeing the connections made, and stuff like that.

Tom: Wow, cool.

Jen: Yeah, it's fun.

Tom: One thing I always admired about you was your patience, because every picture has a certain amount of … you know, political stuff, directors, and ego flying around. I remember you would storyboard these beautiful sequences that they would just piss down a hole somewhere. And you would just go, "Hmm." And I was thinking, like, "God, I would've walked right out of here. I would have quit three times by now." You had the patience of Job. Amazing.

Jen: I probably went out and punched a wall afterwards. I'm sure I let it out somehow. I also think it's because, why do people do what we do? I'm not goal oriented, I'm process oriented. I had worked on a lot of stuff on TV, that if it ever got made, I'm happy. But while you're working on it, you don't necessarily assume it's going to get made. You have to find joy every day doing the job, doing the actual work of the job, whether or not it, as we say, whether or not the bicycle chain is actually attached to a wheel, you're still going to spin. [laughs] But so I enjoyed doing the work and I knew when I was working on *Spirit*, I didn't know how to do feature boards, I had no idea what I was doing at the time. I walked in cold, [had] never done feature boards ever, right? Worked on TV, different animal, different format, different thought process. And I was learning every day, so I was getting something out of it every day, and, yes, the boards got tossed out on a regular basis. And that was also something I learned, because in TV, you never throw out boards. Done—you have one pass, one round of revisions and you're done, that's all you could afford to do. Whereas a feature is twenty, thirty times maybe? And then the scene is thrown out. [laughs]

Tom: Your stuff on *Spawn* was pretty theatrical already. Because HBO was asking for, like, a more cinematic look to the stuff. Who was in charge at *Spawn*?

Jen: It was Eric Radomski. He was the supervising director on *Spawn*. And basically the supervising director of all the shows, and now he's there overseeing Marvel Animation. But he was a cool guy, and the producer was Catherine Winder, who did *Angry Birds*. Yeah, she was super cool.

Tom: HBO's commitment to animation then seemed like they could take it or leave it. They would do a series and then they'd go, "Meh."

Jen: Everybody and their brother was starting an animation studio that time, "Let's try it and see what happens in a couple years, and do a couple shows and see what happens." But I don't necessarily think they wanted to stay in it for a long time.

Tom: Is that where you met your husband?

Jen: I did. I have a funny story about that. So when I first left Hanna-Barbera and jumped over to HBO, I said, "I really want to do storyboards." I talked to Eric [Radomski], and Eric said, "I'm sorry. I got a guy for doing storyboards already." And I'm like,

"Shit! A guy is already doing storyboards." And then he said, "But I got a character design position …" And I said, "Eh, I'll do it. Because, why not? And I know how to do that. So I'll do that. And maybe, maybe … if I'm here, they'll give me storyboards eventually." So I started the job doing the character designs. Then that storyboard artist came in one day. I was like, "That's the guy that took my job," and he's wearing, like, dark sunglasses, and a trenchcoat indoors when he walked in. And I was like, "Why is he wearing shades indoors? I don't know if he's trustworthy 'cause he's wearing shades indoors and also he took my job. But he also really looks like kind of a sweet guy." And we became such good friends. And we became best friends. We worked together for about two and a half years. And then eventually, after two and a half years, we were both happy to be available. Oh well, I guess we might as well start dating. So we got married. And Catherine Winder said that me and him were the best thing that came out of that place.

Tom: [laughs]

Jen: Well, we got married and we're still married eighteen years later. [laughs] And the best thing is, I respect his art. He was a really great story artist, so I said, "I don't feel so bad you took my job, because I could see why they wanted you."

Kung Fu Panda 2, 2011 © DreamWorks Animation LLC.

Tom: There is a thing with professional couples. The usual type of match would be like me and my wife. My wife's job is in the back end of production and I'm at the beginning. So our responsibilities are unrelated. But, when you have animator and animator, or you two are storyboard and storyboard, do you ever feel like you are in competition with one another?

Jen: Never. And I think it goes back to the fact that me and my sisters growing up were all artists. We never competed—it was never a competition thing; and what's good for one, you just smile and celebrate what's happening. So it's good for everybody. It was never a competition thing. And in his case, it was never a competition thing. 'Cause if good things happen to him, if he got work, I was like, "Yay, you deserve it, it's great!" And also he was really good. And he did things differently than I did. So I would watch what he did, and go, "Oh, so that's how you approach a shot, and that's how you draw a character, and that's a cool pose I never would have thought of." And it actually made me better, looking at what he was doing. And over the years, you know couples, they start resembling each other more. Our stuff never looked the same, but each other's stuff sort of crept into the other's stuff. I would draw a pose, and I would say, "That's one of your poses." [laughs] But it never quite looked like what he would do, though.

Tom: What is your favorite part of being a director?

Jen: My favorite part has to be what people tell me, that they are able to do the best work they've ever done. And I think that a job of a director is to get everyone to do their best work. It's not about throwing your weight around and being in charge all the time. 'Cause if you do that, you're going to be beat up, being proved wrong quite a lot. But when people are in an environment, in a situation, [where they] have the information that they need to feel creatively fulfilled and get that rush of, "I am working on something that I'm really happy to see exist," then that makes me happy.

Tom: That is pretty close to what Richard Williams told me.

Jen: Really?

Tom: Yeah, yeah. He said, he says, "Sometimes what's more satisfying than being able to go further than you think you could, is creating a climate for others to do better than they thought they ever could."

Jen: Yeah. Because that's why we're in this business, right? We want to make something that people look at and go, "Wow." And then look at each other and go, "We made that. That didn't exist. We made something that we can be proud of at the end of all the blood, sweat, and tears."

Tom: So now I have to ask, what's your least favorite part?

Jen: The least favorite … I think the least favorite is the horrific weight of responsibility that each of your decisions could affect the livelihoods of many, many people. The buck stops with you, and you have to make those hard decisions. And you know that there will be casualties involved. You know, there may be people's ideas you can't use, or things that could cause someone to lose a weekend with their family, or maybe entire scenes that people work really hard [on] have to be cut out. Those things are really hard to do and you have to make those decisions and make sure the movie's going to be great, and people will have jobs at the end of the day. But that weight of responsibility, it actually goes against the creative process. Because you have to be okay with not having a stake in order to be creatively free. But it's—it's a very exhausting part of the work.

Ron: So there were a couple of times you made people work through the weekend and it was worth it, and maybe a couple of times where it wasn't worth it?

Jen: Yeah. It's like generals of an army—you look at them and go, "We got to take that bridge; a lot of you are going to die. But we got to do it, or we are going to lose the war." That's the role of the leader. You have to ask someone to do the hard work, and it's terribly sad at times.

Tom: There are people who storyboard and they are happy just to storyboard for the rest of their life. There are people who animate, or who character design, and [are] happy to do that for the rest of their life. But when you start directing, you're yielding a certain amount of creative input, because it's not you drawing. It's more about your ability to motivate and inspire your team.

Jen: Right, it's not you doing the work; it's about getting everyone else to do the work.

Tom: Yes. For someone who storyboards so well, how did you handle giving up that responsibility?

Jen: It was very tough actually. Because I think a lot of people when they first start out directing, they end up just trying to do everything themselves, and that's just not what a director is. That just means you're overworking an artist, meaning you. That's not also the best way to motivate people to do the best work.

So, what I ended up doing is finding the parts that I felt like I really needed to do, which may be very surgical little things I just wanted. I saw a moment so clearly I thought, "There's no point in sending someone off to do this; it'll take me a short period of time to just bang it out." So I would try and surgically figure out what parts that I really had to do, but try to outsource, delegate everything else.

And part of it is understanding that it doesn't have to be exactly the way you saw it being done, as long as the point is made. We were talking about before, that there are different styles of directing. There are the directors that will tell you if it's similar to trying to find a place on a map, the destination. He can either say, "This is the address, figure it out." And then there's the directors that will say, "Turn left, turn right, turn left, go 100 feet, go turn right, turn right, turn right, turn left, and then go another 100 feet, and then stop, and then go another 2 feet, and then make a left, and right, and left, and right, and left." I prefer being the "this is the address, figure it out" [type]. Because that is the point of the shot, of the movie, of the character, or that's the point we have to achieve that the audience has to understand. And there are so many people that will do getting to that destination better than you would. And that's a big thing. I think people respect and understand that there are simply people that will get you there better than you would have. You may know where to go, but let everybody else come up with creative solutions on how to get there.

Kung Fu Panda 3, 2016 © DreamWorks Animation LLC.

Tom: **When did you know from the time you were storyboarding, "I could direct"?**

Jen: In TV or feature?

Tom: **I think the first time you ever thought you could be a director.**

Jen: I again [had a] very nontraditional approach to ending up being a director. When I was in TV, my producer was Catherine Winder. I was actually in Australia, working on a live-action movie, 'cause I [had] left HBO, gone to Australia to work on storyboards and illustrations because I wanted to do something different, and I was young and crazy. And then she called me up towards the end of the thing and said, "Hey, how are you doing?" I said, "Oh great. I'm almost done, I don't know what to do and I don't know if I'll stay in live action or come back to animation. Knowing I can't stay here, because I can't live in Australia forever. I miss my family." So she said, "Come back and direct in TV." And I'm like, "Okay … I have no idea how to do that." She said, "Don't worry. You'll do fine." And so, I was pushed. I didn't say, "I want to come back, make me a director and I'll come back." I was told, "Come back and direct and you'll be fine." [laughs] I said, "Okay…" So that's why I directed in TV. And a similar thing happened to me when it was my first time directing in feature animation because on *Kung Fu Panda 1*, Melissa Cobb had set me up to do that two-minute opening sequence, because no one there did 2D animation anymore … Isn't that sad? Like the whole pipeline was gone, they didn't have any of the equipment anymore. They barely had anything to scan anything. So they had to outsource the 2D animation. Melissa said, "Go become essentially a sequence director and just do it because the directors are too busy." So I ran off. What's great training for that was I was a head of story on a film, but as a head of story you don't necessarily go into every department and follow the whole pipeline leading into that. You just kind of stop and peel off. For instance, you're never sitting in lighting dailies as a head of story.

So it was great training for me. And later on, Melissa told me she did it on purpose. She said she could tell my personality type wasn't the kind of person that walks in and says, "I'm going to be the director and blah, blah, blah." I was more like, "I just want to do some cool work and I'm not sure if I can do that …" I'm not the most crazy, overly self-confident person in the world. I need a big push a lot of the time. And so she told me that she did it in order for me to get confidence in myself. That she knew that I wouldn't do a jump like that until I had a preponderance of evidence to prove to myself that I could do it without destroying people's lives. That's kind of what I was doing 'cause I was thinking first of the responsibilities of the job. And the fact that it's such a scary responsibility.

So at the end of the first movie, when both directors said, "We don't want to do another one," they had other things they wanted to do. I think John wanted to do live action, Mark wanted to [do] *The Little Prince*, so they left. Melissa Cobb came to me and said, "You're going to direct the second movie." And it wasn't a "You should direct the second movie" or "Will you direct the second movie?" It's like, "You're going to direct the second movie." And I said, "No …" And she said,

"Yes, you are." And I go, "No, I'm not." And then finally she said, "You can do it." And I said, "I can't do it. I don't know how to do it." I'm like, "Are you crazy? I'm not going to do this." And she said, "You've already done it because that's why I put you on that thing (the 2D prologue) so I can train you to do it. And you were in every meeting as a head of story. You were working with the writers, you were working with every aspect of this, and so you have to do it." So I said, "… Okay."

But I was scared to death. I remember going home and saying to my husband, "Oh crap, they asked me to direct a movie …" It wasn't good news. It was traumatic.

Ron: **In your early period directing, were you learning from mentors? Or from observation of past experiences?**

Jen: Just a bit of everything because as a head of story, and I got to say, I was a very, very included head of story. They brought me into everything, they were very open with everything, so I was able [to] observe everything, down to [the] dynamics of the meeting. I actually think it's easier to learn when they're not staring at you to perform in the meeting. When you're in as an observer in a meeting, you can be very clear on what's going on. You're not clouded by performance anxiety. I would watch meetings where things got done, and it was literally like watching a ping-pong match of colors. You go, that person did that because of this, and that person is saying that because of this. And that person said that, and they're doing this, and they're getting that alliance figured out. I was watching this like a *Game of Thrones* episode—it was so educational.

Ron: **So it was studio politics. It wasn't necessarily what was right for the particular scene, or …**

Jen: I think that essentially that part of directing, the actual craft, was something I already knew. Because I had done head of story on two productions, I'd been working for years on the actual process of animation, I understood what all the departments did at that point. What I didn't know is the politics angle of being a director. That's the thing I had to learn, because it's a very different job. You walk into a meeting and all of a sudden all the eyeballs look at you, and there's huge baggage that everybody has expectations on what you're supposed to be doing. You never would have had that as a head of story. That's the part I had to learn.

Ron: **You were saying some interesting things about being a woman and going to Japan. Maybe you could talk a little bit about that.**

Jen: I was at HBO, and it was *Spawn* and it was my first time going overseas to oversee animation there. It was Madhouse and DR Movie. Madhouse was like this really happy new place. A really cool bunch of people. But I had a mortifying experience for my first time in Japan. This amazing studio, founded by amazing people, all this amazing art everywhere, and then I had a penicillin reaction.

Tom: Oh no.

Jen: I had developed a minor infection, I was taking penicillin. I had never had problems with it before. All of a sudden I'm in Japan, and I suddenly, like, go full-on allergic ICU (intensive care unit)!

Tom: Oh, my God!

Jen: Like, my skin went bright red, you know, and I couldn't breathe. It was [the] middle of the night in a foreign country. So they had to rush me to emergency in the Ginza.

They had to give me all sorts of shots. I was spending my first week in Japan; three of those days were in the ICU in a teaching hospital. But they were all such sweet people, very lovely. Talk about the worst case scenario! That's what happens when you go to meet a bunch of people for the first time.

Tom: Wow.

Jen: But everybody was very supportive and nice about it. But I think that, you know, it was not great. [laughs]

Tom: Did you run into the thing about losing face? When working at an American studio like Hanna-Barbera, which is a lot of old-school animators, when you get tough critique it's no big deal. I had old Disney guys saying, "Idiot! Don't you know how to do this?" And they meant nothing by it. But when you go to Japan or Asia, you have to think about artists losing face. You know you can't say, "this is bad, this is wrong, this stinks," because then they lose face. You have to couch it in a way that's …

Jen: Yeah, you can say, "how about this?" for this suggestion of an idea. And you know, it. Strangely, I think it's cause I'm Asian, but I tend to do that anyway. Even here, I don't walk up to someone and say, "This is crap." I don't tend to do that. I just …

Tom: I remember Iwao Takamoto (1925–2007) at Hanna-Barbera was famous for judging work by saying, "This is good, this is very good, good! Now you … do it again."

All: [laugh]

Jen: Yeah, I mean, even though I was raised here, I did have an Asian family and there was a lot of [influence]. I think part of that is not necessarily being as antagonistic in some situations. I mean you get your point across the same.

Kung Fu Panda 2, 2011 © DreamWorks Animation LLC.

Ron: And with acting, with actors, was it the same?

Jen: It depended on the actor. I directed the second one, so I had a longer-term relationship with most of the leads than Ale had. But then if they were new actors, neither of us had known them. So we would differ to each other. Maybe it was a scene that one of us knew more about than the other because maybe he boarded it. Or maybe I boarded it. And so we would trade off according to who would lead a session. But usually it was the both of us crouched over a little microphone and doing stuff.

Tom: When you're working with an actor, that's usually the protocol. There is only one voice giving instructions to the actor and so—

Jen: Yes, I think it's important … One person would lead a session. Because a recording session is this sort of direct line between the actor and the director.

Tom: Yes.

Jen: Even if you're not in the room, even if you're in the recording booth … the tech area, there is eye contact all between you and the actors all the time. They are constantly thinking, "Am I doing it right?" They do that all the time. So it has to be one person.

Tom: Yes.

Jen: And the whole time, as the director, you're sitting there and you're like a little sheepdog, going to look at the sheep. It's a similar body language as a sheep dog, when they're tap, tap, tap, tap, tap, tap, tap. That's what you're doing the whole time, a little there, a little there, a little there, poke, poke, poke, that—that's it.

Tom: Yes.

Jen: So that's what you're doing, and you can't do that if there's five people involved. You can't. They [the actors] don't know who to look at.

Tom: Do you like working, like, with the actors?

Jen: I do, I love them. And that's something I never got to do as a head of story. When I first started doing it as a director, I was scared to death because these were all massive celebrities and stuff. But I realized it's just like working with an animator. And there [are] a lot of the same processes of how I'm going to have to go through and figure out what the moment is. How to feel what the character is feeling at that moment. So I would communicate to them like an artist and they get it.

Tom: I know a lot of editors who like it that way.

Jen: … 'Cause they can think. And you need different ideas outside of what you expected. Strange, that I actually think it's faster. If you have five people, yelling and screaming in the room, and the poor editor is trying to cut and … and then they're recutting and recutting and recutting, and they never actually get to a point. Soon you're spending the 3 am sessions with nothing to show for it and everyone's tired. Or you do it the other way where you get someone to think. You can get to a solution much more efficiently. That's what I think.

Ron: Did you use the same editor on both pictures?

Jen: Yeah.

Ron: Did it become more intuitive as it went along?

Jen: Very. Me and Clare Knight have a very easy way of working. I think that editors and directors, it's almost like a marriage. You kind of have to find a good match. If you don't have a way of shorthand, it's a lot harder. With me and her, it's always been very, very smooth. We're both relatively quiet people; we're not the kind of people that yell and scream in a room.

And when we work, it's relatively serene. She has, like, an espresso in her office, and she has candles, and always smells nice, and it's clean. Then we sit in there and it's very efficient, the way we work.

Tom: Have you ever had any examples [of] what you call a happy accident? Something you weren't planning, or you know, something somebody said. And you just go, "That's nice, keep it. Put it in."

Jen: There was in the second *Panda* movie. We were cutting the big emotional revelation moment where Po understands the truth of what happened when he was a little baby, and his mom saved his life. Part of it was in 2D, and then when the truth comes out, it becomes 3D. And the transition used to be one shot longer in 2D, so that it becomes 3D [from] his POV (point of view) of the mother. Although, what's interesting is, Clare was cutting that area and we realized that we didn't really have a particular shot quite long enough. We were looking at it, and she suggested that the reveal is exactly the same moment as the change in medium. They negate each other. So, she said, "Let's shift it, so that the reveal happens earlier and the truth and revelation happens one shot later." So we cut out a shot, and all of a sudden it hit you viscerally. That's one of those things you can't quite quantify. Whether something will make you cry, until you actually do it. And she took out this distracting medium shot in that moment where it's supposed to be emotionally engaged, which was a distraction. She took that out, and all of a sudden the moment worked!

Tom: In *Who Framed Roger Rabbit*, when Jessica was singing the torch song "Why Don't You Do Right." At the very end, where she pulls Hoskins close to her lips by his tie and sings, "Why don't you do right, like some other man ... Doo"—like that. There was a little pause. The shot had background actors wallah. All these actors going groaning in ecstasy, "OOH! uhhUUHHH." Then right in that pause, where she says, "why don't—like some other man," a guy in the back goes "UH!" I remember we were sitting in editorial, and Bob Zemeckis asked, "Is that funny?" It was a complete accident. "Just leave it in, it's funny, it works!" [laughs] It's great when you can catch those little things once in a while.

Jen: I think that animation is such a overcooked process—everything has to be thought out so much that you kind of have to force the accidents and treasure them when they do happen. Because otherwise it could be such a forgone process; everything is so predictable because we can control everything.

Tom: Do you encourage with the actors a certain amount of improv?

Jen: We depend on improv with the actors. A natural way of speaking is not necessarily a natural way of writing. Especially a character that is as prone to outburst as Po. And Jack [Black], he's very much into input, all the callouts, a lot of them are just stuff he made up. But also it's just that they are grasping the reality of the emotion of the moment. If it doesn't feel right, you throw out the script page and figure it out on the spot with the actor.

Kung Fu Panda 3, 2016 © DreamWorks Animation LLC.

Tom: William Shatner used to make me laugh because he was in a radio experience and—part of his humor was his—he would change tempo and speed, so he'd go "Hahaha—who're you talkin' to?" [laughs] And he did it so well. So, like, he would just—he'd make you laugh. It's just like … That's good. [Laughs]

Jen: That's great.

Tom: I want to touch on music. How much does music factor in what you do?

Jen: To me, music is 30 percent of the emotional experience of the movie. That's why we bother to do a scratch music track even when we're looking at the rough version of the movie. We try to do a rough music pass, because you have to have some emotional framework for what you're watching. In fact, it can sometimes fool you into thinking a crappy scene is a lot better than it is, 'cause the music's great. But the music is so important, so, so important. I don't understand why we leave it as late as we do. Mainly because of the availability of the composer, you can't lock up a composer for three years—they got other stuff to do, other movies. But it's so important, and it's so frightening 'cause sometimes, you've lived with a scratch music track forever, and you think, "I think it works." And then you throw it all out and you start over with the real music, and everything feels different.

Tom: Yeah.

Jen: It's terrifying 'cause you think, "Did we break it? Are we delusional? Is this a piece of crap? I don't know." But the music has to go through its process, too. They have to have their sketch, and then their honing, and then their polish and all that stuff. And once they get to it—it feels quite amazing. You now think, "Why did I ever load that scratch track in the first place? It's crap!" [laughs]

Tom: Now that you've done a couple [of] pictures, do you feel like you've evolved a personal style?

Jen: Personal style? That's interesting, because in some ways I think the second one was more my personal style than the third one, because the third one was a collaboration. And so there are sections of the third one that are more me, and sections that are more of Ale [Alessandro Carloni]. I think he was pointing it out some time before that some parts that are kind of epic and emotional and kind of over-the-top action stuff are mine, and the ones that have that cute little character, sweet and funny stuff [are] actually his. But it's kind of counter intuitive again, if you look at us and think that. But the sort of personal stuff that I have is getting to that emotional, sort of pushed emotional point, where I think a lot of people are afraid to go, because they think it's going to be too much for the kids. I think kids can take a lot. I could take a lot when I was a kid, I was watching all sorts of stuff. But to be able to get to that deep emotional sort of … revelation, where you make grown men cry, that's the thing that I like to do.

Tom: I see. Everybody has a pet project they keep in their back pocket … Like, director John Houston wanted to do Kipling's *The Man Who Would Be King* for many years. Do you have something that you'd like to tackle someday? Like, "I really want to do grand opera." [laughs]

Jen: Well, I've always wanted to do an action, live-action movie. That's why I got into storyboarding in the first place. I've never actually done that, because in animation you can push things only so far before you start having people thinking you're traumatizing the children. The thing is, I think something like Panda, I could find things in it that were action packed, and I could get a lot of jollies out of it. But I would love to go full, hardcore action someday.

Ron: I understand you do some drawing on your own, of your own ideas. Are they sketches for movies, or are they just meanderings

Jen: When I say that I've been doing storyboarding since I was five, I've been working on these types of stories since I was five. And so, I do storyboards, very elaborate storyboards. They're kind of aggressive, very violent, action, sci-fi stories. And their entire arcs and all. Everything I've learned, I've put into this. In some ways I think even though I call that my R&D, work is my R&D. Because that's where I get the joy, and in doing all this, I can learn better how to do that … strange. So yeah, I do drawings at home all the time. And they're full-on, full-on stories and stuff, but I'll never pitch them.

Ron: **Would you ever make them on your own? If you had somebody [who] said, "Oh, here's twenty or fifty million dollars, go ahead and make it." Would you want to make it yourself?**

Jen: No. No, isn't that weird?

Ron: **Never?**

Jen: The reason is that they're already done for me. For the viewing audience of one. They're already done up here [points to her head], so there's really no point in taking the responsibility and pressure of someone giving me fifty million dollars and then they have a say. No one has a say on this stuff; it's already done. So I could do that for other things. But for that, it's to be kept here. I think I showed some of that in the class talks and stuff. The only times I ever show it is when I, like, talk to classes. It's not for pitching to a studio.

Ron: **So are they Sam Peckinpah-ish violence? Or is there a moral bent to it? Or a societal statement of some sort?**

Jen: They're actually—it's kind of like this epic emotional family drama with sci-fi biotechnology involved. [laughs]

Tom: **Oh, one of those. [laughs]**

Jen: But the reason why I like it is it frees me from a lot of the narrative constraints, fitting it into a two-hour movie. Or a ten-hour miniseries. Or whether it fits a certain demographic. Or whether it's understandable for moms with kids to see, or anything like that. Of all the several stories, the one I'm mainly working on nowadays is just stepping in and looking at someone's life and understanding what character is built through this particular person's life. And for me that's fascinating, because I take pieces of that all the time and put it into things I'm working on. It just, you know, because you've spent this much brain energy creating a reality—creating entire complex characters and motivations. Informative moments and backstories and weird interactions and completely crazy sorts of scenarios. And all that stuff that on a job, you don't have time to figure out. You've got to come up with stuff like that. And then you go, "Oh, I have that idea." And that's a crazy undercurrent to a character that you don't often see and you can throw that in there. So I do that all the time. I just cull stuff out of there.

Tom: Okay, so now we have to ask the inevitable question. What would be your advice for the people trying to follow you?

Kung Fu Panda 3, 2016 © DreamWorks Animation LLC.

Jen: There's a couple things for me; I've been asked that before by students and it's what I would've found useful. 'Cause when you're young and starting out, you don't have as much experience, and everything is scary. I would say just don't take either the success or the failures personally. It's not about you; it's about the context of that job. So, don't walk into it and get devastated if you get turned down. And don't suddenly get completely chuffed if you're hired for something. Because often it's not about you. So just try and find the thing that you like to do, that you would do anyway, whether or not someone else told you that you had to do it. And if you can find joy in doing that thing, then eventually you will get a job doing that thing. But don't let other people dictate what you end up doing by their tastes. You know, if someone says, "I love you because you do this! You're fantastic!" then you may veer towards doing that. That may not be what you want to do; that may not even be what you're good at. But someone said you're good at it, you must do that more, right? But that sort of—it's all a mirage. You just got to find the thing that you find joy in doing and get joy doing that. And do not be discouraged, or overly encouraged, by what other people say. 'Cause that's how you maintain your core.

Tom: Did you ever want to do something completely different?

Jen: The thing is, every project that I've ever signed up to do has something in it that makes me very happy. Even things that you'd go, "Why would she have worked on that?" Like *Happy, the Littlest Bunny*, 'cause there were things on that that made me happy because I was learning something. So every project that I've done, I'm doing [it] because it's teaching me something. And I've always done this thing where I try to figure out, what am I going to learn this year? What am I going to learn [on] this project? What's my goal? What am I going to get out of this thing? And maybe it was like I ran off to do a live-action movie because I wanted to learn how to draw gigantic architectural things—I had never learned how to do that. And so within five months, I could learn how to freehand gigantic cities. That's something that I didn't know how to do before, but—or the one year I thought, "I want to learn all about military aircraft. Or this year I'm going to learn exactly how to use a motorcycle. [laughs] All that, stuff like that, that's all research and development. And so all the movies, all the projects I've worked on, even though they may not necessarily be exactly, purely what my personal sensibility is ... each one has taught me something significant.

Tom: **Well, I think that about does it.**

Jen: Cool.

Ron: **That okay? Have we not covered anything that you feel that should be included?**

Jen: Oh, I don't know. I mean life is complicated, so I don't know what parts are interesting. [laughs]

10

Carlos Saldanha Interview

Carlos Saldanha, photographer Antelmo Villarreal.

Although I knew many at Blue Sky Studios in Connecticut, I had not had the pleasure of meeting Carlos Saldanha until we talked for this book. I had known of his work as a director (and co-director) of hit films like *Rio* (2010), *Rio 2* (2014), *Robots* (2005), and the *Ice Age* films. His film *Ice Age: Dawn of the Dinosaurs* (2009) became an international sensation. It was the highest grossing animated title internationally and the second highest worldwide at the time of release. We met for the interview when he was out at the Twentieth Century Fox studio. A slight, wiry man with a broad smile, I found him a very pleasant fellow and very enthusiastic about the art of animation. Although originally from Brazil, his years living in the New York City area allowed him the opportunity to cultivate a fine Manhattan brogue, so that it awoke in me the lingua franca of my homeland (Brooklyn).

So like, uh … let's do dis …

Tom Sito

Tom: Thank you for doing this. So, to begin, can you please talk a little bit about your own background and how you came into animation? You're originally from Brazil?

Carlos: Yes, I'm originally from Brazil. I was born in Rio. I came from a very average middle-class family. My dad was in the military. My mom was a homemaker. We traveled a lot because being in the service, my dad had to move around the country. But I got to spend most of my teenager years in Rio. I always loved to draw. Usually if I didn't have anything to do, I'd get a pencil and paper and spend my time drawing characters and little comic strips. I also loved watching cartoons and the Disney animation classics on TV. I remember having all the Disney movies in book form or on record, tiny, colorful little vinyls that told the story of *Bambi, Pinocchio*, and all that stuff. I immersed myself into the world of storytelling and animation. So, I grew up with the old classics. I grew up with the *Looney Tunes* also, all those fun cartoons that people here grew up with.

Ron: Did you ever think you could do this for a living?

Carlos: Not until much later in the game. For me drawing was always a hobby. You know, like after a long day in school, I would come back home and I'd draw a little bit. I'd see something I liked and I would draw it or paint it. But I never had training. I never even thought it would be possible to have any training. But when I graduated from high school I thought maybe I'd go to art school. I was very young, I was just sixteen when I finished high school, so my parents looked at me and said, "Art school? Are you crazy? No, don't go to art school. You're too young to go to art school! What are you going to do with art?"

I also loved computers. I took my first computer class in high school. I was excited about the computer's possibilities, especially video gaming and stuff, 'cause you could do graphics on the computer. I was the Commodore 64 kind of generation. So my parents suggested I pursue that instead and maybe do something related to art later. So I went to computer science school and really loved it. But I remember always catching myself doing graphics. To me it was less about the programming and more about designing fun screen layouts, logos, and pop-up menus. I was more interested in the visual aspects of it than actually the programming part of it. Even though I ended up working as a programmer, working with systems and creating software, I was much more driven to the communication and visual aspects of computer science. I was interested in how the message could appear on the screen in the best way possible.

I worked with it (computers) for a couple of years, while at the same time I was always watching movies. I loved sci-fi movies, and my favorite movie was *Blade Runner* (1982). I loved that movie, and kept wanting to be in that world! Creating worlds like that. Not even talking about animation at that stage. I was more into visual effects. But again, being in Brazil was kind of tough, because there was no market for that. And I didn't even know how to get started.

Then I came upon this compilation tape, I think it was a SIGGRAPH tape. I know it was from some kind of big festival that had a bunch of short films. All CG. When looking at that tape I saw *Luxo, Jr.* (1986). I thought, "This is great! Look at this, the guy made it look real. It looks real, but it has a heart, it has a story behind it. I love this stuff. This is what I wanna do!"

For about a year, I started to look around for the possibilities in Brazil. There were some CG companies in Brazil, especially for big TV networks that were starting to tap into computer graphics. But I couldn't find a way in. And then I talked to someone that said, "Well, there are schools in the US that you can attend and you can see if you like it or not." That's when I learned about the School of Visual Arts (SVA) in New York City. I said, "Um, it sounds like a good idea. Maybe I can go to New York and see what happens."

So, I broke my piggy bank. [laughs] I worked hard to try to get together every cent that I could to come to the US and attend school. I was so crazy! I was only twenty, when I suddenly told my girlfriend, "Let's get married and go to the US, and maybe we'll stay there for three months, four months. Who knows? Maybe we will come back." And she said, "Ok, but I have to stop college." "Yeah, stop for a little while and then we'll come back and you can continue," I told her. So it was one of those crazy things you do when you're young, in love, and you don't think too much. We took the leap and drove our parents crazy. Everybody was saying, "Are you out of your mind? You're going to quit your job and go somewhere you don't know?" I explained, "I have to try this. I got a gut feeling that it's what I love."

I came to New York and I started with classes at the School of Visual Arts. I didn't have money to pay for college. I just paid for that semester, just so I could see if I had any kind of potential. And, you know, the minute that I sat at that computer, that's when I found my passion! I think the software was Digital Arts running on a PC. To me it was the fastest, biggest, meanest machine that I could ever imagine! Nowadays I don't think you can even run Google on that one. [laughs] Yet right there, the minute I sat down on the first day of class, I said, "This is what I want to do for the rest of my life," and since then I've never stopped.

No Time for Love, 1993.

Tom: **How did you first connect with Blue Sky Studios?**

Carlos: Well, when I was at SVA, the continuation class was taught by Bruce Wands. He was the head of the undergraduate program and worked with the graduate program. I remember being very impressed with SVA's facilities. Back home, at college, there were maybe a handful of computers that I had limited access to. There at SVA there were forty computer workstations and I had twenty-four-hour access. A lot of computers and software playing, yet the room was empty. Nobody was using it. I was like a kid in a candy store. I was there from nine in the morning to nine at night every single day of the three months that I planned to stay in the US.

Tom: **So you really jumped at the opportunity.**

Carlos: I was very diligent and organized in a way, just wanting to learn it all. When the teacher saw that it was the end of the class, he said to me, "You've got to continue this and you've got to take the master's program." I said, "How am I going to do it?" I was supposed to go back to Brazil. And he just said, "Well, see if you can stay." I had to get a visa. I have to get paperwork done. I had to get money. I borrowed money from friends. But in the end everything worked out fine. I was accepted into their master's program. There, one of my teachers was Chris Wedge. And that's when the Blue Sky connection really began. He was my teacher of animation, and he ended up hiring me.

Chris Wedge, Carlos Saldanha, and TBD, *Ice Age*, 2002 © Twentieth Century Fox. All Rights Reserved.

Tom: **Okay, let's set aside biography for now, and focus on your technique as a director. You've developed some characters around some pretty well-known actors. When developing a character, do you work with the actors? Are you at the recording sessions?**

Carlos: Yeah, I work with them, and I rely a lot on them to help me. Because I have a pretty good idea what the character is all about. When I design, I create a character thinking about what kind of mannerisms the character has. I would always think of them not speaking, but think of them acting. And that's why I can probably help the actor in saying "so this character is like THIS, and is going to do THIS and THAT." I would give them the broad strokes of the character. Then I would rely on their acting chops to bring it to the next level. You find happy surprises. We have been very fortunate with a lot of our casting.

Tom: **Do you have any examples?**

Carlos: Take Sid (the sloth) in *Ice Age*, for example. John [Leguizamo] had originally given us about a hundred potential accents for that character. A hundred different ways the character might talk. Until we came upon the lisp. Then that became the trademark of the character. John continued to help us with the comedy of Sid. When an actor contributes so much at that level, it makes the character better. It's the kind of stuff that we look for when we work with actors. "What is [it] that you can bring to the character that would make the character better than I imagine?"—that's the question. It's a matter of discovery. We never get it right off the bat. Usually the first few sessions with the actors is more trying to figure out what it's going to sound like, or how it is going to be. Only after that can we really get into the character. We can take the character to the next level.

Ice Age, 2002 © Twentieth Century Fox. All Rights Reserved.

Tom: **Do you bring storyboards in and take them (the actors) through [them]? Or do you just work directly from script?**

Carlos: We do a couple of things. Scripts are good, but there're always revisions and changes so maybe the actor doesn't have time to read everything beforehand. Some actors are very good at doing their homework. They come in with the lines memorized, and that's awesome.

If they come in prepared, that helps me quite a bit. But some of them don't come in prepared, and they have to do it on the fly. That takes a little longer, but it's fine too. And I always try to bring the sequences on storyboards (onto the recording stage) so that they can watch it, so they can see what the situation is. I tell them, "Oh, imagine a glacier and then you are at the bottom of the glacier and then you're doing …" Sometimes it's hard. So I show them the sequence and then talk about it. Then they get to know it. Sometimes I would show some animation tests so that they can see how their character performs.

Tom: **Sometimes I would run into an actor who didn't like to work with a storyboard. They'd tell you, "I don't want to be influenced by the character's acting on the storyboard."**

Carlos: Some of them don't like to; many don't like hearing temp voices. And I try to avoid that too, because I don't want to lead them in the wrong direction. I don't want them to feel obligated to match the temp voice. And some of them don't like hearing their voices. It's interesting. Sometimes when I have the sequences with their voices they get self-conscious. They always say, "Oh, I can do better than that," which is good. [laughs] But I only do it surgically. I only show them stuff when it's really important for them to get the context of what I'm trying to get. Other than that, I try not to show too much.

Tom: **How does music play a role in what you do? When you are conceiving of the idea of a picture, do you already have some music in mind?**

Carlos: Music is huge. I think it's almost fifty-fifty. With the right music you get the moment to play ten times better. The wrong music can destroy the moment. So I take music very seriously. I cannot play anything, and I'm not musically knowledgeable myself. But I love putting music into projects and finding that perfect song. Some projects require more than others, but I think it's a very crucial part of the work.

Tom: **Do you work with a sound designer?**

Carlos: I listen to a lot of stuff and I work with the editor. In all my movies I have the same editor, so over time we developed libraries of music. It's tricky because sometimes you go to the same source, and it's like, "Wait, I already heard that music in *Ice Age: The Meltdown*, and that music I used in *Robots*." So you start to get picky. We are always searching for something fresh, so we spend quite a lot of time listening to sound bites and music, cutting them into the reels, trying it out. He [the editor] does the first pass and sees how I react. Sometimes, depending on the project, we ask the [music] supervisor to come in and help us shape it because we don't have a lot of time. Cutting music takes longer than cutting [story] boards. Finding the right music is very difficult.

Tom: **Many directors say a very important part of their job is choosing an editor and working with him or her, because they spend so much of their time working in close proximity together. So you and your editor have a good relationship?**

Carlos: Yeah, we have a great relationship. Harry [Hitner] is amazing, and it is true, most of my time I spend in editorial. It's quality time because outside of editorial I'm moving around the company, fifteen minutes here, twenty minutes there, an hour here.

It's always jumping from department to department, trying to keep the thing going. When I get to editing, it is a time when I can sit down, look at the movie, and actually make the movie in real time. Like when I need the panels for this, I need a shot here, I need music there. It feels more intimate. You get to see the movie that you are making. I love that part of the process.

Tom: **The other thing that you guys [Blue Sky] do really well is the pantomime scenes. There seems to be a musical quality to your sound effects. With a good sound effect, you get a laugh even without any dialogue.**

Carlos: Yeah, it's tough, too. I think it's a combination of many things: music, sound effects, animation, visuals. When it all comes together, you get a great moment.

Tom: **Who is the voice of Scrat?**

Carlos: Scrat is Chris Wedge. That was one of those happy surprises. We didn't have much time to choose. We were thinking about some big names to make those little sounds. We did do a lot of temp tracks. A lot of what we called "The Blue Sky Players." We have our cast of temp voices at Blue Sky that we keep going to for all these sounds and scratch voices, before we get the real actors to come in. Chris was making all the sounds for Scrat, and it was so good. So why change it?

Ice Age: The Meltdown, 2006 © Twentieth Century Fox. All Rights Reserved.

Tom: **It's much like when Hanna and Barbera were creating the characters of Tom and Jerry. The famous stock scream of when Tom gets hit, "Agghhhh," is director Bill Hanna himself. Apparently, he [Bill] kept trying actors all day, saying, "No, not like that, like this, 'agghhhh!!'" Joe Barbera finally said, "Bill, why don't we just use your scream?"**

Carlos: I think that was exactly what happened with Scrat. We went through a casting but no one sounded as good as Chris.

Tom: **Earlier, you mentioned happy accidents. Do you ever get happy accidents, like either the performance of an artist or, or the way the sequence would come together, you'd think, "Wow, we really have something here"?**

Carlos: Yeah, there is a lot of that in the process; that's part of what makes working on an animated project so special. There are sequences that you struggle with a lot. For example, one that we all struggled with is where we had that sequence of the dodos in the first [*Ice Age*] movie. We worked so hard in that sequence to find comedy and dialogue. It just was not there, to a point that it almost got cut. We didn't know what to do with it. A happy surprise emerged when animators got their hands on it. We started to discover the fun of the characters. The dodos, the quirkiness of the characters, came to life. It became one of my favorite sequences in the movie, one of those happy accidents. I think they do happen, not often, but they do happen. Scrat is one of them, too. Originally we only had Scrat at the beginning of the movie. We had an idea for him in the end, but we didn't have him in the middle, so we added that. He became such a big star that we had to start to create more for him.

Tom: **Now that you've directed several pictures, you know the whole process can be overwhelming. Have you modified the way you schedule your day in terms of pacing yourself? How did you learn to relegate your time?**

Carlos: I don't know if I learned yet! [laughs] I find that every movie that I work on is getting harder and harder. I had this assumption that it would all get easier as I went along. At least some aspects of it have gotten easier. My comfort level has gotten easier with the crew, and with the phases of what to expect and how things miraculously get solved.

Tom: **You're better at letting things go now?**

Carlos: No, not good, no! I might have gotten better at picking my battles. But letting things go is always tough. I know the minute I say, "Approved," it is a point of no return. It's just gone, and I'm like, "ahhhhh, don't go!!" [laughs] So I try to only say that when I really feel it's ready to move on. But sometimes I can't, sometimes the shot is way overdue and maybe there is nothing more I can get out of the actor, or the animator, or myself. Then I feel that I need to let it go. Sleep on it and see. I create a list of what we call CBB, "Could Be Better." Every time a shot moves forward, if I'm not a 100 percent sure, I put a little check mark on it. Eventually at the end of the project I'll have a list of all the shots that I can go back to. We've been very successful at managing that. I need to deal with scheduling and getting things to move forward without sacrificing quality. I'm a quality freak. I'm very "it needs to be perfect." But I did learn that sometimes it's just one shot. It's only two seconds on the screen. Maybe the foot is not a 100 percent in the right position that I thought it should be. Who cares? Nobody is looking specifically at that foot, you know. But again, I understand the importance of the details. I always have a little devil and angel on my shoulder saying, "Let it go! You gotta let go!" "No, no! Work on it!" I'm always role-playing with those two voices in my head.

Tom: **Have you ever been the sole director? Or did you always work with a co-director?**

Carlos: When I worked on *Ice Age*, I was co-director with Chris [Wedge]. On *Robots*, I was again co-director with Chris. Then I jumped to *Ice Age: The Meltdown* and did it all by myself. Then *Ice Age: Dawn of the Dinosaurs*, I had a co-director, Mike Thurmeier, who was one of my top animators and an amazing guy. I always got along with him. He had the kind of personality and talent that fit the director's role perfectly. He was so brilliant all the way through. Chris had trusted me and brought me in on the first *Ice Age* as his co-director so I could also learn and grow. I felt the same way about Mike coming to *Ice Age: Dawn of the Dinosaurs*. It would be a great project for him to come on as a director, to both learn and help me more.

Ice Age: Dawn Of The Dinosaurs, 2009 © Twentieth Century Fox. All Rights Reserved.

Tom: Now that you've done a picture both ways, which do you prefer?

Carlos: I like to direct, but, I really value the co-director role. If you have the right person, it's an awesome collaboration. If you have trust and if you share similar sensibilities or similar philosophies on the project, it becomes an amazing collaboration. I was very fortunate to have had Mike on board.

Tom: How did you and Mike divide up your responsibilities? Some teams like to split up sequences of the film. Others split approvals of the various departments.

Carlos: We did a little bit of both. It depends on the need. I have two editors, so we would split it up. Mike would stay with one half. I would stay with the other. We work together on shaping a sequence. He understood what was happening in my head, in which direction I was going to go. And if he had other thoughts, we would just work towards that, too. We would brainstorm on that. But then I would say, "Why don't you take over that sequence and try to shape it a little bit and then show it to me? I'll give you my notes and you can continue to work and vice versa. I'll show you what I'm working on, and if you have some thoughts, I can work on that too." So we tried to divide and conquer. I trust him so much in animation. I'd say, "Mike, just go over there and take care of it." And he would. Finding the sensibilities and what each can best contribute to the project, I think that's the key to working well together, and I think it worked out great for us.

Mike Thurmeier and Carlos Saldanha, *Ice Age: Dawn Of The Dinosaurs*, 2009 © Twentieth Century Fox. All Rights Reserved.

Tom: **Let's talk a bit about the film *Rio* (2011), because that project occupies a special place in your work history. Is it true that it was a story that originated from you?**

Carlos: Yes. It's interesting because most of the projects at Blue Sky already came with a script, or we were pitched an idea. We were given a base treatment, even though in many instances the movie that ended up being made is not exactly how it came to us. It was the seed of an existing idea. With the exception of maybe *Robots*, which was something that was started at Blue Sky, all the other movies were either based on stories like *Horton Hears a Who!*, from a book, or *Ice Age*, which came as a script from Twentieth Century Fox.

Tom: So where did *Robots* come from?

Carlos: *Robots* was an idea that we had at Blue Sky. We pitched the idea (to Fox), and after the green light it evolved from there. But *Rio*, my next project, was an idea I had since the end of *Ice Age: The Meltdown* (2006). I'm from Brazil and I'm from Rio. I always thought that the city was so photogenic, so great to shoot in. There are so many flavors and the culture is so rich. The music, the colors … Why not try to figure out a movie about Rio? I had that movie in my head, and I said, "Maybe one day I can make it." So I pitched the story and the studio liked it.

I had this dream of making a project that could portray Brazil. I can show some aspects of my culture in animation that would be not aimed only at Brazilians, but for the whole world. The idea was there, but I had to finish *Ice Age: Dawn of the Dinosaurs* (2009), so I couldn't spend too much time on it. Halfway through *Ice Age: Dawn of the Dinosaurs*, they came to me and asked, "Carlos, what about that idea that you had about Brazil? What do you think about it?" I said, "Wow, I have it in some shape or form in my head." I pitched it again and they said, "We want to make that movie, but we want that movie to be our next movie." I said "Okay, but I'm still in the middle of *Ice Age: Dawn of the Dinosaurs*." "Well, maybe you can work on it in your spare time," was their response. I was working on both projects at the same time! Lesson learned. Never work on two projects at the same time. Even though I've done it twice, don't do it! [laughs] It kills you! I did that with *Robots*. I was halfway through *Robots* until *Ice Age: The Meltdown* came along and then they said, "We need *Ice Age: The Meltdown* for 2000 ..." I don't remember the year anymore. So, I say, "Oh yeah, I can do it." I was young and inexperienced. I did it and it worked out fine. Then I said, I'm never going to do this again. In the middle of *Ice Age: Dawn of the Dinosaurs*, *Rio* came to life, and it's like, "How am I going to do them both?" So that's how it got started. But the story did take a few turns. For instance, originally I had penguins in the story. It was a year before those other films—

Development art, *Rio*, 2011 © Twentieth Century Fox. All Rights Reserved.

Tom: *Happy Feet* (2006) and then *Surf's Up* (2007).

Carlos: Yeah, and then after *Surf's Up* they said to me, "You cannot make a movie about penguins." I said, "Oh God!" There was also the DreamWorks' stuff; they put penguins in *Madagascar* (2005). So the penguin idea was out but luckily I had already created some great bird characters that I loved. I said, "Maybe I can make those characters the stars of the story ...?"

Tom: And you don't want to go back to Joe Carioca (the Brazilian parrot that debuted in Walt Disney's *The Three Caballeros* in 1942)?

Carlos: No, you don't. I didn't want to do that at all and not because I didn't like the character. I couldn't do better than that. It is a great character. But I didn't want my characters to be compared with that. So, I had to reshape the story. But still we kept the essence of my original thought. What would be the experience of going through Rio de Janeiro as an outsider? That was the essential premise. When I lived here [America], I would go back to Rio on vacation and get that little bit of a "foreign eye." You see the things that you never noticed before. Things that you took for granted you appreciate more, and the things that you always hated are still there [laughs]. I wanted to find a way to capture that experience, somehow. A fish-out-of-water story, somebody from the outside who comes to Brazil. We did that through the eyes of a bird. Even though he was from Brazil, he never lived in Brazil. It was a bird that went to Brazil and actually found his roots, found his connection to that world. I always liked that aspect of the story.

To the second part of the question, it's been much harder on this one (*Rio*) than for example *Ice Age*. In *Ice Age* it was a world that we introduced. We created a neat little package: these are the characters, this is the world that we want to come up with, this is the story that we want to tell. So I focused more on the creation of that element without the responsibility of trying to be true to anything, or trying to be true to an existing culture.

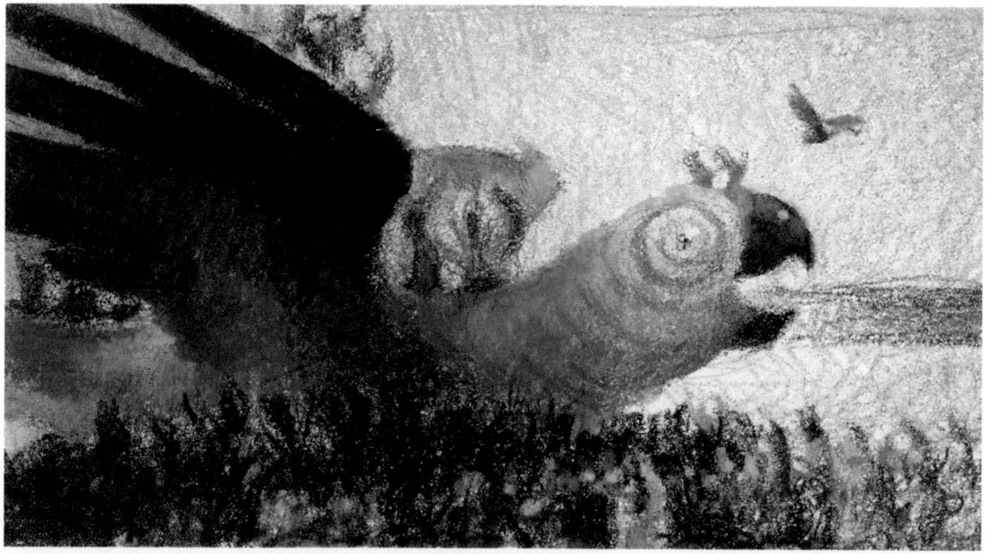

Development art, *Rio*, 2011 © Twentieth Century Fox. All Rights Reserved.

In *Rio* I'm dealing with a world and a culture that exists, a culture that I am a part of, and at the same time a culture that I need to be detached from if I want to convey it to the world. So, I couldn't be focused on what my childhood experience was, because that doesn't always apply to a childhood experience of a kid in France or in the United States. I have to find what are the common aspects of this world, of this culture, that would translate well to a global audience. I have to insert a foreigner's eye into the story. I've always tried to find a balance. What is authentic? What is stereotypical? What is good? What can I understand because I'm from there? What can't I understand? So it's been much more difficult than the other pictures.

Tom: **While dealing with this concept that you are personally invested in, how do you maintain that single vision of yours when bringing in writers, story artists, people who are coming completely from the outside?**

Carlos: The project has been much harder than the other ones because 99 percent of the crew has never been to Rio de Janeiro, or have a very limited notion of what Brazil is all about. It puts a lot more of a burden on me to try to convey what I want to tell, and that has to be reflected in the writing. It's simple things like words. When they try to put foreign words in, they put it in Spanish, but we speak Portuguese. I had to pass my knowledge along without destroying their creative process. It's very hard for them to contribute to the process because I have it all in my head, and I have to find a way to convey even a simple thing like building a sidewalk in *Rio*. I have to explain Brazilians built their sidewalks with mosaics of rocks instead of poured concrete, so it looks different than their idea of a sidewalk, et cetera.

We actually took a small crew to Rio for Carnival (*Carnaval* in Brazilian): the art director, the head of story (storyboards), the writers, the producer, the head of animation. We all went to Rio for a five-day extravaganza. When we arrived we hit the ground running. I tried to take them to the locations that I wanted to shoot, so they could understand the geography. I kept saying, you can't have a sequence here and then all of sudden, two minutes later, be over there. We were talking about completely opposite sides of town, so I drove them to all the locations. Some of the guys went hang gliding. We went to the carnival parade. We managed to do a lot of fun stuff that related to the movie. When we came back, I didn't have to explain the world so much anymore. Now the art director knew the lighting; now they knew the locations. I think it's very important to immerse yourself. To avoid the stereotypes, or if you use the stereotypes, to use them in a proper way so it doesn't become a caricature of what you're trying to say.

Tom: **Have you discovered anything new about Rio de Janeiro through the eyes of your creative team?**

Carlos: Yes. I did. I wanted them all to be like my main protagonist, Blu, the macaw from the Midwest, because they had never been to Rio. Every little thing for me that is second nature, like sidewalks, or the way people dressed, the way people go to the beach, the way people move around, the way the people talk, little things [like] that. Things that I just don't pay attention to, for them, were new. Flavors that they discovered—you know, habits that for me were natural—were awkward. When we all went to the Carnaval parade, we all had to wear a costume and we had to be basically half-naked. We were used to being in the office together with our jackets and coats. Now suddenly we had feathers on and crazy costumes all around us and we're partying and in the parade! It was weird! [laughs]

We all went to the beach one morning just to observe. We took a camera with us so we were shooting people on the beach. I think that broke stereotypes. One of my guys said to me, "Oh no, we can't go to the beach! Everybody's gonna be beautiful and gorgeous and we're gonna stand out." I reassured them, "Guys, don't worry about it. The beach is as democratic as you can think of. You're gonna see the most beautiful person here, and you're gonna see the ugliest one there, or you're gonna see an old lady in a thong. All the extremes will be there." And when we got down to the beach, they [the crew] were having the best time of their lives spotting the different kinds of people. That was something that was much more fun to discover through their eyes.

Tom: **In the process of directing, what was the most bizarre, absurd moment you've had as a director?**

Carlos: I've seen myself in embarrassing situations just for the good of the project. Carnival was interesting, because *Rio* is so close to home. It's so close to my heart that I was terrified of the trip. What if they [the crew] don't like it? If they didn't like it, it could make the process of making the movie tough. How am I gonna get them to do something fun, if they themselves didn't think it was fun? How can they create something beautiful if they didn't think it was beautiful?

But in the end the experience was much more satisfying for them than they ever expected, and Carnaval was a big part of it. I showed them videos, but because they had never been there, they never felt the sensation of being in a parade with 60,000 people watching and cheering and celebrating and dancing from nine at night till five in the morning nonstop. They and I were impressed. You know, I grew up with that stuff, but I never actually had been to a parade.

Tom: **You never danced in the Carnaval before?**

Carlos: No, I never did. My sister did, my friends did, but I never personally did it. So, I was a first-timer the same way that they were. I was terrified that they would not enjoy it. At two in the morning we were standing up, waiting, very hot, waiting for our turn to go parade in these awkward costumes. They're heavy and cumbersome, even a little painful. We were like, "Okay, let's give it a shot!" And then we went in and it was a great moment. It united us. It was towards the end of the trip and at the end we were all celebrating, "We did it! We went through the parade." It was very, very fun. But it was awkward to be next to my story artist, the head of animation, the writers, half-naked, dancing at Carnaval! [laughs]

Tom: It's funny 'cause most animation people probably have their impressions of Rio de Janeiro formed from watching Disney's *Saludos Amigos* or *Three Caballeros*.

Carlos: Yeah, well, it's a completely different place, you know. I tried to make sure that I gave them as much exposure to key elements as possible. You cannot discover Rio in five days, but you can pretty much get a sense of what you are looking for, the vibe that you're looking for, the energy that you're looking for in a movie, colors and everything. It was a great experience.

Tom: How did you approach *Rio 2*?

Carlos: When I started *Rio 2*, I wanted to continue the story. When I created Blu and Jewel, they were the last of their kind. Now I wanted to tell the story of them and their family, their kids, et cetera. I wanted them to find more of their kind. I wanted to evolve their designs and create new characters. I also wanted to get them out of the city.

Tom: How did you approach Blu and Jewel as characters for the sequel?

Carlos: It's what I like about doing a sequel. I know these characters. Now I can evolve them outside their comfort zones. That they don't stay the same. They are growing as well.

Development art, *Rio 2*, 2014 © Twentieth Century Fox. All Rights Reserved.

Tom: In the first *Rio* you showed us your city, Rio de Janeiro. *Rio 2* was more about the Amazon jungle.

Carlos: *Rio 1* was in part the portrayal of a city. The city of Rio itself was a character in the film. Now I wanted the jungle to be a character. When I brought my crew to Rio, they were all like Blu. They were alone and out of their element. For *Rio 2*, I wanted to be Blu. So I went to the jungle myself. I had never been. In fact, for many Brazilians, the Amazon is a very faraway place. I wanted to show it is an amazing place, and worthy of preservation. I wanted to show its complexity of life, its harmony. Trees and animals coexisting. It is precious. When people disrupt it and destroy that harmony, it's gone forever. You cannot simply rebuild it again like rebuilding more buildings in a city.

Tom: *Rio 2* has a lot more music in it. How do you approach directing musical numbers?

Carlos: We started working on it right away. We knew the fun part would be the musical numbers. In the first *Rio* we were locked into a certain amount of physical reality. Being in Rio. Being in Carnaval. Being in the city. But going from Rio to the Amazon allowed us to explore different rhythms. To let our imaginations go. Some places have been stylized, but I wanted people to feel as if they were in the Amazon, as in the first film they were in Rio.

Development art, *Rio 2*, 2014

Tom: Getting back to the *Ice Age* films, *Ice Age: Dawn of the Dinosaurs*, as well as *Ice Age: Continental Drift*, had such great success around the world. It surprised everybody in the Hollywood film industry. I mean, it's a good film, like the other *Ice Age* films. But this film was record-breaking in box office, with most of that coming from outside North America. There were long lines at theaters in Latin America. Why do you think this *Ice Age* struck such a chord with international audiences?

Carlos: I don't know. It's an interesting take on the market. For the longest time, studios always thought about the domestic market more than the world market. But the box office then started to take a turn. The world box office grew much more than I think the US did. Countries where you didn't have a lot of penetration suddenly became huge markets. And now a lot of the movies perform better at the box office outside the US. The *Ice Age* movies are a good example.

Tom: Why do you think that?

Carlos: I think because the movie carries a very universal language. The language of animation. Scrat has that old-fashioned way of doing pantomime with no dialogue. He reached the world without words. Another key for the success of *Ice Age* was how each country found their own talent to dub the voices into their language. They evolved quite a bit. Before that you would find dub artists that would do the voiceovers, and it would be the same kind of voices for every movie. But they're now doing casting in their own countries for the voices of the characters, and that made the movies take an extra leap. They're native. Like in Germany, the character for Sid, Otto, is a superstar, and known there now as Sid. Even though he was a very famous comedian prior to the role, now he worked into his comedy shows a bit of imitating Sid. It created this feeling of a local production, not so much an American production in Germany or an American production in Brazil. So it exploded around the world.

Tom: Do you ever run into a creative block? If so, how do you deal with it?

Carlos: Uh, I do. I can't afford them. Sometimes you have two days to come up with something or you have to solve a problem in the next day or so. I rely a lot on my crew to help when I find that I have a creative block. I try to bring the top heads of the studio together and say, "Look guys, I can't solve this. Any light at the end of the tunnel from you guys? Can you help me out?" And usually, in the brainstorm session, something comes out. Might not be the final solution, but at least it allows me to break out of my block and just find a different path. And sometimes it's a matter of coming up with something new to replace what we can't solve. But I've been very successful reaching out to my creative crew and asking them for help. But I do reach that point, you know, sometimes you're thinking of so many things or you're so stressed that you're just kind of like, "Argh, I don't know what to do!" [laughs]

Tom: I hear you on that. How often do you look at your individual sequence reels instead of the entire movie?

Carlos: I work on the sequences on a daily basis. I usually look at the whole movie maybe once a month, or when I have to prepare for a screening. My goal is to have as much of the movie up on reels as soon as I can, before production starts. But in reality, we have to start production while still finessing the script and the story. It's not the ideal scenario, but our schedules are so tight we usually don't have another option. What we try to do is fast track in production the sequences that we think will stick, and hope the story won't change too much.

Tom: At Walt Disney feature, we used to call that "feeding the beast." Putting sequences into production early so you don't have a lot of artists sitting around idle.

Carlos: Yeah, we're getting that increasingly. Part of it is, I think, because of the successes of our movies there's an expectation. It's the price you pay for maybe doing something right. Even before you start creating, they already have interest in whatever's coming out of your head. So nowadays, with the explosion of animation in the market, they have to start thinking way earlier. When there were only five animated movies a year you could take your time. There was not a lot of competition. Now it's like sixteen movies a year, you know.

Tom: Twenty-one last year (2012).

Carlos: It's insane. You pretty much have more than one movie a month out there. So the markets are going crazy. We've become [a] huge focus of promotional partners because of *Ice Age*. The minute that I said I was making a movie about Rio, we got our groups together and everybody was eager to start.

Tom: As a director, you're not only an artist but also a commander on a battlefield. You also have to be a bit of a salesman and diplomat to deal with the notes from above. How do you handle the studio creative execs?

Carlos: I understand that even though the idea might come from me or the concepts might come from me, once I put it out there and it gets taken, it becomes ours. Not theirs or mine. It becomes a collective project. So I never go into a project with a false impression that, "Close the door. I am creating!" I have to expose myself even more than I wish I could. But at the same time I'm aware of that. I prepare myself when I go into a project, knowing that there will be notes, there will be presentations, there will be conflict. But that also might be valuable. There might be some good discoveries and someone from upstairs could be my ally. I never treat the process as being Us vs. Them. I try to avoid labels and avoid conflict as much as I can, because it damages more than helps. Sometimes there are moments that I wish I didn't have to go through, and sometimes I can't wait for the moment that I can share. But it's a known process. I don't get surprised—"[gasp] Oh my

God, I have to show the movie? Oh my God, I got notes?" [laughs]. I also share the movie with the crew and I know I will get 300 pages of notes from everybody. Some notes are good, some notes are like, "Okay, are you sure you're watching the same movie I'm watching?" But it is important. It's part of the process.

Tom: **Do you ever feel pressured to outdo what you have done before, sort of like Steven Spielberg after *Jurassic Park* (1993)? Every movie of his now has to be more successful than the last.**

Carlos: If you go through the history of many film directors, it's not always consistent. You get some great gems, and then you get some that are not so good. I try to battle it every time, but I'm quite aware of that possibility. I'm very realistic about it.

Tom: **Let's get back to some of the earlier stuff that got you started. Who were some of the artists that inspired you?**

Carlos: I wasn't exposed to art as much as I wish I could have been. I always enjoyed Chuck Jones cartoons and Walt Disney stories. There are animated films that always get stuck in my head. *Bambi* has this whole chunk of my life. The fire in the forest I remember as a kid, when the father comes in and reveals the death of the mother … I like that kind of moment. A coming-of-age moment for Bambi. It always felt powerful to me. Then there's that emotional moment of *Dumbo* and his mom when they must separate. There's all these great visual moments that get stuck in my head. Scary, emotional, or comedic. *Dumbo*, *Pinocchio*, and *Bambi*, that trio of movies, stay much more vivid in my head than, say, for example, *Snow White* or some of the other classics from Disney, like *Sleeping Beauty*. Those don't stick in my head as much as those three movies do, character-wise.

Tom: **Yeah, they kind of reach inside and touch you on an emotional level.**

Carlos: I think so. I love movies, I've seen a lot of them. But, again, I keep going back to the most classic, like *Blade Runner* (1982). I think it's the only movie that I watched over thirty times. [laughs] I still like it today. If I'm flipping through the channels and that movie is playing, I have to stop and watch it. I can't help it. One day, I want to make a movie like that. Sci-fi. Oh, I'm crazy about sci-fi, like *Star Wars*, all that kind of stuff. It's got all the elements that I want.

Ron: **Any other people whose work you admire?**

Carlos: Because I've always been at Blue Sky, I never got too exposed to other studios. I admire a lot of the directors out there. I see what they're doing and try to be inspired by cinematographers and animators. John Lasseter is somebody special. I have a special feeling for him because I remember being inspired by his short *Luxo, Jr.* I remember the first year I was at Blue Sky. I was a newbie and Chris Wedge was very good friends with John. That year there was a big SIGGRAPH convention (annual computer animation society convention). It was my first SIGGRAPH. I was so excited. We came to LA and there was a Disney party. And I was like, "Oh gosh, a Disney party! We can go to a Disney party!" And when we were there, at Disneyland, they had closed down Typhoon Lagoon to the public just for our party. I went with Chris and I remember it was at one of the rides. Suddenly John Lasseter was right there. I was so nervous when I shook his hand. I was thinking, "Wow, this is great! Three years ago when I was in Brazil packing my bags, trying to come to the United States, I never thought I would even pass close to somebody like that!" It was one of those little moments that I still remember, you know, as silly it might be. It was cool. I admire Brad Bird quite a bit, too. I think his projects are brilliant. I remember going to a screening of *Iron Giant* in New York. The movie wasn't fully finished yet, but we got invited because one of our producers had worked on it. Brad was there and I remember going through that experience, "Wow, I wish one day I could have a movie playing …" I admire those guys for the milestones that they set in animation. I can always look at their work and be blown away by what they can do.

Tom: Do you now mentor young people yourself?

Carlos: When I was studying animation at SVA, I started to teach to make my tuition more manageable. I enjoyed it so much I continued it even after I started working at Blue Sky. I always felt it was a great way to interact with the animators and hopefully mentor them in their creative process. Actually, the best part of it was that I was also inspired by their ideas and excitement for the craft. Unfortunately I don't teach anymore, but I feel that at Blue Sky or at the talks I give at festivals I am able to continue to influence or inspire new talent.

Tom: You started as an animator. Do you ever miss animating?

Carlos: I do. Sometimes I catch myself thinking, how would I animate that shot? But now I'm so rusty that I'm terrified of the idea. The animators that I have now are so much better than I was. [laughs] I can remember my thinking process when I went through animation, like the curves and the way to play with the timing. I still have the presets in my head. After a while it just comes to you second nature. You know how to achieve a hand gesture or a head take. I still have those in my head, and I keep thinking, "Will that still work? If I tried to sit down and do it?"

Tom: CG animation today is this kind of technological arms race. Every year, there seems to be new software and programs that are faster and more powerful. How important do you feel it is to be personally on top of the latest gadgetry, or are you at the point now where you can tell the animators what you need?

Carlos: I kind of gave up that quest for knowing everything awhile back, I think maybe on *Ice Age: The Meltdown*, because I couldn't keep up. So I focused on trying to keep the essence of what my knowledge is and not try to work it all out myself. I just let it be up to them, animators and tech support, to discover.

Ron: What you are trying to achieve as a filmmaker is telling good stories. As you mentioned, *Rio* is the first movie of your own creation that really reflects your personal vision. When it comes to story, is there a theme that you are looking to express, some kind of underling concept that you want to show?

Carlos: When I think about a story, I always start thinking about the emotional drive behind it. What is the pathos that you get from the character? How do you relate your life to their lives?

But I always try to take a light-hearted approach to it. I have a hard time conceiving something too dark. Not that I don't enjoy dark stories, I love them, but when I create something in my head, I just don't go there naturally. Tim Burton does it beautifully, and I love his movies. They are a perfect combination of darkness, fun, and emotion. I love his creative take on it. My creative process tends to be much more animated, less dialogue, much more [swashbuckling] fun. A lot of movement, a lot of contraptions, a lot of fun stuff to do. I always look at Charlie Chaplin and Buster Keaton as my reference for animation.

Character design, *Rio*, 2011 © Twentieth Century Fox. All Rights Reserved.

Tom: It's interesting that when we talked about this to Chris Wedge, he talked a lot about giving the audience a good experience. It's something that the audience will enjoy, and then you reiterate that theme in terms of broad audience appeal.

Carlos: I start a project with that in mind. You are making a movie as a collaborative effort with the studio. The end goal for all of us is a successful piece of work that our audience will enjoy. It's important for me to feel like I've made something I can stand behind and believe in. I always feel like the movie is somewhat mine. My creative juices go into it. The movie comes from my head, and from my creative team. But I'm always making the movie for a broad audience, not just America, not just Brazil, but for the world. I'm aware of my responsibilities, both to myself and to the audience.

That's why I'm a super fan of shorts. That's what I tell students when they come to me. I say, "Do a short movie and put your heart and soul into it. That will probably be the only time that you'll make a movie that is 100 percent yours." I still look at my old reels and I think, "Even though it's not perfect, the animation is not great, and the story could be better, it's still my baby. Who cares? It's an ugly baby, but I love my baby!" [laughs] So I have pride in that. I take pride in the struggle. I take pride in being able to do something without a lot of help.

Tom: Is there a short film you've seen in your past that might stand out as a classic?

Carlos: A short movie that I have close to my heart is something that represents a milestone in my creative process and my transition to computers. It was *Luxo, Jr.*, John Lasseter's short. When I saw that movie, in my head all the possibilities opened up. I could create a simple story. I could make inanimate objects come to life and make it look realistic. The fun, the comedy, and the emotion were packed into that little movie. It was short, sweet, and great to look at. Every time I look at that movie I feel a little nostalgia. It's how I got started. This is how I got excited about computer animation. And it gave me enough juice to go after my dream to become a director.

Tom: You have directed several films now. How have you evolved as a filmmaker?

Carlos: Every film you make feels like it's your first. Each time I'm thinking, "Holy shit! How am I gonna do this?" [laughs] It doesn't get easier, because every new movie you want to be better than the previous ones. But I am completely happy with that in myself. I think over the years I have become better at fighting for what I want in a picture. You can't put things in a movie that you do not like, because you are going to have to live with that film for years after. I think I am better at determining what kind of movie I want to make.

Tom: Do you have any closing thoughts on directing?

Carlos: I admire the directors that come from artistic backgrounds, like the guys that came from life drawing, or music, or those kinds of backgrounds. I didn't come from that kind of background. I was never trained on paper. I could never draw too well. To my parents I was Picasso! But for myself, I wasn't like the animators that could draw those beautiful pictures. I could never do it. I was never trained to do it. I always felt a bit embarrassed about it. Originally, I came from a technical background. When I sat down at the computer I could model something or could create something that was in my head without compromises. I just made it. It was easy. I said, "WOW! This is the tool I need to be creative. I don't need to draw.

I need to work on the computer." That is why I was so happy when I discovered computer animation, because I could act on a lot of instinct that was my own. It's a natural ability that might not be as polished or maybe not as perfect technically. But I have a gut feeling, and I made that part of my creative process. I have to trust, even with all the forces that work around all the notes; the crew, and me. I have to make sure my gut instinct remains intact. That's how I became what I am, by simply trusting in what I thought was aesthetically right. And it paid off. All the times that I had to second-guess, everything became mushy and I wasn't as connected to it. So I strive to preserve that first look.

Tom: Well, great, that's wonderful. We are done. *Obrigado.*

Carlos: *De nada.*

Carlos Saldanha, *Rio*, 2011 © Twentieth Century Fox. All Rights Reserved.

11

Kevin Lima Interview

Kevin Lima *Enchanted* © Disney.

When word got out that Kevin Lima was chosen to direct *A Goofy Movie*, a lot of us had the same reaction: "Kevin's a good animator, so he'll make a good director." But Kevin was bringing a lot more to the table than his time behind the drawing disc.

As we all eventually learned, this upbeat, positive guy had a remarkable personal story and a very unusual pathway to success. He not only embodied the essential qualities of the animation journeyman, but touched on a lot of other skills, from character designer to storyboarding to animating. All of these accomplishments added to his quiver of talents, but none of them satisfying his creative goals.

Directing *Goofy* became his revelation. He found that those years spent working his way through the hands-on pipeline of production were the perfect foundation for directing animation. On the relatively low-budget *Goofy* movie, he was given a rare freedom to make most of the decisions, and he loved it.

But Kevin discovered that the talent that would ultimately bring him the most success was not one that he had learned through experience or "pencil mileage," but one that came by pure instinct: his natural empathy with performers.

It's amusing to hear him assert that he had absolutely no training that qualified him to direct a live-action film (*102 Dalmatians*), but in that evaluation he echoes the experience of every director in this book. The qualities of the veteran animation director, from visualizing imagery to expressing a powerful, personal vision, are essential ingredients of success. But no amount of work or practice can supply that elusive ingredient of talent. Kevin has that sensitivity, and sensibility, to create an entrancing performance.

We interviewed Kevin at Pixar Animation Studios.

Bill Kroyer

Bill: When did you first become aware of animation as something that you might see yourself being interested in doing?

Kevin: My interest goes way back. I can't remember a time when I wasn't interested, to be quite honest with you. My mom tells a story about how I went to see *The Jungle Book* with her, and when the movie was over I turned to her and said, "That's what I'm going to do when I grow up!" And she kind of nodded and said, "Yeah, yeah, that's great, Kevin. You just go ahead and do that." I think I was five. And here I am today, having followed that dream. I was one of those rare kids that drew from the time … you know I can't remember not drawing. I can't remember not being creative. I can't remember not wanting to be in animation.

Bill: Where did you grow up?

Kevin: We lived in Pawtucket, Rhode Island, a little mill town just north of Providence. And we were fairly poor. We didn't have much money at all. My mom worked at the toy company Hasbro when I was a kid. I used to ride my bike to the Hasbro factory on a Sunday morning and jump the fence and dig through the trash compactor to see if I could find discarded toys. My grandmother was really influential in that she was the one who was always encouraging me to be an artist. She was the one who spent time with me because my parents were both working. She got me into puppetry pretty early on, so at a very young age—I was about twelve—I became a puppeteer. I made all of my own puppets, I wrote the shows and did all of the voices. So I've always, always had a storytelling streak.

Bill: When did you start figuring out how animation was done?

Kevin: I didn't make films. I didn't have the money to make films. So I went into puppetry pretty heavily. At the age of fourteen I joined a professional puppetry troupe in Rhode Island called *The Puppet Workshop*. I was their intern. I started directing the shows at age sixteen. And then in high school, I had an art teacher, Mr. Venditto, who said, "You know what? You should really follow your love of cartooning and go into animation." He was the one who did the research and found CalArts for me. But my first year of college, I didn't go. My first year out of high school I said, "No. I'm gonna go into theater." I had caught the theater bug. I went to Emerson College in Boston, spent a year attempting to act and said, "This isn't the life for me. I can't do this." And in the second semester of that year applied to CalArts and got in. Basically what I did for my portfolio was design a film. I didn't shoot the film, but I designed the film, designed all the characters, and drew a little storyboard. And it was my only hope. If I didn't get in at CalArts, I didn't know what I was gonna do.

Kevin Lima at CalArts.

Bill: Was it the only place you applied?

Kevin: It was the only place I applied.

Bill: So you show up for fall semester, you've never been there …

Kevin: I'd never animated! I knew the basic principles from having drawn from the Preston Blair animation book, but I had never animated.

Bill: **So how was that year?**

Kevin: You know what? It was a phenomenal group of students, I have to say.

Bill: **It was that second wave.**

Kevin: I was in the class that graduated just as Disney had stopped hiring new talent. I was at the end of the big first Disney push to hire animators. Rob Minkoff was there, Gary Trousdale, Gary Conrad, Chris Bailey, and Kelly Asbury were in the class ahead of me. My classmates were Kirk Wise, Tim Hauser, Dan Jeup, Steve Moore, and Fred Kline. And we were all very determined students. We said to ourselves, "We're gonna be somebody." And it's amazing; you look at that group of people and see how many of them have actually made movies. It's a phenomenal number of successful, talented artists.

Bill: **Talk a little bit about your learning experience at CalArts. You'd never animated. Did you pick it up fast?**

Kevin: I had some draftsmanship skills, so I could draw, a bit, which made it a little easier. But I'll tell you, we all learned from each other. And that was tough. I was talking about this the other day with someone who went to college at Sheridan. They started learning the basics from the first day they showed up at school. A bouncing ball, animating a potato sack, all that stuff. We didn't learn any of that! When we got to school, they threw a cleaned-up scene at you and said, "Inbetween this scene." And most of us had never done anything like that before. So we'd inbetween the scene, shoot it on the Lion Lamb videotape recorder, and we all thought we were geniuses 'cause we could put a line between two other lines. There was one kid in my class, Dan Jeup, who came in knowing quite a bit. While in high school, Dan had written to and started a relationship with one of the nine old men, Eric Larson. So he knew a bunch, and he taught us a bunch. And the upperclassmen taught us a bunch. We really didn't have an animation teacher, per se, and we just sort of struggled through it, learning from each other.

Let's Misbehave.

Bill: **And you made films, right?**

Kevin: We all made films. I think I made three films in my four years.

Bill: So the undergraduates felt you were a reasonably decent animator?

Kevin: I didn't think I was any good. But I thought I could handle it. I got lucky. In my fourth year, we all worked freelance at the Disney studio on a project called *Sport Goofy*. I was assigned Chris Buck as a supervising animator, and he basically put me through animation boot camp. The project was giving us scenes and treating us like we were animators, but very few of us had ever animated professionally.

Bill: When you graduated, what did you do?

Kevin: I went to work on *The Brave Little Toaster*. It's the first full-time job I had in animation, with Jerry Rees directing. It was a bunch of kids like me makin' a film. Joe Ranft was there. Randy Cartwright was there. Rebecca Rees and Brian McEntee were there. And I got really lucky because Jerry let me do some character design. After five or six months of designing in LA, I went to Taiwan for six months.

Bill: Were you animating?

Kevin: I had designed the characters so they thought, "Oh, he knows how to put them together, so let's have him animate." So I animated a bunch of it. My first experience and I'm trying to animate thirty feet a week!

Bill: Thirty feet a week!?

Kevin: That was rough! But it was a grand adventure. I got to go to a new country, something I never thought I'd do. I thought I'd be sitting at Disney in one of those cushy little offices, but nope! Out into the world and making it happen.

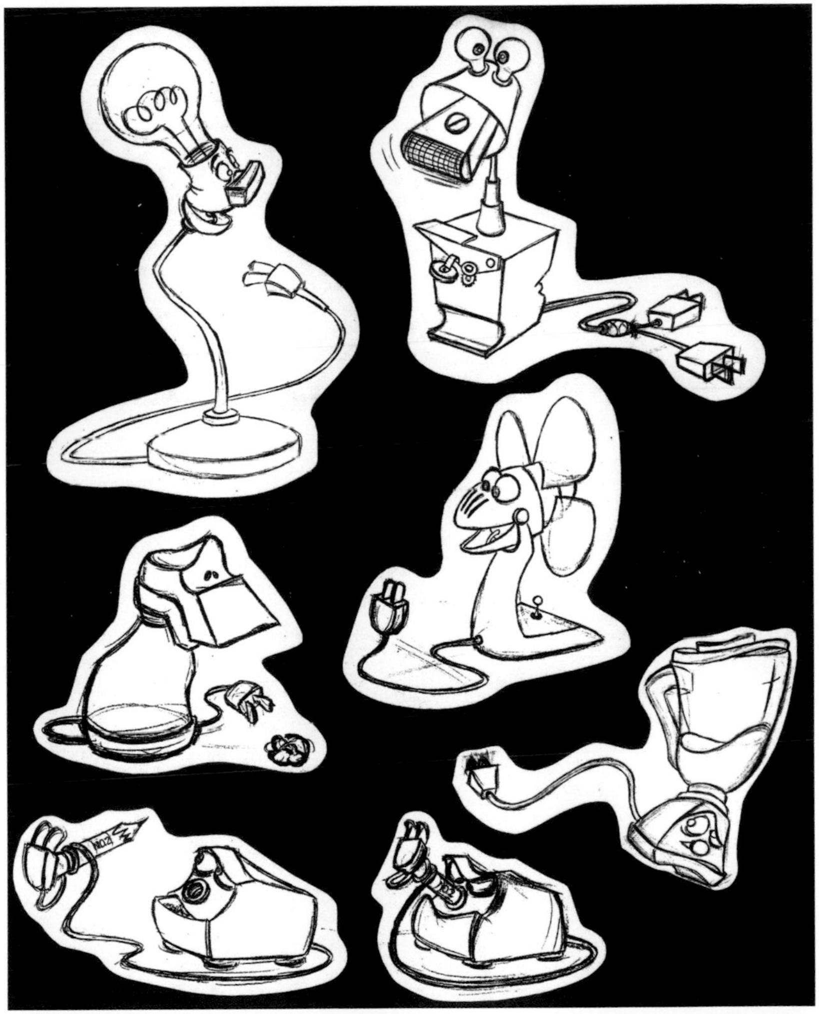

Character designs, *The Brave Little Toaster*, 1987 © Disney.

Bill: So *Toaster* is over, what happens then?

Kevin: *Toaster*'s over, and Jerry Rees is developing future projects at Hyperion, three or four different films, but none of them caught fire. So I went to work on *The Chipmunk Adventure* with the Bagdasarians.

Bill: Oh, that's right, Sue [Kroyer] was there. And …

Kevin: Sue was there, yep. And Glen Keane! And it was a big break for me because I got to animate some Chipette scenes, they're the female Chipmunks, under the tutelage of Glen Keane. It was humbling because I actually thought I knew something at this point. I had been to Taiwan and I had animated thirty feet a week! I'm bringing my scenes to Glen Keane and suddenly you realize, you don't know anything. You're back at square one. I had received such minimal training and I was struggling through, just basically making it up to meet each deadline. Each scene was a brand new experience. I had no chops.

Bill: It's just as valuable to learn what you don't know. To know how far there is left for you to go.

Kevin: To be quite honest with you, I get that lesson every single day. Even what I'm doing right now, directing live action, I realize, "Boy, I just know so little!"

Bill: Did Glen's style, that aspect of entertainment animation, that sophistication, did that start to get through to you at that point?

Kevin: I was overwhelmed working with Glen. His craft, his ability to draw; his ability to act was overwhelming. He could draw anything from any angle and I couldn't do that. The eternal struggle of being an animator is how you take what you see in your mind's eye and have it come through your hand into a pencil onto the paper. How do you communicate it in a way that everyone else understands? I was really lucky having worked with Glen. Not only that every day was a master class in animation, but when he went back to Disney, he said to the management, "You should hire this kid."

Bill: And that's how you went back.

Kevin: Well, I was never there to begin with. I was in that first class at Disney that no one was hired by the studio. So, I just took all the drawings I had done up to that point, put them into a portfolio, and I handed it in, and their reaction was, "Where have you been?" I remember, I was told Ed Hansen, the production administrator at the time, at Disney, asked at a portfolio review, "Whe has this kid been all these years? Why don't we know about him?" Well, I was at CalArts and you looked at my portfolio and you rejected me. That's where I've been! So I was hired to work on *Oliver & Company* as an animator.

Bill: And you were paid an assistant salary?

Kevin: I was happy to be paid at all. And it was slow at the beginning on *Oliver*, so I got a lucky break, and got to do a bunch of character designs on *The Little Mermaid* for directors John Musker and Ron Clements, which was great. Once animation on

Oliver got up and running, I went to work full time as an animator and struggled, and struggled. I was one of those guys that, you know, was doing one point five feet of film a week at Disney.

Bill: Not quite thirty feet a week …

Kevin: And sitting behind that desk, day and night, trying to pull it together. Trying to figure out how to make it work at Disney. I was kind of in trouble. Trying to figure out who I was, and is this really what I wanted? Am I doing the thing that I had dreamed about? Is it what I thought it would be? Only getting to work on this one little sliver of something? As opposed to when I was a kid, designing and directing a whole puppet show, a forty-five minute performance!

Bill: So how long did you stay on *Oliver*?

Kevin: I worked on the whole movie. Then I said, "You know, I'm not having a good time. I'm not happy. I'm not fast. You're not happy with me. Can I do something else?" And that's when Mike Gabriel and Hendel Butoy took me on board *The Rescuers Down Under* as character designer.

Bill: Is that where you met Brenda?

Kevin: No, Brenda and I met at school. I was a senior and she was a freshman.

Bill: But you got married on *Rescuers*.

Kevin: We got married while we were both working on *The Rescuers Down Under*. In 1988. Yeah, designing away and having basically the time of my life, to be quite honest with you, having a really good time. I love to develop character, to have it all come together in one drawing, to not be limited by your ability to act with a pencil! Not just to breathe life into something over many drawings, but to look at one drawing and create a personality. That was easier for me.

Brenda Chapman and Kevin Lima.

Bill: Very directorial.

Kevin: It is. You have much more control over the moment. You're not being handed something and being told what to do. You're there at the birth of something extraordinary.

Bill: So *Rescuers* finishes …

Kevin: I went into development for a little while. Worked a little bit on the very beginnings of *The Lion King* and on a couple of different titles in development. And then *Aladdin* came along and I took on a new challenge and became part of the story team. I became a storyboard artist. I think you can sort of sense a theme here of not being able to stay with one thing for very long. So I traveled from one thing to another to another, and I'd last a good year and a half, two years on each endeavor, then totally burn out and be looking for the next thing. So, at this point I became a story artist on *Aladdin*. I really enjoyed it. I had done character design at the beginning of *Aladdin*, and then I took those characters and started to explore them in a story context. I had gotten to know Howard Ashman a little bit while exploring character designs of Ursula on *The Little Mermaid*. I was really into musical theater, so I approached him and got to know him a bit. On *Aladdin* I was lucky enough to get to storyboard a couple of songs that he and Alan Menken had written for the movie, and that was a great thrill. When that was done I said, "Okay, what's next?"

Character design, Ursula, Kevin Lima, *The Little Mermaid*, 1989 © Disney.

Bill: You're going through director boot camp here. You're animating, you're designing, you're storyboarding …

Kevin: I only realized that at the end of the road. I had no idea I was doing that, collecting a full education, as I was doing it. I realized while working on *Aladdin* that I "wanna do it all!" After *Aladdin*, I had started animating on an Epcot film called *Cranium Command*. While struggling to animate again, I met a Production Assistant on the project, Kevin Traxler, who was producing community theatre. He approached me and asked, "Hey, you wanna direct a show?" So I ended up directing a community theatre version of *Into the Woods*, the musical by Stephen Sondheim and James Lapine. And when it was done, I thought, "Boy, this is so much more exciting and immediate!" And the folks at Disney all came out and saw it. And I said to myself, "Ah, this is my moment." And I went to the executive group, the folks that controlled all of our futures at Disney, and proclaimed, "I wanna direct! That's what I wanna do; that's my next step." And they basically said to me, "You know, Kev, there's no room at the inn. There are no movies for you to direct. We don't have a spot." So I said, "Okay. See you later." And I left, went out into the big world trying to find another inn. I approached Tom Wilhite at Hyperion Studios, where I had worked on *The Brave Little Toaster*, and said, "Hey, do you have anything going on?" And he said, "Yeah, come on! Let's develop some stuff." But nothing ever got off the ground. And then I did some freelance storyboard work for Jerry Rees on a project over at Disney Television. And when Jerry decided not to direct it, they asked me.

Bill: And that was ...?

Kevin: *A Goofy Movie.*

Bill: Back at Disney. Now you get your chance to direct.

Kevin: I'm directing.

Bill: And what crew were they going to give you on that? Not Disney Feature Animation ...

Kevin: No, no. *A Goofy Movie* was a television animation project and I moved to Paris for close to a year to animate that movie.

Bill: That's right, they did it in Paris.

Kevin: We storyboarded the whole thing stateside and then brought it to Paris for production. And I lived there and dealt with the hardships of living in Paris? Come on! You could be in a lot worse places. And I had the privilege of working with a great group of talented people, who I continued to work with on all of the animated projects that I've been on. And we made this little teeny movie for no money and I got my directorial debut.

Bill: You were your own head of story, right?

Kevin: While in the states storyboarding the film, I worked with Brian Pimental, my head of story and between the two of us we tackled a difficult subject. The goal for me was to create a different kind of animated film. I thought: why can't we make a movie that feels like a John Hughes movie? Why can't we do something that's purely character-based with a modern thread, with a modern dynamic between our characters? And it just happens that your lead is Goofy.

Character design, Kevin Lima, *Aladdin*, 1992 © Disney.

Bill: **Because it was a lower budget film, did you have a lot of creative freedom?**

Kevin: Yeah. I really felt like I was running the show. I was a singular director. It wasn't a team of directors, as there had always seemed to be on the Disney features. And in fact, maybe it made it harder for me later on, when I moved up to play with the big boys. I got to decide everything. I got to choose my cast. I got to pick my songwriters. If I was dissatisfied with where the story was going, then I was the one responsible for standing up for it and saying, "This isn't working yet."

Bill: **This is under Jeffrey [Katzenberg], am I right?**

Kevin: Yeah. Jeffrey is still at Disney at this point. And I'd show the film to Jeffrey, usually at 7:30 in the morning. You know, [laughs] it wasn't that bad. I didn't have to come in on Sundays. And he had his notes, but because we were so low budget, he knew there was barely anything he could do. I remember at one point he wanted to change the climax of the film because it wasn't exciting enough for him. So we sat together at the Avid, and it ended up staying exactly the way it was. 'Cause he'd take stuff out and try to move stuff around, and because we couldn't afford to add animation, he agreed, "Yeah, your way is better."

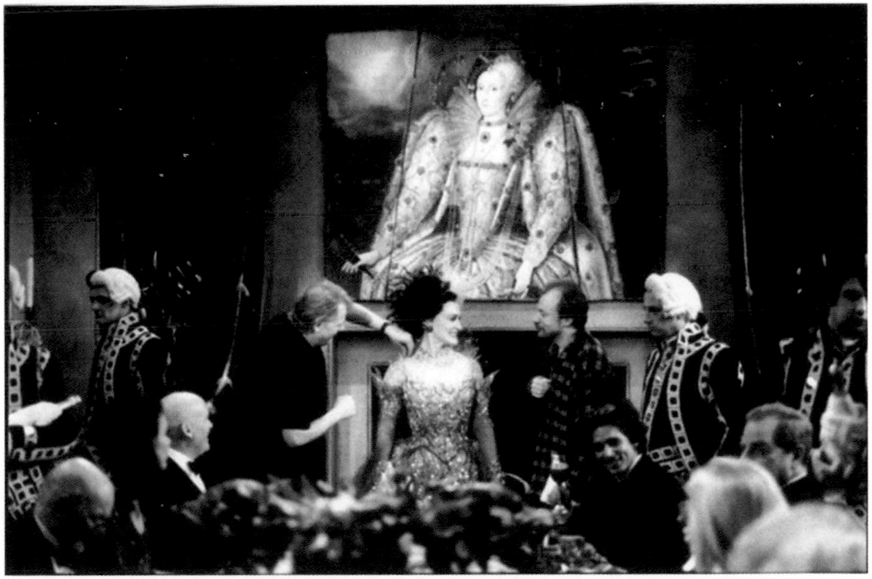

Kevin Lima directing Glen Close, *102 Dalmations*, 2000 © Disney.

Bill: **Language problems in Paris?**

Kevin: No. I have some acting ability. So when I couldn't speak to somebody with words, I would act it out. And it's typically what I'd always done anyway, you know? I even do it when I'm directing live action. So, I talk to Amy Adams and I'm acting like Giselle, and the guys behind the camera are flipping the camera on to catch footage of me going around with my little pinkies up. But that's what I do. I talk to them as actors, and the easiest way is to "become." I was able to wear the character while directing.

Bill: That was your first experience actually directing a crew of animators.

Kevin: That was.

Bill: So your style is more like directing as an actor than directing like an animator.

Kevin: It was. I didn't tell people how many drawings needed to be from "here to here," or "there's not enough cushion." I didn't do any of that. I never tell an actor to put their hand "up here" and then "Let your wrist lead as you slap him across the face!" I would never do that. It's more about the subtext and what's happening inside and how do we take what's happening inside and make it external? How do we communicate ideas? In fact, it's how I became a live-action director. When I was directing Glenn Close in *Tarzan* she said, "You know, you direct more like a live-action director than an animation director. Have you ever thought about doing a live-action film?" I answered immediately, "Sure!" And when *102 Dalmatians* lost its director late in preproduction, and I was out looking for a directing gig, she asked the studio, "What about Kevin?"

Bill: Glenn Close got you the gig?

Kevin: Yep.

Bill: You have no formal training.

Kevin: I have no formal director training. There are days I wish I had a mentor I'll tell ya. There are days I bemoan, "Boy, I wish I had hounded Robert Zemeckis and gotten him to let me sit on the set with him." You hear about all those guys who got their chops directing television and working under some of the best directors in the business and really learned

Tarzan, 1999 © 1999 Burroughs and Disney.
Tarzan® Owned by ERB, Inc and Used by Permission.

some craft. I, unfortunately, had to make it up on the floor. So, I have a different skill set. Part of it comes from being a puppeteer and having acted on stage. Working with actors as I did in community theatre. Directing animators. My skill set is what I've picked up along the way.

Bill: On *A Goofy Movie*, your first experience, how did you deal with art direction and production design?

Kevin: You hire the best people. And have an opinion. [laughs]

Bill: That's a good one-liner.

Kevin: We were at a little bit of a disadvantage with *A Goofy Movie*, because the most seasoned people in the business weren't going to leave their high profile gigs to work on *A Goofy Movie*. We gathered a group of talented young artists who, like me, were in need of an opportunity. As we dove into making the film, we collected all we had learned individually, color theory, camera psychology, how the pace of three scenes put together can mean more than one scene sitting on its own, and put it all to practice.

Bill: So when the movie is over, now you have the director bug?

Kevin: Yeah, I was definitely bitten. At this point, Jeffrey Katzenberg still at Disney before starting DreamWorks Animation, asks me to do *Tarzan*. But he wants me to do it in a new studio that they're going to open in Vancouver, Canada. And I said to him, "Jeffrey, come on. With a new group of folks in Paris we could barely animate *Goofy*. How do you expect me to animate a naked man?"

Tarzan, 1999 © 1999 Burroughs and Disney.
Tarzan ® Owned by ERB, Inc and Used by Permission.

Bill: [laughs]

Kevin: And we were talking about that when Jeffrey left. And Michael Eisner, I think to keep me from following Jeffrey, called me in and said, "We're going to make *Tarzan*. We want you to direct it." So another opportunity comes my way.

Bill: **And when did Chris Buck come on the project?**

Kevin: From the beginning I said, "I want to direct *Tarzan* alone." And they said, "We don't do that here at Feature Animation. We always have a team. It's too much work for one person to do." And I looked around and thought, "Who can I stand being with for four or five years? Who would be a good match?" In the same way that you choose your wife, this is gonna be your professional wife, and you're gonna live with this person; you're gonna have to share a vision. It's hard enough for one person to have a vision. How do two people share a vision? I knew that I wasn't gonna be able to give up any piece of the process, you know? I knew that I was gonna want to look at every piece of art and be a part of the discussion on everything. So I was thinking, who is that guy? I had worked with Chris twice before and we were friends, so I thought, "he and I could do this." We've always shared a sensibility. We've always had great, honest conversations about so many different topics. So I asked him. And I said, "But this is how it's got to work. We're both going to be involved in everything."

Bill: **What was the toughest part of that movie? You went to Africa.**

Kevin: That was not the toughest part of making the movie. Yes, we went to Kenya and Uganda and sat with the mountain gorillas in the Bwindi Impenetrable National Park.

Bill: **Worth the trip?**

Kevin: It awakened my sense of the natural world around me and I realized while I was trudging through the jungle that the world could be a character within the movie in a way that I'd never really thought about before. And while in Uganda, Dan St. Pierre and I started the conversation about Deep Canvas, a process created specifically for *Tarzan*. All those conversations started in Africa. We talked about, How do you put the characters in the world? How do you create a sense that you could step through the picture plane into the world; that you weren't watching it from afar? Maybe that conversation would never have happened if we hadn't gone on that trip. Sure, we could have animated gorillas; we could have looked at footage of gorillas and figured that out. But to actually feel what it was like to be in that place and step on that ground, influenced so much. Jane's entrance in that movie, of being totally out of sorts, comes from our trip. 'Cause we were trudging through the jungle and it was difficult.

Bill: So you're given an assignment to picture it, but it's not an original vision yet. You need to find the vision …

Kevin: The vision started with the book by Edgar Rice Burroughs. But each participant, each collaborator, has to find their own original vision. Getting back to what was the most difficult part of making the film for me. I wanted to direct. But so did everyone else on the picture. Every storyboard artist wants to direct. Every layout artist wants to direct. Every animator wants to direct. Every artist involved wants to direct his piece of the film. He doesn't really want to be directed. I'm gonna be in trouble for saying this, aren't I? [laughs] So, you're fighting ten different people all wanting their imprint on the material, and you're trying to create one vision for a movie. And I got in trouble time and time again, struggling against that. Because I said, "No, no, no. I'm the director. I get to have it my way. I hold the vision for this movie. I can't expand this acting moment because it will throw off the rhythm of the scene. The gorillas can't be purple because it will destroy the sense of realism. I can't let the story go in that direction over there, because it will totally feel like a canker on the side of a movie that's moving in this direction." So I fought to hold onto the directorial vision of the film a lot.

Bill: Was Chris feeling that same struggle that you were feeling?

Kevin: I don't know if he felt it as viscerally as I felt. Looking back at the animation process through the live-action lens, one of the hardest things is pulling together three or four different people to create one character. The designer, the animator, the cleanup artist, the voice talent. Your character is split in four different directions. And I think it's really the job of an animation director to get all of those disciplines synthesized.

Glenn Close, Kevin Lima, *102 Dalmatians*, 2000. © 2000 Disney.

Bill: Did you guys ever crash and burn on *Tarzan*?

Kevin: We didn't have a story crash and burn. We had our struggles, but we never threw out half the film and started over. I think I got lucky because *The Lion King* stage show was going on at the same time we were producing *Tarzan*. So all those eyes that were typically worrying at your movie were distracted by their new toy. And that new toy is shiny and exciting, and sparkly, you know? And it's more in their wheelhouse. The theater is where they all came from. Most of our leadership came from the theatre, so they were thrilled to be back on the boards. *Tarzan* also happened in the moment when Jeffrey left the studio. Jeffrey is trying desperately to pull away talent. Disney is trying desperately to hold onto talent. So our movie got incredibly expensive. I think we have the honor of being the most expensive 2D animated film ever made.

Bill: *Tarzan*? Really?

Kevin: I'm pretty sure, or at least that's what I was told. Because of the studio's need to not have Jeffrey succeed, artists who were making four thousand dollars a week are now making ten. And that money has gotta come from somewhere, so they added it to *Tarzan*'s budget.

Bill: That's tough.

Kevin: Yeah, I won't take off my shirt and show you the scars. [laughs] The real hardship of that movie was, how do you hold onto a creative vision when the costs are escalating—and escalating in the middle of production?

Bill: Everybody comments how scenes and sequences can be perceived differently as they move through the pipeline. When you finally see it in final color with effects, there's a different vibe to it. Did you have any wonderful surprises or perplexing disappointments in your first big movie?

Kevin: We had an idea to do a song in which the apes took over the human camp, and it turns into this big *Stomp*-esque number. And we thought, "Ah, this will be hugely original. No one's ever done this before in animation!" And we wrote a song with Phil Collins, and we were all really thrilled and happy. And then as it moved through the process, I started to get this pit in my stomach that it wasn't gonna be what I had hoped, that it wasn't gonna be a highlight. We had trouble boarding it. We had this song we loved, we had this idea we thought could be really great, but we had a lot of trouble boarding it. And, tonally, I realized when it was in color, in the final film, that it just didn't speak in the same voice as the rest of the movie.

Bill: But the balance of course is that it was a tremendously successful movie.

Kevin: Yes, the movie did incredibly well.

Bill: So, now you've done a big movie …

Kevin: Yep. And I'm still not satisfied. [laughs]

Bill: You're hoping that Hollywood will call …

Kevin: And it just happens that the stars aligned again for me.

Bill: Glenn Close …

Kevin: That was the Glenn Close recommendation I spoke about earlier. She recommends me to direct *102 Dalmatians* and I thought, "Okay, this is gonna be good because, you know, she'll look out for me. She'll help me." I talked to her about it. I said, "You know, I've never been on a live-action set. I've never done this before. I appreciate you giving me this recommendation, but what I really need is for you to be my teacher."

Bill: You said that to Glenn Close?

Kevin: I did.

Bill: And she said?

Kevin: She said, "I believe in you, let's do it."

Bill: Did she teach you a lot about directing?

Kevin: She taught me a lot about how to interact with actors in the moment on the set. She didn't teach me about cameras or lights or all that other technical stuff, which was also TOTALLY alien to me. In fact, I just sort of said to everyone supporting me, "I need your help." I hired a DP and I said to him, "You know, I've never done this specific process before and need you to educate me." So my first film became my training ground.

Bill: That's a gigantic step from animation director.

Kevin: It was big.

Bill: The whole nomenclature is totally different.

Kevin: Everything about it is different. Everything about it. I mean, what's totally different is that everything leads to this one moment in time, in which you capture something. Whereas in animation, it's not a single moment; it's multiple moments in time that you're hoping will all come together at the end. So it's a completely different sensibility.

Bill: What did Glenn Close tell you about working with actors on the set that was valuable to you?

Kevin: I don't know if there was any specific one thing. What she really taught me was to treat every actor as an individual, understand what that actor needs in that moment. You have to figure out what you need to be for each actor. Do you need to be a therapist and just listen, do you need to be a father and give unconditional love, do you need to be a disciplinarian and, you get it. And what they need may be different on different days. She taught me to look at each actor as an individual and be able to tell when he or she walks on the set, what the dynamic is, what the temperature is for that day, how to change your approach. Don't be totally locked down to only one way of doing something. Treat the process like it's an organic, growing, ever-changing relationship. And I think I already had a little bit of that going on. I think that's what she saw in me during the *Tarzan* voice recording sessions. That I could see when she was struggling with a scene as Kala, and I could make a suggestion that an actor would understand. I could make an acting-based comment as opposed to asking for a result. Which a lot of animation directors do. "It's kind of slow, could you speed it up? Or, "Could you give me another one that's different?" I was asking her for motivations. I was asking her, "Okay, now I want you to come in and I want you to kill the person across from you."

Bill: [chuckle]

Kevin: And she'd come in with a fury. Because that was the subtext of the scene. "I want to KILL you!"

Bill: Do you think those directorial suggestions would be applicable to working with animators as well?

Kevin: For sure. And I was doing it. I didn't know I was doing it. I didn't realize it. I didn't have the formal training to know that actors think in action verbs. And that the scene is made up of a series of action verbs strung together to create conflict and emotion and shape a scene. I didn't know any of that. But I was doing it. So maybe I was lucky in some ways to have picked up some of that. From my year acting at Emerson College and some of it must have come from the years of puppetry I did way back when.

Bill: I imagine you boarded the film, right?

Kevin: We boarded a lot of *102 Dalmatians*. And I found that boarding is one of the tools that I bring over from animation. Being a visual thinker I have to board the film in order to understand the characters and arrive on set prepared to talk to the actors. The boarding is not just about layout for me. It's not just about how the scenes link together, and how the cutting works from scene to scene. It's about, "Who is that character in the moment and how does that character live through the body of the film?" It's hard for me to get that strictly from the written word. I don't know how, honestly, to dissect a script in that way—in the way that an actor would, because I don't have that training. My training is to dissect the film and gain understanding through storyboards. I learned from *102 Dalmatians* ... that I have to hold onto the pieces of the animation process that make me successful. I can't let go of those things. They're an important part of who I am as a live-action director. And with *Enchanted*, I storyboarded the entire movie! I storyboarded the movie to understand the characters and their motivations.

Bill: An animation director, when they storyboard, they're automatically thinking of staging, sort of predeciding how that scene is going to be staged and shot in the end. But in live action, how much of that do you find you bring over to the set? Do you actually think, "Oh, I know I'm going to shoot from this angle," or do you shoot the coverage and then decide later?

Kevin: No, I bring all of it to the set and then I'm ready to let it all go. That's one of the big differences between *102 Dalmatians* and *Enchanted*. On *102 Dalmatians* I held onto that blueprint. I think it made that movie somewhat cold and predictable. I let go of it on *Enchanted*. If I saw something happening between my actors, or staging that happened in the moment, I totally just let it go and redirected or reimagined the specifics of that scene in that moment. And having boarded it allowed me that confidence, because I had the storyboarding to fall back on, you know? You're not standing out there empty with nothing. The homework is done; now you can move forward from that place.

Bill: On *102 Dalmatians*, you were brought in after somebody else was taken out. But Enchanted wasn't that way. They came to you in the early stages, right?

Kevin: I begged for it. I had to beg for that movie.

Bill: And how did that come about? How did you find out that it existed out there?

Kevin: My agent Adriana Alberghetti told me about it. She said, "It's the perfect movie for you." And I complained, "Oh, I don't know, it has

Enchanted, 2007. © 2007 Disney.

animated characters in it and I need to be moving away from animation." And I read it, and my first response was, "Well, I'm not sure about it. It seems like, you know, sort of a familiar romantic comedy." And I was full of hesitation.

Bill: **Really?!**

Kevin: Honestly! And my agent scolded me, "You're a fool! You need to read it again." So I read it again, and I realized that it was the perfect vehicle for me. It was emotional. It was surprising. And what I found in that second read that didn't exist in the script at the time was that it could be a love letter to everything Disney.

Bill: **Right.**

Kevin: And I said to myself, "This would be the 'in' for me." I love animation. It courses through my blood. I can make a love letter to the one thing I wanted to do since I was five years old.

Bill: **And you knew animation.**

Kevin: I knew it!

Bill: **And it couldn't have been made by a director who didn't know animation.**

Kevin: It's true! And they tried to make it with two other directors before me. It always fell apart. And I think it fell apart because there was a level of cynicism about their approaches. When I dove in, I said, "I'm gonna let all that cynicism go." *Shrek* had happened and had succeeded poking fun at Disney, and I said, "Just let go of all that, and let's embrace our love of everything Disney. Let's just say that we love it, and not be embarrassed to say that we love it, and see where it goes." The executives were scared to death. What I had to do is what we would typically do at Disney Animation: I filled a whole floor of a production building with storyboards and artwork. I hung up all the art we had produced, I got photo clippings for the live-action sections, and I pitched the entire story and I sold them the movie. I used the animation process of beat boarding the film, which is to put together the story of the movie before you even make the movie. You make it in static drawings first, then you make it again, with the camera recording.

Bill: **But they paid for the art department?**

Kevin: I was a little sneaky with this. I used the idea that if we wanted to have the film by a certain release date, I was going to have to put together the animation before we shot the live-action. Animation takes a certain amount of time to produce and if we wanted to complete the animation by a certain date, we needed to start storyboarding now. The studio was still unsure they wanted to make the film, so I used that storyboarding money, not just to put together the animated section, but to sell them the entire movie.

Bill: **Where did you do the animation?**

Kevin: It was animated by James Baxter's company, James Baxter Animation, in Pasadena.

Bill: **What a lucky choice that was.**

Kevin: Lucky? I'm not sure luck had anything to do with it. His company was, by far, the best choice for this gig. Couldn't have had a better character animator than James in charge.

Bill: **The key to that movie was finding Amy Adams. I think when most people hear that story they think, "Who would believe that any girl could be that sweet …"**

Kevin: Right …

Bill: **Did you know you needed somebody like that?**

Kevin: They wanted me to hire a star. And I said, "No." Just being bull-headed I said, "No, no, no. This is one of those moments, like casting Julie Andrews as Mary Poppins, where you get to hire someone that the world doesn't yet know about. And they believe in the character 100 percent." You're not carrying a tabloid story about your lead actress while creating a character who exudes purity.

Amy Adams, Kevin Lima, *Enchanted*, 2007 © Disney.

Bill: **Right.**

Kevin: So I said, "I'm gonna go look for an unknown." And they said, "Okay, you go look for someone, but we want this actress over here to do it." And Amy came in for an audition.

Bill: **She had already done *Catch Me If You Can*?**

Kevin: She had. She came into the room and I think I had a 103-degree temperature, I was really sick that day. And we were doing fifteen-minute auditions, just moving people in and out and getting a taste of each of them. Amy walked into the room and I suddenly perked up. You just know! You just have this intuition that it's going to happen. And I invested in her in that moment, and we spent forty-five minutes together and I knew I had found Giselle. I knew: there she was. And I took the tape back to the studio and said, "This is the girl we're hiring." They said, "Okay, we'll watch it, but we want that girl over there." And I said, "Wait 'til you see it!" Dick Cook, then Chairman of the Walt Disney Studios finally saw the audition, and he said, "Go ahead, Kev, hire her. I understand what you're trying to do."

Bill: Casting is a big part of directing, right?

Kevin: It's the biggest part of live-action directing. Casting is everything. I think that's true of animation as well. I think the casting, the coming together of the vocal performance and the animator, if you can get that right, if you can get the chemistry of that right, then you've captured something magic.

Bill: Is there a secret?

Kevin: I don't know if there's a key to casting. What I tend to do is never work on the script thinking about an actor. Never, never. I try to keep it as wide open as possible. And I sort of think of it like, and I learned this from Peter Weir, he talks about his concept of the "Wanted" poster. That you create the "Wanted" poster in the writing, and as it progresses you're starting to think visually. I'm a real visual thinker, so I start to see the character. I board some stuff before I even get the actor, so I've already got a little bit of a mental picture of what I'm going for. Then I wait for that person to walk into the room.

Bill: And …

Kevin: And then I arrest them and I make them do the movie!

Bill: I think when an animation director sees a scene like that Central Park extravaganza in *Enchanted* they think, uh … that would be a big thing to keep …

Kevin: [laughs] Under control?

Bill: Yeah. Number one, is it as big and complex as it looks? And number two, in your animation experience, is there an equivalent to that kind of intensity?

Kevin: I think a scene like that has almost direct correlations to animation. And what I've learned in animation is that there's a great number of people who are coming together to make a moment in time, across many, many different disciplines, happen. And the only way to control it is to have done your prep. It's about being prepared for when each person comes to you and asks a question. It's easy to walk into a scene with three or four people and control the dynamic of those people without extensive prep. It's harder when you've got 400. So you have to really have planned out the scene. Because it was a song, it follows a process very much like animation, in that you record the song beforehand, you storyboard the song, you decide how many characters are in each scene, you know? You've gone through the boards with your choreographer, you've gone on location, you've figured out how many brides and grooms for this section, how many construction workers for that.

Bill: **You worked with Phil Collins on *Tarzan* ...**

Kevin: I did.

Bill: **And then you had this big musical live-action picture. Is there a difference in working with composers in live action or animation?**

Kevin: I don't treat it any differently. One of the things I do is treat everything like it's possible. I treat everything like it's an animated film, to be quite honest with you, and then I figure out how to do it in live action. The storytelling is the same; the planning is the same. It's just when you get in front of the camera it takes a different set of tools to capture it.

Bill: **Are there types of films or types of stories you want to tell from now on?**

Kevin: I feel pretty open. I love this idea of creating worlds that don't exist. I love this idea of creating characters that don't exist. You know, that's really where most of my focus goes. Whenever something comes out of me, it's all about bringing together those worlds and things that seem impossible. It doesn't mean it's the only thing I'll ever do. I'm actually looking forward to the challenge of just two actors in a room. 'Cause in some ways you can't hide behind any of the flash. The truth has to be there in the moment, and you either capture it or you don't.

Bill: **Two actors in a room will still have a visual effects supervisor.**

Kevin: [laughs] It probably will. The thing that is the hardest between the two mediums for me is the fact that you don't ever get to go back if you fail. You don't ever get to go back and do it again. In animation, I always felt like there was a safety net. If we didn't get it this time with the actor in the booth, we'll go back and rewrite it and come and get it again. That doesn't happen very often in live action. So, you gotta make sure it's there on the day and the dynamic is happening. That's the big, big difference: that you don't really have that ability to keep returning to the same scene. So you've gotta be sure, when you walk into the room, that you can make it happen.

Bill: **_Enchanted_'s a movie that definitely reflected the balance of your specialties.**

Kevin: *Enchanted* was a big example of that for me, in that I was embracing what I loved. And not trying to be someone I'm not. Letting the inspiration come from somewhere deep inside of me is when I've been the most successful. It's such a strange thing to think that somehow it all comes from outside forces, from life's experiences. When I finished *Tarzan*, I hadn't seen my dad in twenty-five years. My parents were divorced when I was nine; my dad disappeared when I was twelve. And I have so many father issues that have worked their way through my films. Goofy and Max in *A Goofy Movie*. Tarzan and Kerchak, the alpha gorilla. And these things just kept coming back. And I thought, "Boy, if I meet my father, if I heal that relationship, I might lose all of that." And what I realize is that the damage was done and you could never heal it. It still follows you, and it still exists within what makes you who you are. But I was so worried, and in that moment I realized I don't need to worry about that stuff anymore.

Bill: **Did you meet him again?**

Kevin: He actually contacted me.

Bill: **Was this after the movie?**

Kevin: I think someone had told him I was working on *Tarzan*. And he started trying to figure out where I was and what I was doing, what I had done. And then he wrote me a letter. And here I am, having a baby and releasing a movie at the same time. Actually both of those things happened on the same exact night. I had my daughter on the night that *Tarzan* premiered in theatres. I'm not kidding. So my dad wrote me a letter. And my first instinct was, "What does this guy want?" 'Cause I only knew him as this father who had abandoned his family. It took us a couple months to figure out how we were gonna meet. He was living in Florida. We met in Orlando. I was staying on the Disney property promoting *Tarzan*, and he came down and we had a meeting. We had a meeting; that sounds so official, doesn't it? We came together. It was fine. And I realized how tough he had had it. I had no idea, you know? He was at one point homeless, and he had been sober at that point for about five years.

Bill: **He was not working?**

Kevin: He held down a job. He was trying to pull his life together. Two years later he died of a brain tumor. So it got me wondering whether or not people know these things are happening and somehow they're trying to pull their life together and make amends.

Bill: So you didn't continue to see him?

Kevin: We kept a relationship going for those two years. I think that relationship sort of formed me in many, many ways. Because as a kid, I escaped into the world of the arts, a world I could control, a world I could build. Here I am as a director, building worlds, creating a sandbox that I invite others to play in. That was very instrumental in making me the artist I am today.

Bill: That is pretty important.

Kevin: Yep. When my mom—we're getting so personal here—When my dad left, my mom sort of fell apart, and we became a welfare family. The whole thing with forcing my way through the front door of the Puppet Workshop is about earning money for my family. Yet finding a place where I could be fulfilled, because I wasn't getting any of it at home. At school, I was the kid who was called the faggot, because I played with puppets and because I drew. So, I just kept building these worlds, you know? It taught me that I had to take care of myself, that I had to go after everything I wanted. Each step in the process, moving from student to professional, growing as an artist, was all about me going after what I wanted. It was about me saying, "I'm going to direct a feature animated film." And going to the right people and saying, "This is what I'm going to do next." And the only way that's going to happen is to ask for it. It's about putting yourself out in the world and saying, "I want it."

Bill: That's the distinctive thing about you. Every director we meet has a different path. With some people, it just seems like they were in the right place at the right time. Other people have a lot of trouble. A lot of knock down, get up. You just kept asking.

Kevin: And when they said, "No," I said, "Okay, I'm gonna go find it somewhere else." With enough headstrong chutzpah to say, "It's gonna happen somewhere." And the whole thing is getting back up on the horse. It's about when you fail, saying, "Okay, how do I learn from this? How do I not let it hold me down?"

INDEX

C

D

E

F

T

U

V

W

Y

Z